Ideologies of American Fore

A comprehensive account of ideology and its role in the foreign policy of the United States of America, this book investigates the way United States foreign policy has been understood, debated and explained in the period since the US emerged as a global force, on its way to becoming the world power.

Starting from the premise that ideologies facilitate understanding by providing explanatory patterns or frameworks from which meaning can be derived, the authors study the relationship between ideology and foreign policy, demonstrating the important role ideas have played in US foreign policy. Drawing on a range of US administrations, they consider key speeches and doctrines, as well as private conversations, and compare rhetoric to actions in order to demonstrate how particular sets of ideas – that is, ideologies – from anti-colonialism and anti-communism to neo-conservatism mattered during specific presidencies and how US foreign policy was projected, explained and sustained from one administration to another.

Bringing a neglected dimension into the study of US foreign policy, this book will be of great interest to students and researchers of US foreign policy, ideology and politics.

John Callaghan is Professor of Politics and Contemporary History at the University of Salford.

Brendon O'Connor is an Associate Professor at the United States Studies Centre at the University of Sydney.

Mark Phythian is Professor of Politics in the School of History, Politics and International Relations at the University of Leicester.

Edited by Inderjeet Parmar, *City University*, and John Dumbrell, *University of Durham*

This new series sets out to publish high-quality works by leading and emerging scholars critically engaging with United States Foreign Policy. The series welcomes a variety of approaches to the subject and draws on scholarship from international relations, security studies, international political economy, foreign policy analysis and contemporary international history.

Subjects covered include the role of administrations and institutions, the media, think tanks, ideologues and intellectuals, elites, transnational corporations, public opinion, and pressure groups in shaping foreign policy, US relations with individual nations, with global regions and global institutions and America's evolving strategic and military policies.

The series aims to provide a range of books – from individual research monographs and edited collections to textbooks and supplemental reading for scholars, researchers, policy analysts and students.

For more information about this series, please visit: www.routledge.com/series/RSUSFP

Ideologies of American Foreign Policy

John Callaghan, Brendon O'Connor
and Mark Phythian

LONDON AND NEW YORK

First published 2019
by Routledge
2 Park Square, Milton Park, Abingdon, Oxon OX14 4RN

and by Routledge
52 Vanderbilt Avenue, New York, NY 10017

Routledge is an imprint of the Taylor & Francis Group, an informa business

British Library Cataloguing-in-Publication Data
A catalogue record for this book is available from the British Library

Library of Congress Cataloging-in-Publication Data
Names: Callaghan, John (John T.), author. | O'Connor, Brendon, 1969– author. | Phythian, Mark, author.
Title: Ideologies of American foreign policy / John Callaghan, Brendon O'Connor, and Mark Phythian.
Description: New York : Routledge, 2019. | Series: Routledge studies in US foreign policy | Includes bibliographical references and index.
Identifiers: LCCN 2018045193 | ISBN 9780415474306 (hardback) | ISBN 9780415474313 (pbk.) | ISBN 9780429019241 (e-book)
Subjects: LCSH: United States—Foreign relations—1945–1989. | United States—Foreign relations—1989– | United States—Foreign relations—Philosophy.
Classification: LCC E840 .C32 2019 | DDC 327.73009/04—dc23
LC record available at https://lccn.loc.gov/2018045193

ISBN: 9780415474306 (hbk)
ISBN: 9780415474313 (pbk)
ISBN: 9780429019241 (ebk)

Typeset in Sabon and Frutiger
by Apex CoVantage, LLC
Printed by CPI Group (UK) Ltd, Croydon CR0 4YY

Contents

List of figures

Notes on authors

John Callaghan is Professor of Politics and Contemporary History at the University of Salford. His publications include: *The Labour Party and Foreign Policy: A History* (2007); *The Retreat of Social Democracy* (2000); *Cold War, Crisis, and Conflict* (2003); *Socialism in Britain Since 1884* (1990).

Brendon O'Connor is an Associate Professor at the United States Studies Centre at the University of Sydney. He has published books and articles on anti-Americanism, US foreign policy and US welfare policy.

Mark Phythian is Professor of Politics in the School of History, Politics and International Relations at the University of Leicester. He is the author or editor of some dozen books on aspects of security and intelligence, co-editor of the journal *Intelligence and National Security* and a Fellow of the UK Academy of Social Sciences.

Acknowledgements

In the course of writing this book we have had the opportunity to present our ideas and test out our approach at a number of international conferences. We would like to take this opportunity to express our gratitude to all those panel and audience members who engaged with us and provided comments on the work in progress. In particular, we would like to thank those who attended and participated in discussions at panels organised around this book at the Society for Historians of American Foreign Relations conference in Falls Church, Virginia, the International Studies Association conference in New Orleans and the American Political Science Association conference in Boston. We would also like to thank Claire Maloney at Routledge for her support and guidance in seeing the book through to publication and Lusana Taylor for her work as copy editor. Brendon O'Connor would like to thank the United States Studies Centre for supporting this book and Conor Wakefield for his diligent research assistance work.

1 The question of ideology

This is a book about ideology and its role in the foreign policy of the United States of America. Specifically, it is about the way United States foreign policy has been understood, debated and explained in the period since the US emerged as a world power, on its way to becoming *the* world power. It is therefore about ideas, but ideas of a particular character. The ideas, values, opinions and beliefs in question are those that are held by significant groups and that exhibit recurring patterns. These sets of ideas compete with rival ways of understanding by seeking to control political language and plans for public policy; they do this in order to justify the political arrangements that they deem necessary for the realisation of their objectives.

We start from two premises. First, that ideologies facilitate understanding by providing explanatory patterns or frameworks from which meaning can be derived. As Michael Freeden puts it, ideologies

> map the political and social worlds for us. We simply cannot do without them because we cannot act without making sense of the world we inhabit. Making sense, let it be said, does not always mean making good or right sense. But ideologies will often contain a lot of common sense.[1]

The more complex the context, the more important ideological understanding becomes; it serves as a tool-kit via the application of which everything can make sense. Arguably, no context is more complex than the landscape confronting the foreign policy decision-maker, where uncertainty is the norm. For example, key but complex questions confronting US foreign policy decision-makers in the 1960s included: what are the aims of Soviet foreign policy? How do we understand revolutionary nationalism in the developing world? What is the nature of the Sino-Soviet split? Are we losing influence over an increasingly integrated Western Europe? The answers to these questions were inevitably arrived at and understood via the filtering mechanism of ideology. Hence, the study of the relationship between ideology and foreign policy is important.

Our second premise, though, is that the role of ideology in US foreign policy is understudied and only poorly understood. In part, this reflects the fact that the nature and functions of ideology are themselves often poorly understood. It also reflects the extent to which academics have baulked at giving ideas a prominent role in the study of foreign policy because their influence is hard to measure precisely. In the field of political science tracing the exact consequences of ideas on policies and outcomes is seen as complicated and messy. We would argue, however, that just because such a tracing can be contested and difficult that does not mean it is not worth attempting. Our aim in this book is to demonstrate the important role ideas have played in US foreign policy. Drawing on a range of US administrations we consider key speeches and doctrines, as well as private conversations, and compare rhetoric to actions in order to demonstrate how particular sets of ideas – that is, ideologies – from anti-colonialism and anti-communism to neoconservatism mattered during specific presidencies. This, then, is the rationale for this book; to bring what otherwise risks being a neglected dimension into the study of US foreign policy. But before we go on to discuss the role of ideology in US foreign policy we should begin with a discussion of ideology itself.

UNDERSTANDING POLITICAL IDEOLOGY

Ideology is a much misunderstood term that tends to be misused and underutilised in academic scholarship. The stigmatising of ideology is not entirely surprising given that from the time of the Russian revolution ideologies have been presented (and caricatured) as pernicious closed systems of thought designed to explain the world according to the dictates of a single, totalising theory. Communism and fascism were the prime examples. In this reckoning, ideologues – the high priests of such 'political religions' – sought to change the world in accordance with abstract visions of the world both as it was supposed to be and as it was destined to become. Much of the violence of the twentieth century derived from the attempt to fit or socially engineer societies into these ideologically prescribed moulds. Thinking of ideology in this way would clearly suggest that while the Soviet Union was based on and guided by ideology, the US (and the liberal West more broadly) was not.[2] This depiction was at the heart of the 'end of ideology' thesis.[3] In this version, ideology was always explicit, systematic, coherent and rigid.[4] Hence, conservatism, liberalism and even socialism were said to be un-ideological in so far as they eschewed such totalising ambitions and embraced more open, flexible, sceptical and pragmatic ways of thinking about the pros and cons of piecemeal change.

This no more than reflects how the experiences of fascism and communism in the twentieth century led to ideology becoming strongly associated with extremes and with rigid dogma and brutality. The word itself became suggestive of something inflexible, dangerous and threatening. It developed into a term of abuse, with its implied opposite being sensible, pragmatic behaviour and dispassionate analysis. Although the origins of the term are usually traced to Antoine Destutt de Tracy,[5] who wished to create a branch of study concerned with the study of ideas, ideology soon became associated with distortion, deception and propaganda. The influential writings of both Karl Marx and later Karl Mannheim created the ever-popular dichotomy between ideology and truth. Mannheim agreed with Marx that a non-ideological standpoint could be identified. Whereas Marx thought this standpoint was that of the proletariat, Mannheim believed it could be occupied by the intelligentsia. For anyone familiar with debates about epistemology, or anyone who has studied the course of twentieth century politics, Mannheim's appeal to a political truth that goes beyond ideology has no more support today than the Marxist-Leninist case for 'scientific socialism' as the standpoint of the proletariat. Nevertheless, despite the naivety and philosophical and experiential sophism of the position, the negative framings of the term ideology associated with Mannheim and Marx remain. As Terry Eagleton contends: "Roughly speaking, one central lineage, from Hegel and Marx to Georg Lukács and some later Marxist thinkers, has been much preoccupied with ideas of true and false cognition, with ideology as illusion, distortion and mystification."[6] For Marx, ideology was the smokescreen that legitimised the capitalist system and communism was the post-ideological scientific truth that was there to be uncovered by the forces of history (this being in Marx's term the difference between false consciousness and true consciousness).

It is not surprising that the pejorative conception of ideology has left a negative legacy, placing 'scholarly blinkers' on how the term has come to be viewed.[7] Ironically (given Marx's view that communism was post-ideological), this negative view of ideology was compounded a hundred times over by the experience of Marxist ideology in practice in the form of communist states. As Michael Freeden has observed, "the emergence of these totalitarian ideologies reinforced the widespread view of ideology as doctrinaire, dogmatic, closed, and inflicted on an unwilling populace."[8] A similar view of ideology as totalising drives the more recent post-structuralist critique of ideology. As Eagleton points out: "If the 'end-of-ideology' theorists viewed all ideology as inherently closed, dogmatic and inflexible, postmodernist thought tends to see all ideology as teleological, 'totalitarian' and metaphysically grounded. Grossly travestied in this way, the concept of ideology obediently writes itself off."[9] Freeden makes a similar point noting that:

> An 'ism' is a slightly familiar, faintly derogatory term – in the United States even 'liberalism' is tainted with that brush. It suggests that artificially constructed sets of ideas, somewhat removed from everyday life, are manipulated by the powers that be – and the powers that want to be. They attempt to control the world of politics and to force us into a rut of doctrinaire thinking and conduct . . .[10]

One consequence of this is the promotion of pragmatism over ideology. Today Realism in International Relations is often claimed to be a system of describing the way the world works that is non-ideological (claims that sound rather like those made by scientific Marxism in an earlier era).[11] Conservatives, most notably Russell Kirk, have contended that the conservative (pragmatic) mind is the exact opposite of the ideological mind which seeks, unrealistically, to bring heaven to earth. Here ideology is conflated with a utopianism that can be both dangerous and naive. American liberals never seem to tire of calling their conservative opponents from Goldwater through to George W. Bush 'ideological', while painting themselves as more practical and pragmatic (a rhetorical stance particularly favoured by Barack Obama during his time as President). As Eagleton has written, "nobody would claim that their own thinking was ideological, just as nobody would habitually refer to themselves as Fatso. Ideology, like halitosis, is in this sense what the other person has."[12]

Hence, it is important for us to separate actuality from caricature in thinking about the role of ideology; to take ideology seriously. In most instances, ideologies are not all-embracing, self-sufficient dogmas (totalitarian ideologies were the exception to the rule in this respect), but rather systems of ideas competing for the attention of citizens and this requires of them significant flexibility and adaptability. We can see these attributes very clearly with reference to one of the most successful of all ideologies, liberalism.

Though the term 'liberalism' was not coined until 1815 and did not become associated with a political party until the mid-nineteenth century, we can trace its roots to the Reformation and the writings of seventeenth century thinkers such as Thomas Hobbes and John Locke. At the core of this new thinking was the idea of individual rights. The individual was said to be possessed of natural rights – for example, the right to acquire and own property – and the ability to reason. Upon this foundation Locke argued for government by consent and toleration of opposing (religious) viewpoints. Good government in this view protected the rights and liberty of the individual and concerned itself only with "life, liberty and estate" (property). Liberty was understood as the absence of external constraints. Good government was essentially minimal government, permitting the individual maximum freedom to pursue his own interests as he saw fit. Later thinkers built on these foundations to stress the possibility of social progress through a questioning and empirical approach to knowledge and scepticism in relation to received truths, whether religious or otherwise. Social progress was possible, in this view, on the basis of reason and the removal of obstacles in the form of dogma, privilege and superstition. In the American War of Independence and the French Revolution such thinking led to the assertion of universal rights, the legal and political equality of citizens, and the foundation of government on the basis of consent. Adam Smith applied elements of this reasoning to political economy, arguing that as the individual was the best judge of his own interests the most efficient allocation of resources would result from removing barriers to the exercise of individual liberty. This also pointed to the virtues of minimal government and sweeping away all forms of arbitrary interferences such as those associated with monarchy, aristocracy, privilege and earlier systems of wealth creation such as mercantilism. But by the end of the nineteenth century many liberals had come to question the idea that liberty was simply the absence of external constraints. An increasing number of liberals saw that state intervention was necessary to supply correctives to the evident failings of markets. By the middle of the twentieth century this type of liberalism, emerging in the US via Franklin Delano Roosevelt's New Deal,[13] reinforced by John Maynard Keynes' analysis of chronic unemployment, was comfortable with a welfare state, macro-management of the economy and a state which disposed of some 40 per cent of the national income, much to the disgust of other liberals like Friedrich Hayek.

Hence, varieties of liberalism have shared core concepts such as the primacy of individual liberty but promoted very different analyses of political economy and policy conclusions, demonstrating its flexibility and adaptability. With regard to foreign policy, the liberal ideology has similarly developed over time from an early focus on free trade to one, from the late nineteenth century, concerned with creating a rules-based international system with institutional forms of arbitration (courts and tribunals), even extending to quasi-forms of world government – the most prominent example being the United Nations. Contemporary liberals have continued this domestic-international nexus with the focus at home on the welfare state project while, on the international stage, the key questions have included how far intervention should go in order to 'protect', what methods should be used, and who the legitimate agents are and under what circumstances. At one extreme in the twentieth century was the humanitarian interventionist liberal camp that supported the wars in the former Yugoslavia in the 1990s and, in some cases, in Iraq in 2003; at the other were the Jeffersonian liberals who wished to focus on free market relations and believed that the ideal government was the least interventionist both domestically and internationally. The challenge for analysing the impact of liberal ideology on US foreign policy lies in the fact that various dimensions (economic, political, international) and historical versions (classical, modern, social) of liberalism are used by politicians when it seems useful to their cause. This is to be expected and thus when analysing the influence of liberal ideology it is crucial to carefully analyse the particular character of the liberal ideas being invoked.[14]

Other ideological ways of thinking, like socialism and environmentalism, have demonstrated similar abilities to change and adapt over time. The tenacity of these ideologies derives from their relationship to the lived experience of societies (and of the groups within them) as well as the institutions that they develop. They survive by continuing to incorporate, defend, promote and contest the dominant belief systems. Typically, beliefs are developed and articulated in their most sophisticated form – as systems of thought – by intellectuals and elite groupings. But they achieve social potency because of their ability to connect with the values and beliefs of broader publics. An ongoing dialogue between these different levels of articulation of the same ideology is evidence that the beliefs in question appear to explain and give meaning to the world to large numbers of people.

Political ideology, therefore, can be usefully thought of as a set of ideas, beliefs, opinions and values that exhibit a recurring pattern, held by significant groups that compete to control political language and public policy.[15] Individuals can be self-conscious advocates of particular political ideologies, but this is not necessarily true of most people. Those who are self-consciously ideological tend to be disproportionately found among political activists and educated elites – the very people who dominate the decision-making process in modern politics. Even in these circles political ideologies can exercise an emotional as well as a cognitive hold on their advocates. Indeed, ideologies generally contain both affective and cognitive elements and exist both in the conscious and unconscious mind. Every political system on earth makes use of flags, rituals, anniversaries, foundation myths, historical narratives, anthems and a host of supporting cultural symbols to buttress and express officially sanctioned beliefs designed to represent the origins, development and greatness of the nation. At the same time, most nations have experienced internal division along lines of ethnicity, language, class, region, religion and other enduring group identities.

Ideologies struggle to control political language. They invent new words and concepts and contest the meaning of established vocabularies. Their conscious advocates compete for popular support and pay close attention to the ways in which ideas are consumed, much in the way advertisers have learned to sell products, often using the same techniques of market research and expecting little more from the public than companies expect from their customers. Ideologies also assist politicians in the legitimisation of policies by, for example, associating the policies with approved, sometimes consensual, values and beliefs – such as the need to defend freedom, democracy, human rights, individual choice, equal opportunity and the like. While the meanings of political concepts are never completely unambiguous – except when the political struggle to fix meaning results in a temporary victory for one side or another in the political process – they often bear the stamp of the national political culture. Ideologies are useful as ways of organising, representing, mobilising, legitimating, interpreting and expressing politics precisely because they are flexible enough to adapt to change.

If ideologies are understood as belief systems organised around a malleable set of core concepts we are much more likely to see the role they play in political life. As we noted at the beginning of this chapter, ideologies impose a pattern, some form of structure, a narrative, a set of concepts, catch-phrases and terms that enable us to interpret and respond to events. As Freeden says, without this "we remain clueless and uncomprehending, on the receiving end of ostensibly random bits of information without rhyme or reason."[16] Therefore ideologies, "order the social world, direct it towards certain activities, and legitimate or delegitimate its practices. Ideologies exercise power, at the very least by creating a framework within which decisions can be taken and make sense."[17] Freeden also emphasises the importance of the emotional appeal of ideologies, as does Gerald Gaus, who writes that, unlike philosophical enquiry, ideologies seek to offer "an emotionally and psychologically compelling package of beliefs, commitments and values."[18] This need to simplify, to legitimate, to connect to current issues, and to forge emotional connections between large groups of people, makes ideologies much more practical and action-oriented, and by their very nature much cruder systems of thought. All this is illustrated, for example, in the authoritarian populism developing within grass-roots American conservatism which, beginning with hegemonic anti-communism and racism in the 1950s, succeeded in fashioning a broader ideological appeal, against 'big government' and the moral decay of the nation, as the post-war 'Keynesian welfare state' faltered in the 1970s .

To summarise, we can say that ideologies provide decision-making frameworks without which political action cannot occur. From the vantage point of professional politicians, ideologies are instruments of power, but they can also be vehicles of dissent and opposition, "instruments of enabling and empowering choice, from the viewpoint of members of an open society."[19] They are power constructs in their capacity to determine agendas, prioritise ideas and policies, marginalise alternatives, and promote the interests of specific groups within society.[20] They can be an element in the 'soft power' exercised by states.[21] Ideologies have influence because "they have practical import, because they are adopted by significant numbers of adherents, and because their ideas have hit a sensitive spot" in national, sub-national and international consciousness.[22] This is made possible by the fact that they are relatively easy to communicate, unlike much of the political philosophy from which many of their core concepts are derived.

FIGURE 1.1 Key factors influencing policy-making

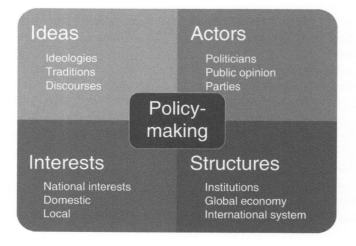

FIGURE 1.2 Ideology and American foreign policy: a three-tiered approach

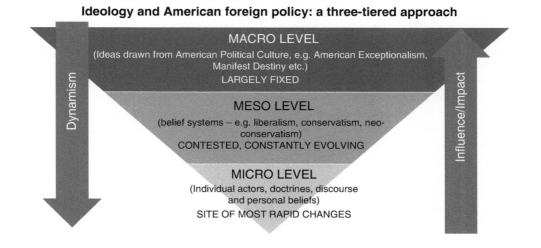

IDEOLOGY AND FOREIGN POLICY

Although ideology has a significant impact on foreign policy decisions we should not lose sight of the fundamental point that other factors are also very important, particularly the roles of structures, actors and interests. This reality is represented in Figure 1.1, above. If we view ideas, actors, interests and structures as completely discrete and separate categories, then the figure can be seen as oversimplified. However, what Figure 1.1 aims to acknowledge is the overlapping nature of these categories by showing them not as distinct but rather as porous entities gathered around policy-making. What is ultimately most important to understand is the interaction between these categories and their combined impact on shaping policies and events.

In what follows we can imagine the development and impact of ideology on foreign policy thinking as operating across three porous levels, or tiers, as represented in Figure 1.2.

The macro-level is where we find the hegemonic values and beliefs of American political culture. At this level we are dealing with a broad but often vague sets of ideas. However, these ideas are no less important or powerful just because they can be emotional, simple and repetitive. These are the ideas that not only promote liberal democracy in the US (and beyond) and constitute its civic nationalism, but also invest it with a moral superiority. Though the political culture changes, and is contested from within, these hegemonic values persist over relatively long periods of time and only change very slowly. The types of beliefs and traditions we are looking at here are those associated with the notions of American exceptionalism, American idealism and ideas related to American greatness. These values and myths are consciously and subconsciously at the core of American nationalism. This conception of ideology undoubtedly borrows from the Frankfurt School and Clifford Geertz, but in the US context also draws significantly on the work of scholars such as Seymour Martin Lipset and Walter Russell Mead, as we discuss in the next section. Macro-level ideas are used regularly by presidents in set piece speeches, such as inaugural and state of the union addresses. They are also commonplace in times of war and international conflict.

The meso-level is where we have the political system proper, where ideas are elaborated more systematically. At this level conscious efforts are made to contest control of policy and language to better mobilise voters and supply politicians with ideas used to make public policy. This is the world of party politics, lobbies and think-tanks. It is a world of civil society groups, but it is also a world of state-private networks where civil society groups have enjoyed the direct and indirect support of the American state.[23] Ideology at this level is more explicit and systematic than it is at the macro-level. Its purveyors are not only consciously seeking to connect with popular values and beliefs, but also to shape them and find coalitions that will support the goals of policy. Ideologies, as Michael Freeden's work emphasises, are dynamic bundles of ideas that make sense of daily politics and offer broad policy solutions to the big questions of the day. While they have a central core of meanings, they are also evolving and developing in a constant effort to remain salient in a changing world. Such ideological competition is a key feature of the meso-level. The key meso-level ideological actors (parties, think-tanks, intellectuals and unions) are engaged in crafting and shaping the development of meso-level ideologies (such as liberalism, conservatism, neoconservatism, etc). This is a more dynamic process than at the macro-level, reflecting the flexibility of ideas like liberalism and conservatism.

At the base is the micro-level. Ideological analysis here focuses on the reasoning of significant political actors in the foreign policy arena. In other words, the focus is on the policies, doctrines and political discourse of presidents and other administration principals in the foreign policy arena which feed into the higher two levels. Ultimately, it is the interaction between the levels that is critical to understanding how ideology functions in political life. Few would doubt the need to legitimate foreign policy in an age of democracy; indeed, foreign policy insiders from George Kennan to Zbigniew Brzezinski have complained about the problems democracy poses for foreign policy in a political system as open and fragmented as that of the United States. But it has to be emphasised that this legitimising function is only possible when the dominant values and beliefs are successfully mobilised and appealed to in the defence of policy. This means that to be successful, politicians must draw upon dominant beliefs and values within their society. They cannot invent legitimising values and beliefs to suit themselves. Many would concede this point but remain sceptical about the impact of ideology on the policies that are actually pursued. There are those who think that ideology is simply for the hustings, the set-piece speech and the public declaration. In our view they are wrongly confining it to the functions of window-dressing and self-conscious manipulation of 'the public'. Such a view does not easily explain something that we demonstrate throughout this book, why the thoughts of political actors – as revealed in the minutes of meetings, private correspondence, diaries and official documents – continue to mirror the ideological tropes which characterise their publicly expressed beliefs. Nor does it explain why foreign policy insiders have complained about the tendency in US foreign policy for 'idealism' to displace a more 'realistic' approach.[24] If idealism has got into the system the obvious explanation is that politicians have put it there.

Liberal ideas appear at the macro-, meso- and micro-levels as they move up and down the model. At the macro-level, liberal ideas are often used in a more strident and less consistent manner in the service of American nationalist rhetoric. Indeed, all presidents are drawn to use the terms 'freedom' and 'liberty' – key liberal notions – to celebrate and promote America's contribution to the world. Most crucial to our model is the argument that presidential administrations tend to use ideas from the macro- and meso-levels in combination with each other; thus it is often the case that meso-level ideologies, particularly realism, are drawn upon by various administrations to moderate such macro-level ideologies as nationalism and idealism.

We can see something of this intersection of ideas at the different levels in relation to the question of US support for democracy and democracy promotion as a foreign policy goal. Focusing on this question also underscores the shrewdness of Michael Hunt's warning that the question of the role of ideology in US foreign policy is a "big and slippery subject."[25] Support for democracy, often expressed in the language of support for 'freedom', lies at the very heart of US foreign policy discourse. The George W. Bush administration's September 2002 National Security Strategy of the United States revived interest in the question of the place of democracy promotion within US foreign policy. This emphasised that the US had to accept both the need for pre-emptive war in the changed security environment of the early twenty-first century and the importance of democracy promotion to US foreign and security policy. Building on the logic of Francis Fukuyama's *End of History* thesis[26] and the core tenet of the democratic peace idea,[27] the Strategy explained, with reference to Russia and China, that, "America will encourage the advancement of democracy and economic openness in both nations, because these are the best foundations of domestic stability and international order."[28] It went on to invoke the sentiments of the US Declaration of Independence and promote a sense of mission arising from the exceptional historical experience of the US in explaining that: "Freedom is a non-negotiable demand of human dignity; the birthright of every person – in every civilization . . . Today, humanity holds in its hands the opportunity to further freedom's triumph . . . The United States welcomes our responsibility to lead in this great mission."[29]

From the time of the Truman Doctrine, the language of 'freedom' has been central to US foreign policy discourse, as has 'national security' which provided for the defence of freedom.[30] 'Freedom' was often used to conflate the benefits of capitalism and democracy. Earlier, in the 1920s and 1930s, US foreign policy had often been couched in terms of 'democracy'. However, the Cold War-era shift from an emphasis on 'democracy' to one on 'freedom' was not without significance. Clearly drawing on the grand narrative of US history, in the Cold War context 'freedom' was held to be constantly under threat, requiring vigilence lest its beneficiaries find it overturned and themselves subjected to its polar opposite – slavery. Given its place in US history, this term did not need to be explicitly stated, the implication that this was the antonym of freedom was well enough understood. As Anders Stephanson has noted, in the ideology of US foreign policy:

> Freedom (or 'liberty') is understood as independence, as not being dependent on the will of any outside power. This state is natural, something innately given. Any loss of freedom, any movement in the direction of dependence, is defined as 'slavery'. Such dependence/slavery does not have to be actual: the very threat of arbitary imposition on the still independent self is a form of slavery because it is a constriction, a diminution of autonomy. [31]

As Daniel T. Rodgers has noted: "Freedom in mainstream postwar talk was not this or that list of rights. It was bigger and vaguer. It was the obverse of the twentieth century's new totalitarianisms; it was, in a word, everything that fascism and communism were not."[32] But it was more then this. As a speech act, the utilisation of 'freedom' served a wider purpose. As Rodgers explains:

> Every abstraction conflates; that is the essence of open, accordion-like phrases. But none of the earlier metaphors of politics had been employed so deliberately to bundle in a word the institutions of the status quo – or so fully efface the boundary between economic and political life. One of the strengths of American political talk had been a sense that the keywords of politics must somehow be different from those which undergirded the mere 'expediences' of economic relations . . . But now, under the rubric of Freedom, capitalism and democracy were finally, confidently folded into a common entity.[33]

There was little respite for this, "single, powerfully flexible noun" [34] in the years after the proclamation of the Truman Doctrine in 1947, as it was adopted to give meaning to "the unnerving events of the late 1940s in the clarifying language of the past", bestowing on "the nation's new quasi-war posture and its nervous armament drive the legitimating mantle of the war just won."[35] It drew its potency from its all-pervasiveness; its lack of specificity. In this, it shared something with 'national security', that other ubiquitous concept in post-1945 US foreign policy. Like 'freedom', 'national security' drew its power from an antonym that was too obvious to need stating. As Emily Rosenberg has explained:

> Even advancing the *need* for national security implied its potential lack. Fears about insecurity (personal and social, as well as international) were already rampant in postwar American life. Amid postwar uncertainties, who could argue for insecurity? 'National Security,' a term without historically negative connotations, was a consensus-builder; it became the key word in an enormous peacetime expansion of state power.[36]

In our three-tier model, freedom is constantly used in American political discourse to mean a myriad of different things. This is how ideas work at the micro-level; at the meso-level the term is claimed by American liberals and conservatives alike as they employ particular understandings of freedom to buttress their ideological contentions; at the macro-level, freedom is a common-sense ideal that America, above all other nations, is defending and at times spreading.

American exceptionalism as ideology

This focus on one of the grand themes that has endured in US foreign policy discourse leads us to a focus on the single most significant macro-level theme, that of American exceptionalism, from which the democracy impulse flows. The idea of America as a new beginning planned by God had Puritan roots in the first New England settlements, reflected in names such as Providence, New Haven and Bethlehem. However, for some the *idea* of America as an exceptional land even pre-dated its settlement. For example, Peter Conrad has written of how:

> Before America could be discovered, it had to be imagined. Columbus knew what he hoped to find before he left Europe. Geographically, America was imagined in

advance of its discovery as an arboreal paradise, Europe's dream of verdurous luxury. After the discovery, the political founders of the United States were its inventors. They too, like the explorers, constituted America as a promised land, a conjuration of the liberal hopes or aristocratic fears of Europe. They saw the new kind of state they were creating not as a fact but as a formula, not a natural growth of history but the actualization of an idea. As the Gettysburg Address puts it, America was created in homage to a proposition.[37]

As a national consciousness developed during the eighteenth century the *idea* of America became cemented, as did the related idea of Americans as a chosen people.[38] As one prominent Connecticut clergyman put it in 1777: "We in this land are, as it were, led out of Egypt by the hand of Moses."[39] These notions had material roots in the advantages of geography and economic potential of the New World. Herman Melville's novel *White-Jacket*, protesting against the 'British' practices of flogging miscreant sailors, provides a good mid-nineteenth century articulation of this sense of providence:

And we Americans are the peculiar, chosen people – the Israel of our time; we bear the ark of the liberties of the world. Seventy years ago we escaped from thrall; and, besides our first birthright – embracing one continent of earth – God has given to us, for a future inheritance, the broad domains of the political pagans, that shall yet come and lie down under the shade of our ark, without bloody hands being lifted. God has predestinated, mankind expects, great things from our race; and great things we feel in our souls. . . . And let us always remember that with ourselves, almost for the first time in the history of earth, national selfishness is unbounded philanthropy; for we can not do a good to America but we give alms to the world.[40]

This national mindset has it that it was America's destiny to fill and subdue the virgin continent by expansion to the West. Success in this enterprise reinforced claims of exceptional potency and privilege, and so the perceived differences between the Old and New Worlds continued to amplify. A famous passage from J. Hector St. John de Crèvecœur's *Letters from an American Farmer*, first published in 1782, provides perhaps the best characterisation of this emerging sense of exceptionalism:

What, then, is the American, this new man? . . . He is an American, who, leaving behind him all his ancient prejudices and manners, receives new ones from the new mode of life he has embraced, the new government he obeys, the new rank he holds. . . . Americans are the western pilgrims who are carrying along with them that great mass of arts, sciences, vigour, and industry which began long since in the east; they will finish the great circle. . . . The American is a new man, who acts upon new principles. He must therefore entertain new ideas and form new opinions. From involuntary idleness, servile dependence, penury, and useless labour, he [the American] has passed to toils of a very different nature, rewarded by ample subsistence. This is an American.[41]

As the republic developed, the process of westward expansion and notion of 'Manifest Destiny' gave added weight to this vision of America, with the settling of North America (including parts of what were Mexico) held to constitute the progress of liberty and the right to a continental dominance that was sanctioned by God and history.[42]

The US Constitution itself was, of course, couched in universal truths and the colonial revolt that preceded its drafting saw the spread of ideas proclaiming America's special mission. "We have it in our power", said Thomas Paine, "to begin the world all over again."[43] In historian Arthur M. Schlesinger Jr.'s phrase: "Experiment gave ground to destiny as the premise of national life."[44] Protected from world affairs by its geography, preoccupied with conquering the North American continent, unable to play a significant role in the power politics of Europe and with no interest in doing so, within the newly-constituted United States "the theory of the elect nation, the redeemer nation, almost became the official creed."[45]

This is the context for novelist G. K. Chesterton's observation that; "America is the only nation in the world that is founded on a creed. That creed is set forth with dogmatic and even theological lucidity in the Declaration of Independence."[46] In saying this Chesterton was echoing earlier thinkers, such as Ralph Waldo Emerson and Abraham Lincoln, who had referred to the country's 'political religion'. Emerging as it did from an anti-colonial revolt, the US had no feudal past and the political religion that it adopted – expressed in its quasi-sacrosanct Constitution – drew powerfully from the liberal Enlightenment and a religious sense of its own innocence in a corrupt world. This position has often been referred to as America's 'civil religion' because of the liturgical zeal given to an oft-repeated set of ideas that are presented as uniquely American. Samuel Huntington went so far as to call this an ideology, which he termed "Americanism." For Huntington:

> It is possible to speak of a body of political ideas that constitutes 'Americanism' in a sense in which one can never speak of 'Britishism,' 'Frenchism,' 'Germanism,' or 'Japaneseism.' Americanism in this sense is comparable to other ideologies and religions. To reject the central ideas of that doctrine is to be un-American . . . This identification of nationality with political Creed or values makes the United States virtually unique.[47]

Similarly, Seymour Martin Lipset creatively borrowed from Richard Hofstadter's definition to claim that the US's "fate as a nation" has been "not to have ideologies, but to be one."[48] Writing in 1996, Lipset could still identify five living components of this dominant American creed that he called the ideology of "Americanism": liberty, egalitarianism, individualism, populism and laissez-faire. These beliefs commanded popular support throughout the twentieth century, claimed Lipset, and identified the nation with a specific set of ideas and values that made the US a uniquely ideological society.[49] Lipset also stressed that, since the birth of the republic, Americans have exhibited a stronger religious commitment than most Christian countries and have done so as devotees of numerous, predominantly Congregationalist, sects. This has been a powerful contributing factor in shaping the country's voluntarist, egalitarian, populist and democratic culture and one that has reinforced, and been supported by, social and political individualism. Religion, then, has contributed to 'Americanism', an Americanism for Lipset that counts as an ideology on a par with other political ideologies.[50]

This has produced a moralistic people who have a greater need than most, it is argued, to believe that God is on their side in any conflict. In 1900 in a Senate debate over US control of the Philippines, Indiana Senator Albert Jeremiah Beveridge declared, in tones that would be echoed by presidents for the next century and beyond, that God "has marked the American people as His chosen nation to finally lead in the regeneration of the world. This is the divine mission of America, and it holds for us all the profit, all the glory, all the happiness possible to man. We are trustees of the world's progress, guardians of its righteous peace."[51] Such rhetoric and beliefs are still heard regularly a century later in a significant departure from most industrialised societies in which messianic religious rhetoric is far less common in politics.[52]

Politicians in general know that it is easier to mobilise public opinion if the enemy is believed to be evil, but the tendency in the US to make this appeal is reinforced by the evangelistic element in Americanism.[53] Deep inside the nation's sense of itself as special is the conviction that it has been singled out by God or providence, by destiny or history, or simply by its democratic credentials, to do good on earth. Involvement in conflicts has generally reinforced these beliefs.[54] An elevated rhetoric of national mission along these lines has been occasionally employed by most, if not all, of the administrations covered by this book, illustrating that this national mission is rooted deep within the political culture rather than simply being the culture of a particular party or period of history. Being an ideology, anyone who embraces this civic nationalism can, in theory at least, become an American; but failure to adhere to the country's dominant values is regarded as 'un-American', and a rejection of the 'American Way'.[55]

In this context, then, American nationalism, "constituting itself not only as prophetic but also universal",[56] emerged as a contradictory claim of unique virtue and opportunity on the one hand, and universal leadership on the other. America was both uniquely blessed and also the model which the rest of the world must follow. The resulting tension has been played out in US foreign policy. As Walter Russell Mead has written: "The belief that the essence of American nationality lies in dedication to universal principles is constantly at war with the idea that Americanism belongs exclusively to the American people and must be defended against alien influences rather than shared with mankind."[57] It has also meant that American nationalism could either regard the world beyond its shores as corrupt and impervious to the American Way, or as the pliable object of "regenerative intervention" by the US.[58] The period covered by this book has been dominated by the latter sentiment.

By the time of the 1901 census the US was by some measures – for example, coal, textile and steel production – the biggest industrial power in the world, as well as the world's greatest source of food.[59] Its future world role had been forecast for some time, notably by William Gladstone in 1878, who foresaw the US replacing Britain as "the head servant in the great household of the World."[60] By 1902 the distinguished English journalist W. T. Stead could write about "the Americanization of the world" and pronounced the US "the greatest of world-powers."[61] Even before the First World War the future security of Australasia was seen to depend on the USA, rather than Britain, with the First Lord of the Admiralty, Winston Churchill, conceding as much in March 1914.[62] But all this was potential, not to be fulfilled for another few decades. The greatest industrial and agricultural power soon also became the greatest financial power and was in many ways the greatest cultural influence in the world by the 1920s. In 1945, finally, the USA added to these credentials the distinction of being the world's greatest military power, in part a consequence of the atomic monopoly it held at the end of the Second World War.

In this sketch of the multifaceted expansion of America we can see why a culture of self-reliance, acquisitive individualism, immigration and anti-statism put down such strong nationalist roots. Collectivism in America – as measured by trade union membership, adherence to socialism in any of its variants or the strength of mutualism in any of its political forms – was particularly weak. European socialists were among the first to comment on this apparently abnormal development; the biggest capitalist economy in the world had signally failed to produce a socialist movement of commensurate size.[63] Americans have embraced de Tocqueville's idea that the US was qualitatively different in a wholly positive way as a key part of their national mythology; in contrast non-Americans have been more inclined to see proclaimed differences as a double-edged sword with the US representing both the hopes and dreams of a better life (and world) and a dystopia and harbinger of a global nightmare.[64]

With regard to foreign policy, the belief in American exceptionalism has been most commonly expressed since the early twentieth century via the idea of Wilsonianism; the idea that the US should (and does) use its power and influence to help order the world so that it is made 'safe for democracy'. Wilsonianism built upon a foundation of American ideals and values that can be traced back to John Winthrop's 'city on a hill' sermon proclaimed aboard the *Arabella* to immigrants heading for a new life in America in the 1620s. During the twentieth century Wilsonian ideas were, in turn, taken up by a number of liberal (and some would argue conservative) presidents. However, it is important to bear in mind that Wilson's most well-remembered set of ideas – his Fourteen Points[65] – was ultimately rejected by the US Senate with the US thus rejecting membership of Wilson's special project, the League of Nations. What does the idea of Wilsonianism, which will be discussed more fully in the next chapter, tell us about ideology and the role of ideas in the period covered by this book? It illustrates how powerful ideologies are often entwined with national traditions and myths. Wilson's ideology drew heavily on American nationalism in a way that concealed it (nationalism has often been claimed to be alien to America, a claim that is clearly erroneous[66]). Wilsonianism draws on nationalist and liberal traditions in American thought and then adds to those traditions, reflecting the iterative way that ideologies develop. The failings of Wilsonianism reflect the contested space that ideas compete within in the US: Wilson's Fourteen Point plan was defeated by Senators like Henry Cabot Lodge who had a conservative vision of internationalism that did not involve membership of the League of Nations. The plan was also defeated by isolationist views that were both conservative and progressive; the isolationists feared that the League of Nations would draw the US into the entangling and messy affairs of other nations and thus rob it of its 'exceptional' nature.[67] These opponents of US membership of the League of Nations had different ideological convictions and interpretations of America and its role in the world, but their ability to defeat Wilson's proposal reflects the often complicated role that ideas play in policy-making. However, as David Steigerwald argues, the development of the UN and post-Second World War order can be seen as a vindication of Wilsonianism, reminding us that ideas have a life and power that often go beyond the times when they were first constructed or deployed.[68]

AIMS AND STRUCTURE

Our aim in writing this book is to set out the significance of ideology to the making of US foreign policy. This does not involve, or require, an administration-by-administration history of US foreign policy, a number of which already exist. Rather, it requires a focus on the ideas that became dominant and guided the foreign policy of administrations and on how these were challenged and supplanted as the dominant idea, and how all of these ideas drew on macro-level ideas rooted in American political culture. In providing this, we follow the pioneering work of Michael H. Hunt, whose study of *Ideology and US Foreign Policy* was first published in 1986. Hunt's major contribution has been to clearly set out the importance of certain ideas in US foreign policy, from America's founding through to the late twentieth century. His understanding of ideology is similar to ours, viewing it as "an interrelated set of convictions or assumptions that reduces the complexities of a particular slice of reality to easily comprehensible terms and suggests appropriate ways of dealing with that reality."[69] Hunt recognised that in the historiography of US foreign relations, "the power and persistence that ideology acquired has not been sufficiently appreciated"[70] and proposed rectifying this state of affairs by looking at the "elite's private musings and, more important, the public rhetoric by which they have justified their actions and communicated their opinions to one another and to the nation."[71] In many ways, this approach mirrors our own. Speeches in which foreign policy visions and programmes are articulated are clearly an important source of information. But these are tailored to multiple audiences, and often framed so as to place the foreign policy initiative under enunciation within the broad legitimating cloak of US political culture. Hence, it is important to consider these in the context of the guides to presidential and administration thinking that exist in internal memoranda, private telephone conversations and discussions, captured either by recording device or in contemporaneous minutes or diaries. Memoirs can be another important, albeit more problematic, source of such personal deliberations.

This is not to deny the importance of public rhetoric, but to see merit in comparing public and private expressions of thinking wherever possible. We certainly do not see the public use of ideology in explaining and justifying foreign policy decisions as simply reducible to acts of cunning window-dressing designed to deceive (which would represent a return to the pejorative understanding of ideology). Instead we agree with Hunt that:

> Public rhetoric may seem peculiarly suspect as evidence to be taken at face value. The cynical would contend that carefully staged public appeals are occasions not for frank and nuanced expression but for cant intended to fool the gullible and mask true intentions. One might argue that rhetoric is a form of persuasion, that to treat it instead as confession would be profoundly mistaken.
>
> But such a skeptical view may be too clever by half. Public rhetoric is not simply a screen, tool, or ornament. It is also, perhaps even primarily, a form of communication, rich in symbols and mythology and closely constrained by certain rules. To be effective, public rhetoric must draw on values and concerns widely shared and easily understood by its audience . . . Interpretive naiveté may reside not in taking rhetoric seriously but rather in failing to listen carefully for its recurrent themes and values.[72]

Although Hunt's focus on the role of rhetoric and ideas in foreign policy is important, his approach focuses on historical themes and contains little mention of the concept or word 'ideology' beyond his introductory and concluding chapters. Hunt argues that three sets of ideas have been crucial to shaping American foreign policy: American greatness, a notion of racial superiority and a particularly American view of revolutions. Hunt devotes a chapter to each of these notions and provides excellent narrative histories of how these ideas have shaped and impacted American foreign policy ideas and actions. However, his three ideological drivers of American foreign policy have far more purchase on American foreign policy in the nineteenth century than the twentieth. Hence, we build here on foundations laid by Hunt by focusing on the twentieth century and examining how nationalism has combined with liberal, realist and neoconservative ideologies to shape and challenge US foreign policy from the early twentieth century to the early twenty-first. In particular, our greater focus on the Cold War period allows us to consider at length the power of anti-communism and its relationship to other core ideas in framing US foreign policy choices.

What follows is divided into seven chapters. In the next chapter we look at ideology and US foreign policy in relation to US leadership in two world wars and into the early years of the Cold War. The Truman, Eisenhower and Kennedy administrations elaborated the consensus which dominated US foreign policy thinking in the 1950s and early 1960s, on which we focus in chapter three. The following four chapters each focus largely on a single administration in charting the evolving relationship of key ideas to the conduct of US foreign policy across the later Cold War period, including the period of the 'Second' Cold War of the 1980s, and onto the radically changed post-Cold War international landscape. Across all these chapters there is a focus on the place of ideas of freedom and democracy in the making and application of American foreign policy and in shifts in emphasis with regard to these. Chapters four and five consider the place of ideas in the foreign policies of the Johnson and Nixon administrations and focus in particular on the use and meanings attached to the idea of 'freedom' in relation to Vietnam and the evolving Nixon Doctrine, incorporating one of the themes introduced by Hunt – the "perils of revolution."[73] Chapter six discusses the role of ideology in shaping the policies of Ronald Reagan and his administration in light of popular perceptions that ideology was extremely important in the beginning but less influential over time. A popular scholarly narrative is that more 'sensible' policies towards Gorbachev's Soviet Union emerged in the second term of the Reagan administration as ideology was put aside.[74] We argue that ideology in fact played a role throughout the Reagan presidency, although different ideas came to the fore at different times. Chapter seven discusses the impact of ideology on US foreign policy during the George W. Bush presidency. Here, we examine the ascendancy of neoconservative ideology and the role this played in the Bush administration's decision to go to war in Iraq in 2003. Each of these chapters is intended to demonstrate the ever-present influence of ideology on US foreign policy, addressing major questions in a manner that gives due weight to the role of ideas in the development of US foreign policy over the last hundred years. Finally, in concluding our study chapter eight considers how the analysis provided here can be extended to focus on the question of the domestic legacies of the ideological crusades that have been a characteristic of US foreign policy.

NOTES

1 Michael Freeden, *Ideology: A Very Short Introduction* (Oxford: Oxford University Press, 2003), p.2.
2 David. E. Apter, (ed.) *Ideology and Discontent* (New York: The Free Press, 1964).
3 Daniel Bell, *The End of Ideology: On the Exhaustion of Political Ideas in the Fifties* (New York: Collier Books, 1962).
4 See Hannah Arendt, *The Origins of Totalitarianism* (New York: Harvest Book, Harcourt, 1966), pp.468–473 for a Cold War-informed assertion of this idea.
5 Michael Freeden, *Ideologies and Political Theory: A Conceptual Approach* (New York: Oxford University Press, 1996), p.14. See also, Willard A. Mullins, 'On the Concept of Ideology in Political Science', *American Political Science Review*, Vol.66, No.2, 1972, pp.498–510.
6 Terry Eagleton, *Ideology: An Introduction* (London: Verso, 1991), p.3.

7 Freeden, *Ideologies and Political Theory*, p.15.
8 Freeden, *Ideology*, p.90.
9 Eagleton, *Ideology*, p.xii.
10 Freeden, *Ideology*, p.1; E. J. Dionne, *Why Americans Hate Politics* (New York: Simon and Schuster, 2004).
11 Typical of this mindset is the Realist assertion that it sees the world as it is, not as it ought to be. Erik Owens, 'Searching for an Obama Doctrine: Christian Realism and the Idealist/Realist Tension in Obama's Foreign Policy', *Journal of the Society of Christian Ethics*, Vol.32 No.2, 2012, pp.93–111.
12 Eagleton, *Ideology*, p.2.
13 One of the most obvious and open set of exchanges in American political history in this regard occurred during the 1932 presidential election contested by Roosevelt and President Herbert Hoover. Roosevelt sought to claim the term 'liberal' to mean, among other things, government assistance to the unemployed and dubbed his anti-interventionist opponent a "conservative" among other epitaphs. Hoover forcefully retorted that he was the true liberal and that Roosevelt was hijacking this proud ant-statist tradition.
14 For a discussion of the "layers of liberalism", see Michael Freeden, *Liberalism: A Very Short Introduction* (Oxford: Oxford University Press, 2015), pp.37–54. See also, Duncan Bell, 'What is Liberalism?' *Political Theory*, Vol.42, No.6, 2014, pp.682–715.
15 Freeden, *Ideology*, p.32, p.55.
16 Ibid., p.2.
17 Ibid., p.11. See also Michael Freeden, 'Stormy Relationships: Ideologies and Politics', *Journal of Political Ideologies*, Vol.3, No.1, 1998, pp.5–11.
18 Freeden, *Ideology*, pp.69–70; Gerald F. Gaus, 'Liberalism at the End of the Century', *Journal of Political Ideologies*, Vol.5, No.2, 2000, pp.179–199, at p.193.
19 Freeden, *Ideology*, p.127.
20 As Freeden argues; ". . . the main feature of ideologies is the morphological act of decontestation, of prioritizing among options, of accepting or ruling out paradigms that interpret political reality, of competing over the legitimate meanings assigned to political language, of pronouncing not on which political values are true or false, but on which conceptual combinations are available to be applied to the understanding and shaping of the political world." Freeden, *Ideologies and Political Theory*, p.551.
21 Joseph S. Nye, *Soft Power: The Means to Success in World Politics* (New York: Public Affairs, 2004). Nye uses the term ideology only three times in this book, but it is clear that his argument – namely that states can get what they want by virtue of others admiring and adopting their values and by their ability to set agendas by means of their cultural strengths - applies to some ideologies: "If a country's culture and ideology are attractive, others more willingly follow." p.10.
22 Freeden, *Ideologies and Political Theory*, p.41.
23 On state-private networks see, for example, Helen Laville and Hugh Wilford (eds.), *The US Government, Citizen Groups and the Cold War: The State-Private Networks* (Abingdon: Routledge, 2006); Scott Lucas, *Freedom's War: The American Crusade Against the Soviet Union, 1945–1956* (New York: New York University Press, 1999); and Inderjeet Parmar, 'Engineering Consent: The Carnegie Endowment for International Peace and the Mobilisation of American public Opinion, 1939–45', *Review of International Studies*, Vol.26, No.1, 2000, pp.35–48.
24 George Kennan, *American Diplomacy* (expanded ed. London: University of Chicago Press, 1984), pp.55–107; Zbigniew Brzezinski, *The Choice: Global Domination or Global Leadership* (New York: Basic Books, 2004), pp.198–209.
25 Michael H. Hunt, *Ideology and US Foreign Policy* (New Haven, CT: Yale University Press, 1987), p.xi.
26 Francis Fukuyama, *The End of History and the Last Man* (London: Hamish Hamilton, 1992), an expansion of the argument originally put forward in Francis Fukuyama, 'The End of History?' *The National Interest*, No.16, Summer 1989, pp.3–18.
27 For a collection of different perspectives on the democratic peace proposition, see Michael E. Brown, Sean M. Lynn-Jones and Steven E. Miller (eds.), *Debating the Democratic Peace* (Cambridge, MA: MIT Press, 1996).

28 George W. Bush, *The National Security Strategy of the United States of America* (Washington, DC: The White House, 2006), p.4.

29 Ibid., p.5.

30 For an analysis, see Denise M. Bostdorff, *Proclaiming the Truman Doctrine: The Cold War Call to Arms* (College Station, TX: Texas A&M University Press, 2008). Andrew Preston traces the rise of the concept of national security back to the New Deal politics of the Roosevelt administration in his 'Monsters Everywhere: A Genealogy of National Security', *Diplomatic History*, Vol.38, No.3, 2014, pp.477–500.

31 Anders Stephanson, 'Liberty or Death: The Cold War as US Ideology', in Odd Arne Westad (ed.), *Reviewing the Cold War: Approaches, Interpretations, Theory* (London: Frank Cass, 2000), pp.81–100, at p.85.

32 Daniel T. Rodgers, *Contested Truths: Keywords in American Politics Since Independence* (Cambridge, MA: Harvard University Press, 1998), p.215.

33 Ibid., p.216.

34 Ibid.

35 Ibid., p.215.

36 Emily S. Rosenberg, 'The Cold War and the Discourse of National Security', *Diplomatic History*, Vol.17, No.2, Spring 1993, p.281.

37 Peter Conrad, *Imagining America* (London: Routledge, 1980), p.3.

38 There is already an extensive literature which acknowledges the role of idealist thinking and messianic language in American foreign policy, and a great deal has been written tracing such perspectives to the origins of the country. See, for example: Walter Russell Mead, *Special Providence: American Foreign Policy and How It Changed the World*, (New York: Knopf, 2012); Robert W. Tucker and David C. Hendrickson, *Empire of Liberty: The Statecraft of Thomas Jefferson* (London: Oxford University Press, 1992); Hunt, *Ideology and US Foreign Policy* and his 'Ideology' in Michael J. Hogan and Thomas G. Paterson (eds.), *Explaining the History of American Foreign Relations* (2nd ed. Cambridge: Cambridge University Press, 2004), pp.221–240; Walter A. McDougall, *Promised Land, Crusader State: The American Encounter with the World since 1776* (New York: Houghton Mifflin Company, 1997); Anatol Lieven, *America Right or Wrong: An Anatomy of American Nationalism* (New York: Oxford University Press, 2004).

39 Nicholas Street, *The American States Acting over the Part of the Children of Israel in the Wilderness and Thereby Impeding Their Entrance into Canaan's Rest* (East Haven, 1777).

40 Herman Melville. *White-Jacket*, (New York: Harper and Brother, 1850).

41 J. Hector St. John de Crèvecœur, *Letters from an American Farmer* (New York: E. P. Dutton, 1957).

42 Anders Stephanson traces the influence of the idea of Manifest Destiny in US foreign policy in his, *Manifest Destiny: American Expansion and the Empire of Right* (New York: Hill and Wang, 1995).

43 Thomas Paine, *Common Sense*, in *The Thomas Paine Reader*, edited by Michael Foot and Isaac Kramnick (London: Penguin Books, 1987), p.109. See also, John Keane, *Tom Paine: A Political Life* (London: Bloomsbury, 1995), Ch.5.

44 Arthur M Schlesinger, Jr., *The Cycles of American History*, (New York: Houghton Mifflin, 1999), p.17.

45 Ibid.

46 G. K. Chesterton, *What I Saw in America* (San Francisco: Ignatius Press, 1990).

47 Samuel Huntington, American Politics: The Promise of Disharmony (Cambridge, MA: Harvard University Press, 1981), p.23, p.25.

48 Seymour M. Lipset, *American Exceptionalism: A Double-Edged Sword* (New York: Norton, 1996), p.18. The original quote from Hofstadter sees this as the case in America's "earlier days." Richard Hofstadter, *Anti-Intellectualism in American Life* (New York: Knopf, 1963), p.43.

49 Lipset, *American Exceptionalism*, p.19.

50 Seymour M. Lipset, 'American Exceptionalism Reaffirmed', in Byron E. Shafer (ed.), *Is America Different? A New Look at American Exceptionalism* (Oxford: Clarendon Press, 1991).

51 Albert J. Beveridge, 56th Cong., 1st sess., *Congressional Record*, 33 (9 January 1900), p.711. Available from: http://wwnorton.com/college/history/ralph/workbook/ralprs30.htm.

52 Contemporary examples of this rhetoric in American politics are easily found: in a Republican Party primary debate in 2015 candidates were asked what advice they had received

from "God." Senator Marco Rubio replied: "I believe God has blessed our country. This country has been extraordinarily blessed. And we have honored that blessing. And that's why God has continued to bless us. And he has blessed us with young men and women willing to risk their lives and sometimes die in uniform for the safety and security of our people." Governor John Kasich replied that "the lord is not picking us. But because of how we respect human rights, because that we are a good force in the world, he wants America to be strong." Jack Jenkins, 'What The GOP Candidates Meant When They Were Talking About God At Last Night's Debate', *ThinkProgress*, August 7 2015, https://thinkprogress.org/what-the-gop-candidates-meant-when-they-were-talking-about-god-at-last-nights-debate-9f557986fe91#.108f4u5aa.

53 Huntington, *American Politics*, p.154; Andrew Preston, *Sword of the Spirit, Shield of the Faith: Religion in American War and Diplomacy* (New York: Random House, 2012); Lieven, *America Right or Wrong*; John B. Judis, *The Folly of Empire: What George W. Bush Could Learn from Theodore Roosevelt and Woodrow Wilson* (New York: Scribner, 2004); Peter Singer, *The President of Good and Evil: Questioning the Ethics of George W. Bush* (New York: Plume, 2004).

54 See, Will Herberg, 'America's Civil Religion: What it is and Whence it Comes' in Russell E. Richey and Donald G. Jones (eds.), *American Civil Religion* (New York: Harper and Row, 1974); Shafer (ed.), *Is America Different?* esp. the chapter by Andrew M. Greeley, 'American Exceptionalism: The Religious Phenomenon', pp.94–115; and Robert N. Bellah, *The Broken Covenant: American Civil Religion in Time of Trial* (New York: Seabury Press, 1975).

55 This ideology, which the Republicans have often sought to (falsely) claim as their own, was represented in a particularly shrill manner by President Barack Obama's enemies who frequently questioned his commitment to American exceptionalism. In reply, time and again Obama used the liturgy of exceptionalism and providence to express his foreign policy aspirations. For example, during his 2012 Democratic Convention speech he pronounced that America keeps its, "eyes fixed on that distant horizon knowing that providence is with us and that we are surely blessed to be citizens of the greatest nation on earth"; in 2013, justifying possible intervention in Syria, he stated: "Terrible things happen across the globe, and it is beyond our means to right every wrong. But when, with modest effort and risk, we can stop children from being gassed to death, and thereby make our own children safer over the long run, I believe we should act. That's what makes America different. That's what makes us exceptional. With humility, but with resolve, let us never lose sight of that essential truth." Barack Obama, 'Remarks by the President in Address to the Nation on Syria', White House, Washington, DC, 10 September 2013, https://obamawhitehouse.archives.gov/the-press-office/2013/09/10/remarks-president-address-nation-syria.

56 Stephanson, *Manifest Destiny*, p.xiii

57 Walter Russell Mead, 'The Jacksonian Tradition', *The National Interest*, No.58, Winter 1999/2000, pp.5–29.

58 Stephanson, *Manifest Destiny*, p.xii.

59 Philip S. Bagwell and G. E. Mingay, *Britain and America: A Study of Economic Change, 1850–1939* (London: Routledge and Kegan Paul, 1970), pp.158–164; Clark C. Spence, *The Sinews of American Capitalism* (New York: Hill and Wang, 1964).

60 William E. Gladstone, 'Kin Beyond the Sea', *North American Review*, September 1878. Tocqueville in the 1840s had prophesised that American and Russia would be the great powers of the future. In the 1830s Hegel had called America the "land of the future" although because of its newness he thought it did not deserve the attention of historians or philosophers. Charles C. Verharen, '"The New World and the Dreams to Which It May Give Rise": An African and American Response to Hegel's Challenge', *Journal of Black Studies*, Vol.27, No.4, 1997, pp.456–493.

61 William T. Stead, *The Americanization of the World, or the Trend of the Twentieth Century* (New York: H. Marckley, 1902), cited in Geoffrey Barraclough, *An Introduction to Contemporary History* (London: C. A. Watts and Co, 1966), p.69, p.70.

62 Barraclough, *Contemporary History*, p.67.

63 As observed by W. Sombart, *Warum gibt es in den Vereinigten Staaten keinen Sozialismus* (Tubingen: Mohr, 1906), translated as *Why is There No Socialism in the United States?*

64 Lipset, *American Exceptionalism*; Brendon O'Connor (ed.), *Anti-Americanism: History, Causes, Themes* (4 vols. Westport, CT: Greenwood, 2007); Ziauddin Sardar and Merryl Wyn

Davies, *Why Do People Hate America?* (Cambridge: Icon Books, 2002); Lieven, *America Right or Wrong*.

65 Hunt, on describing the Fourteen Point plan, says this "consummately ideological document carried to new limits the old American commitment to an active international policy in the name of national greatness and liberty for all men. It looked forward to an era of Anglo-Saxon cultural supremacy and Anglo-American diplomatic cooperation." Hunt, *Ideology and US Foreign Policy*, p.134.

66 Lieven, *America Right or Wrong*; Michael Freeden, 'Is Nationalism a Distinct Ideology?' *Political Studies*, Vol.46, No.4, 1998, pp.748–765 at pp.748–750. Like us, Michael Hunt sees American nationalism and America's most powerful ideologies as intertwined. Hunt, *Ideology and US Foreign Policy*, p.189.

67 Those steadfastly opposed to the Treaty in the Senate like Norris, La Follette and Borah appealed to the Jeffersonian belief that: "The pursuit of greatness abroad killed reform and narrowed liberty at home." As Borah argued: "Involvement in foreign struggles and arms races would only encourage despotic and militaristic tendencies at home." Hunt, *Ideology and US Foreign Policy*, pp.135–136.

68 David Steigerwald, *Wilsonian Idealism in America* (Ithaca, NY: Cornell University Press, 1994).

69 Hunt, *Ideology and US Foreign Policy*, p.xi.

70 Ibid., p.125.

71 Ibid., p.15.

72 Ibid.

73 Ibid., Ch.4.

74 Melvyn P. Leffler, *For the Soul of Mankind: The United States, the Soviet Union, and the Cold War* (New York: Hill and Wang, 2007); Robert G. Patman, 'Reagan, Gorbachev and the Emergence of "New Political Thinking"', *Review of International Studies*, Vol. 25, No.4, 1999, pp.577–601.

2 The age of ideology in foreign policy

The twentieth century was the 'age of ideologies' because it was the age of mass politics. Most of the ideologies that dominated the period – nationalism, socialism, communism, conservatism and liberalism – were born in an earlier epoch.[1] Even fascism was synthesised from much that came before it. Every age has required explanations of the world that are able to justify decisions and promote actions. But in the twentieth century it was increasingly necessary, and possible, to conduct politics in such a way that masses of people could be mobilised in support of politicians' goals. Some of the more important dictatorships of both left and right felt this need as much as the democracies. Massively destructive wars, involving whole continents, world economic crises, civil wars and revolutions may have "destroyed rational certainties and made Europe receptive to irrational thinking" and susceptible to the appeals of the political extremes, but the age of ideologies was never identical to the age of totalitarianism and political extremism and it was certainly not confined to Europe.[2] As Bracher observes, the conditions that supported the ideological age affected the entire political spectrum. There was an unprecedented need for legitimacy, for the justification of governments, movements and policies. There also existed the means to manufacture this legitimation. Never before had political leaders had access to the multiple forms of mass communication as they did in the twentieth century. Such access was a function of mass education and literacy as well as inventions like radio or innovations like the mass circulation newspaper. The need and ability to communicate with broad masses of people encouraged simplification, but this had more significance than the function of spreading the message as far as possible. It was also a reflection of the high levels of certitude that existed among intellectuals and political activists in the early twentieth century about their ability to understand the social world and bend it to their requirements.

What has been said about 'the ideological style of politics' applies with particular force to the foreign policy of the most powerful liberal democracy of the twentieth century, that of the US. What Kedourie says has particular force in America:

> Interest, expediency, or the necessities of the case are not sufficient to justify political action . . . a constant effort must take place in order to reconcile actions with first principles . . . By means of high philosophical words rulers can better control the ruled, who are ensnared by their literacy, and obtain their active support or their passive acquiescence.[3]

High principles rather than *realpolitik* are invoked to explain and justify policy and the public is thereby socialised to judge foreign policy by the same criteria. But it is far from obvious that the politicians merely invoke these principles in bad faith.

WOODROW WILSON'S VISION

It was under Woodrow Wilson's leadership that the US entered the ideological contestation of the twentieth century on a world scale. He left a lasting impression. Wilson sought to reform the world order, no less. His ambition was to make the world anew in America's self-image. The world was to be reconstructed on the basis of independent nation-states united by liberal-democratic values and open markets. These states would be able to make and abide by global rules constructed in their own global forum. Under Wilson the US entered the Great War of 1914–1918, in its later stages, in order to 'make the world safe for democracy'. Wilson supposed the US wielded the power, moral as well as material, to stand up to both the old predatory imperialism – exemplified by authoritarian, militaristic and expansionary Germany – and the anti-capitalist extremism of the Bolsheviks. Bolshevik anti-imperialism promised to destroy the institutions and values on which America itself was founded. Liberal-capitalist values had been dominant in the US from its beginning and America's economic successes in the nineteenth and early twentieth centuries had only served to strengthen them.[4] Some thought their future health within America depended on the world being converted to the American way and, lacking a formal empire, the US had made known its preference for the 'Open Door' since John Hay's 'notes' to the Great Powers over their policies in China. The US had made efforts before 1914 to protect that principle against the incursions of imperial powers. The advocates of 'free trade' always depicted it as a universal blessing, if only vested interests would listen to reason. Wilson was of this persuasion, had made a major cut in American tariffs one of his top priorities in 1913, and took it as axiomatic that the world would benefit from a conversion to his own commitment to liberal internationalism. He never doubted that American values were of universal application for the betterment of mankind.[5]

Many liberal Europeans agreed with him by 1917, and so did those moderate socialists who led the French and British left, as well as their counterparts in Germany.[6] Wilson had popular appeal and was greeted by cheering crowds wherever he went on his brief European tour immediately after the war. In Milan, London and Manchester he delivered speeches denouncing the balance of power doctrine, militarism and imperialism and appealed directly to the labour and socialist movements.[7] On the eve of the Peace Conference Wilson made America synonymous with a programme of reforms which raised hopes across the world. He achieved this with the help of a propaganda campaign conducted with growing confidence during the period of America's neutrality. The world was put on alert, however, when America entered the First World War in April 1917 and in January 1918 Wilson outlined America's war aims in a speech to Congress. As he said on that occasion: "Not once, but again and again, we have laid our whole thought and purpose before the world, not in general terms only, but each time with sufficient definition to make it clear what sort of definitive terms of settlement necessarily spring out of them."[8] The programme of the world's peace, he said, "is our programme, and that programme, the only possible programme." It was to consist in "open covenants of peace, openly arrived at", instead of secret diplomacy; absolute freedom of the seas; and the removal of all economic barriers, bringing an equality of trade and an association of states dedicated to its maintenance. Wilson also talked about "a free, open-minded and absolutely impartial adjustment of all colonial claims, based upon a strict observance of the principle that in determining all such questions of sovereignty the interests of the populations concerned must have equal weight with the equitable claims of the government whose title is to be determined." There was to be "a general association of nations" set up "for the purpose of affording mutual guarantees of political independence and territorial integrity to great and small states alike." Whereas Lenin argued that nothing short of the socialist revolution could change the system generating imperialism and imperialist conflict, Wilson offered rational reforms to make the world more like America. His programme represented the "moral climax" of the "final war for human liberty", he said, because it offered "the principle of justice to all peoples and nationalities and their right to live on equal terms of liberty and safety with one another, whether they be strong or weak."[9]

Even before he became president, Wilson had "published and lectured extensively on the theme that the US government was not a mere series of random institutions, but a growing network of power structures that after the war of 1898 was prepared to lead the world into a glorious future."[10] Raised a Presbyterian covenanter, Wilson believed righteous nations – first and foremost the United States – held a special relationship with God. He never wavered from these views and when he began to focus American efforts to end the war, from May 1916, he used his speeches to Congress to reach the world with his vision of a future in which American self-interest and the universal values of mankind were identical. The evidence shows that he succeeded, in that he inspired support – identifying the US with "peace, liberty, and democracy" and a new world order of independent nation-states – even in the most remote corners of the globe.[11] People understood that Wilson addressed the world, rather than Europe, because much of what he stood for amounted to a critique of the Entente as well as the Central Powers. His global appeal derived from his repeated talk of the equality of nations and the importance of the consent of the governed. At this time, most of the world consisted of colonies, semi-colonies and dependent territories and Wilson's language challenged the legitimacy of this state of affairs. The fact that his views on colonial self-determination were actually much closer to the official British rationale for Empire – namely that long periods of trusteeship were necessary before many peoples could graduate to self-government – did not weaken the impact of his message. Nor did his, or the USA's, record on race, or its history of military intervention in Central America and the Caribbean. Wilson's words took flight, as powerful rhetoric often does, and distant people – people he knew nothing about – took up his words for their own purposes. But he had competition for these 'hearts and minds'.

Just after the US declaration of war, the post-Tsarist Provisional Government in Russia declared in favour of the self-determination of nations. By the time Wilson's Fourteen Points were composed the Bolsheviks had exposed the secret treaties implicating the Allied Powers in multiple, self-interested annexationist arrangements. Wilson's first explicit reference to colonies in his Fourteen Points speech has been seen as a riposte to the Bolsheviks, designed to retrieve the ideological initiative.[12] From February 1918 Wilson took up their language of 'self-determination' but gave it his own inflection, stressing democracy and government by consent as the basis of a stable post-war order, rather than the violent overthrow of imperialism projected by the Bolsheviks. Wilson's secularised preaching had the advantage because what mattered in the colonial world was the fact that the leader of the most powerful state in the world had publicly questioned the legitimacy of the existing imperial arrangements. The Bolsheviks could not compete with that.

Manela shows in his case studies of Egypt, India, Korea and China that the literate minority in the colonial world were well served by "the machinery of global communications" which, together with the US administration's propaganda agencies, delivered Wilson's rhetoric to its door.[13] It was a rhetoric that stimulated, reinforced and expanded their own political goals and led nationalists to numerous campaigns and organisational initiatives at home and overseas. Wilson's admirers in the colonial world were persuaded that America was uniquely motivated by its founding ideals, rather than imperial interests, even though it had racial and colonial issues of its own, which some of them were fully aware of. They also knew of America's origins in anti-colonial revolt and saw its subsequent progress as something to be emulated.[14] By the end of the First World War nationalist agitations had grown stronger in much of Asia and the Middle East. The failure of the Peace Congress to realise the heightened expectations of the nationalists caused disillusionment. But Wilson had permanently altered "the norms and standards of international relations", establishing the "self-determining nation-state as the only legitimate political form throughout the globe."[15] The nationalist movements did not go away, rather they took on a new momentum, with socialist and communist currents entering the ideological mix. As the Chinese nationalist Sun Yat-sen said, "Wilson's principles, once set forth, could not be recalled."[16] But there was now a struggle in which one side – the communists – argued that imperialism would only give way when compelled to do so, while the other talked of imperial trusteeships and League of Nations' mandates for the eventual self-government of dependent peoples, once the Western powers had sufficiently raised the economic and political standards of the peoples concerned under an indefinite imperial stewardship. The imperialists nevertheless were thus increasingly obliged to stress the provisional nature of their empires. Even the League's mandates system – invented and administered by the imperialist powers themselves in 1919 – implied criticism of imperialism and supported its continuance only on the new basis of a legitimacy that stressed the interests and development of the subject peoples.

Detailed examination of the League's operation, especially with the hindsight afforded by post-1945 decolonisation, suggests that the system did indeed set agendas for future imperial retreat.[17] But at the time of its adoption it was easy to depict it as imperialist 'business as usual'. By the 1930s aggressive, expansionist imperialism was in the ascendancy and the established imperial powers were confronted with both an external threat from this source and colonial movements undermining imperialism from within. Colonies, dependent territories and Dominions still represented over 77 per cent of the world's territory and contained something like 69 per cent of its population. Communists and many anti-communists alike thought they were essential to Western prosperity. Upstart imperialist powers in the shape of Nazi Germany, Fascist Italy and militarist Japan embarked on a ruthless expansion in the 1930s in demonstration of this conviction.

The Wilsonian vision of a world of liberal, economically interdependent nation-states observing the same international laws seemed remote by the end of that decade but it was a vision that some Americans still supported as an ideal. But those who turned their backs on it were in the ascendancy. The turn to isolationism, as it is often regarded, with the refusal of Congress to ratify the Treaty of Versailles in 1919, is somewhat misleading, however, given America's subsequent activities in respect of naval treaties, disarmament proposals, the Open Door in China, its dominance of the Western Hemisphere and its interventions in the management of German reparations. Nevertheless, the expansive internationalism of Wilson was certainly rejected. The ideological dominance of liberalism in the US supported more than the conviction that America set international standards for freedom and democracy; it had always been accompanied by anxieties that its special advantages could be imperilled by overseas entanglements. Anti-interventionists had often argued the latter case ever since Washington's valedictory speech in 1796 warning of "the insidious wiles of foreign influence" and the "frequent controversies" of Europe "essentially foreign to our concerns." They also expressed scepticism about the readiness of other countries to follow the American way. Opponents of Wilsonian internationalism could also argue that a largely self-sufficient America, protecting itself with tariffs and immigration controls and bounded by the world's greatest oceans, had no need of foreign alliances and extravagant overseas commitments that would certainly cost money and might consume lives and endanger American institutions. American values could spread by force of example, by means of commerce and growing economic interdependence, rather than politics. These anti-interventionist views prevailed under Presidents Harding, Coolidge and Hoover in the 1920s and early 1930s. The Wilsonian vision seemed dead in America particularly after the Smoot-Hawley tariff of 1930 raised US tariffs to levels not seen since the 1820s and other countries retaliated with tariffs of their own.

ROOSEVELT'S WORLD VIEW

Even after Hitler's accession to power in Germany in 1933, anti-interventionism continued to dominate public opinion and both Democratic and Republican parties. This remained the domestic context at the end of Franklin Roosevelt's first term as president, a term preoccupied with the domestic aspects of the Great Depression crisis. Roosevelt himself was in the Wilsonian tradition, however, and promised to lower tariffs on a bilateral basis. Having been appointed Assistant Secretary of the Navy by Wilson in 1913, in which capacity he served throughout the First World War, Roosevelt ran for the vice-presidency in 1920 on a broadly Wilsonian ticket. The return to isolationism, signalled by Warren G. Harding's landslide victory in 1920, still showed no sign of weakening in 1937 when Roosevelt, now president, made a major foreign policy address in the heart of the isolationist Midwest.[18] It was prompted by Japanese aggression in northern China (and the Neutrality Act, then recently passed by Congress). Roosevelt referred to a "reign of terror and international lawlessness" that had started some years before. His major point was that it was pure delusion to imagine that "if those things come to pass in other parts of the world . . . America will escape." It would not. There was no escape from "international anarchy, international instability . . . through mere isolation or neutrality." There was a degree of "interdependence about the modern world" which made isolation impossible, especially when political and economic upheavals were spreading, as they were in 1937. Roosevelt said: "There can be no stability or peace either within nations or between nations except under laws and moral standards adhered to by all." But the new aggression was not simply a question of broken laws and treaties, it was a question of "world economy, world security, and world humanity." The "contagion" of war was spreading, according to the President, and "quarantine" was necessary to contain the danger. Already he was talking about the world, rather than the problems of this or that region within it but for those in Europe hoping for American practical support Roosevelt's warm words seemed to be all that was on offer.

Until 1939 there was consensus in America about avoiding involvement in a European war. But there was deep division, often bitterly expressed, over domestic policy, with the Republicans opposing the New Deal as a type of socialism. It involved, they said, a

swollen Federal bureaucracy, an expansion of restrictive rules and regulations on business, increased taxes, unprecedented welfare programmes, the growth of organised labour
and an undermining of the US constitution as Federal government grew at the expense
of Congress, the states and the Supreme Court. Republican gains in the mid-term congressional elections of 1938 helped to block further reforms but Roosevelt's opponents
maintained their critique of state interventionism throughout the period of his presidency,
including the war years when an even more powerful impetus was given to the statist
forces Republicans opposed.

Though the US remained officially neutral until the Lend-Lease Act of March 1941,
no one imagined that it had any sympathies for the Axis Powers. On the day Britain and
France declared war on Germany, Roosevelt made known America's interest in "a final
peace which will eliminate, as far as possible, the continued use of force between nations"
and declared that "even a neutral has a right to take account of facts" and "cannot be
asked to close his mind or close his conscience." By the summer of 1940, with the fall of
France, it was clear to policy-makers that it was in American interests to keep Britain in
the war. Roosevelt now took up the cry of democracy imperilled, asking what the future
held, "for all peoples and all nations that have been living under democratic forms of
government – under the free institutions of a free people." These were ideals that had
been declared "decadent" by "self-chosen" leaders, advocates of force who wanted to
"overrun the earth." What did they know, he asked, of "the conception of the way of life
or the way of thought of a nation whose origins go back to Jamestown and Plymouth
Rock." Conversely, those who came from that "ancient stock" and those who had come
to America more recently, could not be indifferent "to the destruction of freedom in their
ancestral lands across the sea." Isolationists might imagine America as an island, but most
Americans, asserted the President, would find such a prospect "a helpless nightmare", a
prison no less. It was necessary to proclaim certain truths:

> Overwhelmingly we, as a nation, and this applies to all the other American nations,
> we are convinced that military and naval victory for the gods of force and hate would
> endanger the institutions of democracy in the Western World – and that equally,
> therefore, the whole of our sympathies lie with those nations that are giving their life
> blood in combat against those forces.[19]

It was an election year and soon after his victory over Wendell Willkie, Roosevelt unveiled
the scheme that would become known as Lend-Lease, at a press conference in which he
asserted the identity of national self-interest in aiding Great Britain and "the survival of
democracy as a whole in the world." Weeks later, on 29 December, in one of his 'fireside
chats', Roosevelt once more invoked Jamestown and Plymouth Rock against the Axis
Powers – three nations openly proclaiming war against the American way of life and
aiming for "world control." Survival in a world so dominated would reduce America to
a "permanently . . . militaristic power on the basis of war economy", he said. "The plain
facts are that the Nazis have proclaimed, time and again, that all other races are their
inferiors and therefore subject to their orders." Their agents were active inside America,
assisted by American citizens, "many of them in high places, who, unwittingly in most
cases, are aiding and abetting the work of these agents." There were "American appeasers" who misjudged the nature of negotiated peace with the dictators, a new order in
which "there is no liberty, no religion, no hope" – "an unholy alliance of power and pelf
to dominate and enslave the human race." And yet even now Roosevelt knew that he

could not recommend sending an American expeditionary force beyond US borders. The point was to win support for aid to Great Britain, to turn America into "the great arsenal of democracy."[20]

It was only a week later that Roosevelt delivered his State of the Union message to Congress in which he repeated the argument that America needed to maintain its rights and peaceful commerce and had fought wars in the past for these very ideals. He depicted the war raging on four continents as "armed defence of democratic existence" and warned that defeat would result in the loss of "all the resources of Europe and Asia, Africa and Australia." America's interest was in a world founded upon the four essential human freedoms: freedom of speech and expression, freedom of worship, freedom from want and freedom from fear, which meant such a reduction in armaments as to eliminate successful acts of aggression. This was no utopia but "a definite basis for a kind of world attainable in our own time and generation."[21] His third inaugural address, on 20 January 1941, was an ode to democracy and American democracy in particular, which he called the foundation of "an unlimited civilization capable of infinite progress in the improvement of human life":

> The destiny of America was proclaimed in words of prophecy spoken by our first President in his first inaugural in 1789 – words almost directed, it would seem, to this year of 1941: 'The preservation of the sacred fire of liberty and the destiny of the republican model of government are justly considered . . . deeply . . . finally, staked on the experiment intrusted to the hands of the American people.'[22]

Roosevelt had not made the war ideological, of course; its ideological character had been proclaimed by all the participants, not least the Axis Powers, and stemmed from the character of the regimes they had established in their own countries. Nevertheless, Roosevelt contributed to the construction of the war as a 'world war' well before the USA entered it, in his repeated references to the global isolation of the US, should the dictators have their way, and in his Four Freedoms rhetoric referring to the better world that could be made after the war.[23] Clearly, his arguments were designed to refute the opponents of intervention, many of whom were mobilised by the America First Committee, but they already reached out to the rest of the world. When Roosevelt and Winston Churchill met in August 1941 they issued a press release stating certain common principles which expressed "their hopes for a better future for the world." It was obviously designed to reflect the values of their own countries and to have global appeal. The Atlantic Charter, as it became known, became a statement of war aims, even though the US had not yet entered the war. It asserted that neither country sought any form of aggrandisement, territorial or otherwise; they wanted no territorial changes separate from "the freely expressed wishes of the people concerned"; they respected "the right of all peoples to choose the form of government under which they will live"; they wanted to restore "with due respect for their existing obligations" – a clause insisted upon by Churchill – "to further the enjoyment of all states. . . . of access, on equal terms, to the trade and to the raw materials of the world"; they desired "the fullest collaboration between all nations in the economic field"; that all men in all lands could live in freedom "from fear and want"; and that all men could use the seas and oceans without hindrance. They even referred to "the establishment of a wider and permanent system of general security" which might provide the basis for the "essential" disarmament of nations.[24] It was not very different from the ideals Wilson had stood for in 1917.

Roosevelt used incidents involving German U-boats to continue alerting the American people to Nazi ambitions to control the high seas and imperil American commerce. It was, he said, pure folly to imagine Nazi control of Europe coexisting with the survival of freedom in the Americas. But, perhaps to bring home the lesson more forcefully, he stressed that the Nazi fifth columns were already at work – a point repeatedly made by members of the administration in reference to the America First movement.[25] Agents and dupes of the Nazis were present throughout the Western Hemisphere, they contended. "Conspiracy has followed conspiracy", Roosevelt told his radio audience on 11 September 1941, in Bolivia, Argentina, Uruguay and Colombia – the instances could be multiplied. These were not disconnected episodes but "determined step[s] towards creating a permanent world system based on force, terror and on murder."[26] In response Charles Lindbergh, spokesman for America First, fulminated against the warmongering of "the English, the Jews and the Roosevelt government." In common with other prominent non-interventionists, such as Father Coughlin, the radio priest, Lindbergh warned of the spread of Godless communism following a Nazi defeat. But in the wake of the Japanese surprise attack on Pearl Harbor on 7 December, and after hearing Roosevelt's address to a packed joint session the following day, it took Congress just 33 minutes to declare war on Japan. By contrast, Congress had kept Woodrow Wilson waiting a week in April 1917.

Throughout the war certain themes recurred in Roosevelt's speeches.[27] The problem of being allied to the Soviet Union was not one of them. Freedom and security of property were indivisible, according to the President. The United Nations – "an association of independent peoples of equal dignity and equal importance" – was struggling for the values of the Atlantic Charter, values that applied to "the whole world." It was engaged in a struggle to save America's own "democratic civilization" for the world. The sons of the New World were "fighting to save for all mankind . . . the principles which have flourished in this new world of freedom." Once that was achieved it would be necessary to fight for the perpetuation of the same ideals. There would be no American retreat from the world when the war was over.[28] The conquered peoples liberated from fascism would be restored to the four freedoms, "choosing their own governments in accordance with the basic democratic principles."[29] America had learned, Roosevelt said in his fourth inaugural address, less than three months before he died, that it could not live alone, at peace, and that its own well-being was dependent on the well-being of other nations far away.

Until the middle of 1942, however, the news concerning the progress of the war was far from good, especially in the Far East where Japanese advances evicted the European colonial powers with apparent ease. Ever since the declaration of war against Germany on 3 September 1939 the British had been keen to project their own Empire, in propaganda designed for the USA, as essentially benign. In so far as British imperialism existed at all, it existed to guide the peoples concerned to democracy and prosperity. The British merely held trusteeships with this mission in mind. This was the established view in Britain and was not much different from the views of Woodrow Wilson and Roosevelt when it came to specific cases such as the peoples of the African Crown Colonies. There was nevertheless doubt in America about Britain's enthusiasm for decolonisation, the competence of its management of the colonies under its control, and its dealings with nationalist opinion in those countries. American scepticism was well known in London and "there was something approaching unanimity in the American public's attitude about the 'colonial question'" throughout the war. American newspapers and magazines rarely had anything favourable to report about empires, whatever their positions on other matters.[30] The British knew this and generally trod carefully. Clashes nevertheless occurred, as when

Churchill insisted on watering down a commitment to free trade in the Atlantic Charter, because of the British commitment to the system of imperial preference, as adopted in 1932. Tensions came to the fore when Churchill informed the House of Commons that the third point in the Charter did not apply to the British Empire. The right of all peoples to choose the form of government they lived under applied only to "the nations of Europe under the Nazi yoke", not the British colonies. As Churchill explained to Leo Amery, Secretary of State for India, it was not intended that "the natives of Nigeria or East Africa could by a majority vote to choose the form of Government under which they live, or the Arabs by such a vote expel the Jews from Palestine."[31] The leader of the Labour Party, Clement Attlee, a member of Churchill's War Cabinet, publicly rejected Churchill's view by telling the *Daily Herald* that the Charter embraced "coloured peoples as well as white."[32]

More to the point, Churchill's views were rejected in the US. With the Japanese military advances of early 1942 American opinion was quick to conclude that the war was going badly in the Far East at least in part because of the lack of support for the Allied cause among subject peoples, perhaps attracted by the Japanese slogan 'Asia for the Asians'. Even *The Times* correspondent in Singapore commented (18 February 1942), after the collapse of that supposedly impregnable fortress, that Britain's 120-year dominance of the region had produced no more than "a thin and brittle veneer" of imperial bonding beneath which "the vast majority of Asiatics were not sufficiently interested in the continuance of this rule to take any steps to ensure it." The refusal of the Indian National Congress (INC) to give the Allied war effort its full support underlined the problem. By June one poll showed that 56 per cent of Americans felt that the British could be described as "oppressors" because of their exploitation of their colonial possessions.[33] The INC agreed and even when the Japanese were at India's borders its leaders demanded a British commitment to independence before consenting to join the anti-fascist struggle. The majority of American newspapers sympathised with the INC position.[34] A commitment to Indian independence might make India a more effective fighting machine and send a positive message to subject peoples everywhere about the Allied cause. The Atlantic Charter had to be upheld. As early as May 1941 Cordell Hull had urged the British Ambassador to Washington, Lord Halifax, to find a settlement that would make India a "full and equal partner."[35] Hull and Sumner Welles, Roosevelt's friend and roving diplomat, had both contributed to the chorus that stressed America's commitment to a post-war settlement based on free trade, equal opportunities and a world of free and independent states. Gandhi appealed directly to the US to support India's cause. Chiang Kai-shek, America's ally in China, added his voice to the demand that India be given "real political power" in a "message to the Indian people" delivered at the height of the crisis caused by the collapse of Singapore. It was at this point that Roosevelt wrote directly to Churchill pressurising the latter to convene some sort of constitutional convention analogous to the Continental Convention of 1774. He also despatched a personal representative to India in the shape of Colonel Louis Johnson.

The rhetoric of the Atlantic Charter was thus far from 'empty'. The American press was determined that the war was not being fought to maintain the imperial *status quo ante*. As in 1917–1919 the hopes and aspirations of nationalist movements had been stimulated by the belief that American power was in favour of self-determination.[36] Pressure had been brought to bear on the British. The Atlantic Charter was 'political' and was informing both thoughts and actions. Churchill himself was happy to invoke it against Soviet demands for the recognition of the USSR's 1941 frontiers (involving incorporation of eastern Poland, the Baltic States, Bukovina, Bessarabia and the gains made in the war against Finland), as did Assistant Secretary Adolf Berle when it looked as if Britain would accede to Stalin's demands. Gandhi invoked it when he appealed to Roosevelt and Roosevelt made clear that it applied to all the peoples of the world in a speech he gave on George Washington's birthday in 1942.[37] Of course, the practical problem of fighting the war efficiently raised colonial issues to a peak in the spring of 1942 and it is arguable that they never attained the same saliency again. Public opinion in America remained supportive of Indian independence, for example, but was content by 1943 to leave the timing to the British and the post-war settlement. Sympathy for the nationalists waned somewhat after the INC refused compromise and embarked on the Quit India campaign in August 1942. Roosevelt's pressure on Churchill to relent over India probably peaked in the spring of 1942.[38]

But the Allies' stance on colonialism continued to matter to Roosevelt because, "he was convinced that the pressure of nationalism in the European empires was the most serious threat to the post-war peace."[39] Soviet Ambassador to the US Maxim Litvinov even told Stalin in June 1943 that Roosevelt was not just a staunch anti-fascist but one who expected to "benefit at the expense of the British empire."[40] There is no doubt that Roosevelt was a genuine enthusiast for self-determination and a scathing critic of colonialism, and remained so long after his interest in the Indian case waned. He engaged in an "unceasing public and private campaign aimed at eliminating the European empires and setting the colonial world on the road toward independence."[41] He held talks with nationalist leaders, he criticised the British and the French for obstructing the path to independence at presidential press conferences and he invoked places like Indochina and Gambia as instances of "plain exploitation."[42] He wanted international trusteeships and timetables for independence administered by the UN. The British rejected these proposals outright but redoubled their efforts to promote a persuasive alternative strategy. The alternative they stressed was colonial 'development'. In December 1942 a major propaganda effort was devoted to this end at the 8th conference of the Institute of Pacific Relations at Mont Tremblant in Canada, where Labour and Conservative politicians joined forces with administrators and experts such as Lord Hailey in selling colonial 'development' by the imperial power as the alternative to Roosevelt's ideas for internationally policed trusteeships.[43] The development policy was later expressed in the Colonial Development and Welfare Act (1944). By this time Roosevelt's enthusiasm for international trusteeships administered by the new international authority (the UNO) had domestic opponents too, such as the military, keen to acquire island bases in the Pacific of their own. Yet as late as March 1945, weeks before his death, Roosevelt was telling a State Department official, in words he had used before, that there were 1.1 billion "brown people" in the world "ruled by a handful of whites." The goal, he said, "must be to help them achieve their independence – 1,100,000 potential enemies are dangerous." He then added, "Churchill doesn't understand this."[44]

By 1943 between 70 and 85 per cent of Americans supported the country's post-war involvement in world affairs and opinion polls showed that the public overwhelmingly favoured some sort of League of Nations with police powers.[45] This mood for a lasting international role embraced both political parties and forced isolationism to the political margins. Roosevelt let others – like Wendell Willkie and Henry Wallace – make the running on the UN and had little of detail to say about it, possibly with Wilson's mistakes at the back of his mind. But as the United Nations took shape it was the Americans who pressed hardest for a conception of the new body as a "cultural and ideological community", while the Russians focused on security and the British stressed its role in achieving military and economic stability.[46] The Charter of the new body began with an assertion of human rights and the equality of nations and made much of its commitment to the principles of trusteeship and the development of self-government in dependent territories. The founding conference of the UN in San Francisco in fact largely ignored the issue of colonies. But it soon became apparent that Churchill was not alone in underestimating nationalism in the colonial world. As in 1919, so in 1945 Ho Chi Minh petitioned the great powers for support for Vietnamese self-determination – and was ignored again. This time a Vietnamese Declaration of Independence consciously mimicked its American forerunner: "All men are created equal; they are endowed by their Creator with certain unalienable rights; among these are Life, Liberty and the pursuit of Happiness." However, evidence of disillusionment was soon visible. Indian independence leader Jawaharlal Nehru publicly doubted that the US represented any real difference in principles from the imperial powers even as the Philippines became formally independent in July 1946 and the old empires were restored in South East Asia. American flags were burned in the Bombay and Calcutta riots of February 1946, though opinion polls showed that two-thirds of American citizens continued to favour Indian independence.[47] A period of confusion concerning American policy had opened up since the end of the war, which we will return to later.

First we should recognise that the anti-imperialism expressed so often in Washington – by Hull, Sumner Welles, Henry Wallace, Harold Ickes, Wendell Willkie and many others during the Second World War – was not confined to words. A key objective of American policy during the war was to establish a world economy based on open access to global markets and resources, a world of free trade intolerant of the protectionist practices that had come to dominate in the 1930s. The identification of open global markets as an American national interest was a clear conviction of most leading members of the Roosevelt administration. We have seen earlier expressions of it in Hay's Notes and Wilson's Fourteen Points. Roosevelt had wanted the Atlantic Charter to reflect such preferences. It has been argued that Open Door imperialism, driven by persistent expansionism, has been one of the dominant forces in American foreign policy throughout the twentieth century.[48] It was a policy with popular roots, not just because a citizen's material self-interest could be connected to the state of the world, but also because the ideal of open markets, liberal economic principles and antagonism to protectionism could be 'de-contested', as Michael Freeden would put it, by their association with ideals of democracy, freedom, self-determination and anti-imperialism – ideals deeply rooted in American political culture. Certainly, in the Second World War there is no doubt that post-war planners in Washington were persuaded that America's domestic well-being depended on a liberal, stable, rule-based, global economy. The war saw the American economy virtually double in size and it was questionable whether economic growth could be sustained and a repetition of the Great Depression avoided unless world trade could be restored on the basis of open global markets.

Zealots of free trade like Hull were convinced that America and the world would benefit if the system of imperial preference, adopted by the British at a moment of weakness in 1932, could be prised open. The sterling area which had emerged from that decision was the largest trading bloc in the world. It discriminated against nations, like the US, that were outside the imperial preference system. Hull saw the Ottawa Agreements that had set up imperial preference as "the greatest injury, in a commercial way, that has been inflicted on this country since I have been in public life."[49] He consistently campaigned for lower tariffs throughout the 1930s, and though the times were against him he could point to the Reciprocal Trade Agreements Act of 1934 as a step in the desired direction.[50] Although Hull was ignored and bypassed by Roosevelt on most matters, he was supported on this issue by Sumner Welles and State Department policy-makers such as Herbert Feis, William Phillips, Leo Pasvolsky and Stanley Hornbeck, as well as influential figures elsewhere in the administration such as Adolf Berle, Henry Morgenthau and Harry Dexter White – the last two at the Treasury. They connected free trade not only to prosperity but to world peace and stability. The inter-war crisis, on this reading, was the result of deflationary and protectionist beggar-my-neighbour policies that shrank world trade, created mass unemployment and the growth of poverty and provided the platform for fanatics and militarists advocating wars of territorial expansion. These themes connecting prosperity, peace and open markets "would become commonplace among advocates of liberalised trade" during the war.[51]

The Second World War itself was depicted as the consequence of the destructive syndrome which Hull and his co-thinkers had identified. The war also brought about America's economic recovery from the Great Depression and led to its rapid economic expansion. It enabled US planners, as the Great War had done after April 1917, to draw up plans for a new world order, one that linked American security and prosperity to open markets and international law, much as Hull had demanded since the 1930s. As American economic and military power expanded relative to all the other participants in the war, American views came to dominate discussions. The Soviet Union, by contrast, was materially devastated by the fighting, dependent on reparations and preoccupied by security on its western borders. Britain, which was dependent on American assistance from the beginning of the conflict, was the first to experience US economic ambitions. The opening of the sterling area emerged as an American objective in the Lend-Lease agreement, which Britain signed in February 1941. It came up again in the Bretton Woods negotiations of 1944 and in the negotiations for a British loan from America which the sudden cancellation of Lend-Lease prompted in 1945. Yet throughout the war the British supposed that continuation of imperial preference was essential to the national interest, as post-war economic recovery was hard to envisage in London without it.

The anti-imperialist rhetoric which accompanied these discussions between the two nations, according to the economist Roy Harrod, one of the British participants, was evidence of "current American mythology about British Imperialism" which depicted the British as clever Machiavellians, whose scheming ways always gave priority to maintenance of the Empire.[52] These suspicions were present throughout the war. A chorus of congressmen and newspaper comment could be relied upon to claim that Lend-Lease was being used to subsidise British imperial objectives. Britain was allegedly undercutting American exporters to Latin America.[53] It was, according to Roosevelt's roving personal envoy Pat Hurley, using Lend-Lease to undermine democracy and bolster imperialism in the Middle East.[54] The British were, after all, trade rivals of the US and men like Harry Dexter White and Lauchlin Currie, the *de facto* manager of the Lend-Lease programme in 1941–1943, kept this in their minds. Lend-Lease was manipulated so that Britain was unable to build up its reserves to make them adequate for post-war needs – a policy Roosevelt endorsed in January 1943.[55] The policy seems to have been based upon an inflated reading of Britain's economic strength, the Americans believing, as Harrod put it, that "Britain had shown herself a mighty Power with great economic reserves" and would have little problem reconstructing when the war was over.[56] Such wilful ignorance was many times deeper when it came to depicting Soviet strength in the late 1940s, as will become evident. But the Roosevelt administration's internationalism, hegemonic by 1945 in Congress, consistently envisaged a leading role for the US in building the post-war political order and as the war came to an end it was equally determined to reshape the global economy. It was to do so by emphasising the desirability of the Open Door, the principles of national self-determination and the institutionalisation of liberal democracy in the defeated Axis countries and those liberated from their control.[57]

GLOBAL CONFLICT RESUMED

The Soviet Union and the spread of its power into central Europe by 1945 represented a major contradiction to the professed goals of the US war effort. Roosevelt and Churchill had been forced to work with Stalin in overcoming the Axis – indeed the Soviet Union had borne by far the heaviest burden and paid the highest cost in the defeat of Nazi Germany, the Allies' top priority. Roosevelt had hoped that friendly relations with the USSR would allow it to play a leading role, along with the US, Britain and nationalist China in policing the post-war settlement. He had played down differences with Stalin to that end, ignoring Churchill's concerns about Soviet domination in Eastern Europe, especially Poland. More than that, in the war against evil the Soviet Union had been depicted in wartime propaganda as a force for good. Public ignorance of Soviet criminality in Poland, the Baltic states, Bukovina and Bessarabia in the aftermath of the Nazi invasion of Poland was virtually total, as was Western ignorance of the extent of Soviet devastation at the hands of Nazi Germany. But as victory over Hitler drew closer, suspicion and hostility towards the Soviets began to surface.

In the 1944 presidential election the Republican candidate, Thomas Dewey, attacked both New Deal institutions and Roosevelt's alleged betrayal of Poland. These issues were tied together by the argument that the administration and the Democratic Party had become the home of communists and fellow-travellers. Congressional concern about Stalin's domination of Eastern Europe and violation of the principles of the Atlantic Charter was already being expressed by Republican Senator Arthur Vandenberg, while others feared that the Yalta Accords amounted to a betrayal of that region. Nevertheless, the Declaration on Liberated Europe issued at Yalta in February 1945 ostensibly committed the Soviet Union to free elections and democratic government in the countries it liberated. But by the following month it was already clear that Stalin had ignored these principles in Romania by establishing a minority communist government there. By the end of the war the Soviet Union was the *de facto* power as far west as Berlin. Large communist Parties had emerged in Italy, France, Greece, Yugoslavia and Czechoslovakia. Communists had emerged as a force throughout Asia.

It appeared to many that the Soviet Union, having enlarged its territorial power in Europe, could not be stopped from further encroachments unless the US took a tough line. Republicans in particular argued that Roosevelt had appeased Stalin and betrayed Eastern Europe. Even with contemporary hindsight some historians maintain that Roosevelt's policies sought "the dissolution of the British Empire" and reduction of the role of France while overlooking Soviet imperialism and its effects on the balance of power in Europe.[58] Harry Truman, who became president on Roosevelt's death in office in April 1945, weighed the evidence provided by Soviet behaviour – there was very little useful intelligence on Soviet policy – and was ready to confront the Soviet Union by the beginning of 1946 over Stalin's refusal to allow free elections in Eastern Europe. Fourteen months later Truman was able to make a sweeping declaration of intent with regard to Soviet ambitions with the full support of Congress. The pretext was the need to assist Greece – plunged into civil war – and Turkey, subject of Soviet diplomatic pressures. Britain had declared its inability to continue supplying aid to both states and Truman was advised to step into the space left behind. In a speech to Congress Truman predictably, if misleadingly, talked of assistance as imperative if Greece were to survive as a "free nation." A "militant minority", exploiting human want and misery, generating political chaos, making economic recovery impossible, was threatening the "very existence of the Greek state." This "terrorist" body of "several thousand armed men, led by Communists", as Truman called the army of the Greek Left, representing at least half of the nation, would prevent Greece from becoming "a self-supporting and self-respecting democracy" – something it had never been – unless stopped now. But here was the larger point; the last war had been fought against aggressive countries "which sought to impose their will, and their way of life, upon other nations": "We shall not realize our objectives . . . unless we are willing to help free peoples to maintain their free institutions and their national integrity against aggressive movements that seek to impose upon them totalitarian regimes."[59]

The fact that Stalin showed little interest in the Greek communists or that the forces of order in Greece were far from democratic was not allowed to affect the simplicity of Truman's message. Poland, Romania and Bulgaria were examples of the violation of the Yalta agreements:

> At this present moment in world history nearly every nation must choose between alternative ways of life. The choice is too often not a free one.
>
> One way of life is based upon the will of the majority, and is distinguished by free institutions, representative government, free elections, guarantees of individual liberty, freedom of speech and religion, and freedom from political oppression.
>
> The second way of life is based upon the will of a minority forcibly imposed upon the majority. It relies upon terror and oppression, a controlled press and radio, fixed elections, and the suppression of personal freedoms.
>
> I believe that it must be the policy of the United States to support free peoples who are resisting attempted subjugation by armed minorities or by outside pressures.
>
> I believe that we must assist free peoples to work out their own destinies in their own way.[60]

In acting in this way, Truman said that the US would be giving effect to the Charter of the United Nations. Observers could see immediately that global commitments were implicit in this new ideological turn of foreign policy. The US was setting itself up for a world-wide struggle. Its opponent was defined as an alien creed and way of life imposed by minorities with the aid of a foreign power, the Soviet Union. How had it come about that this stance commanded such rising public support?

THE GROWTH OF ANTI-COMMUNISM IN AMERICA

Soviet behaviour is part of the answer as it became clear that its domination of Eastern Europe was to be long-lasting, if not permanent. In the face of this there were also clear continuities in rhetoric between Roosevelt and Truman with regard to America's mission and the sort of adversaries it faced at home and abroad. Truman's tone of urgent crisis was also a factor in stirring public opinion. John Foster Dulles once suggested that to sustain public interest in a "vigorous" foreign policy: "Mass emotion on a substantial scale is a prerequisite. The willingness to sacrifice must be engendered. A sense of peril abroad must be created."[61] General Douglas MacArthur made a similar point in retrospect, when he complained in 1957 that for ten years: "Our government has kept us in a perpetual state of fear – kept us in a continuous stampede of patriotic fervor – with the cry of grave national emergency."[62] Fear was the great mobiliser of opinion. Truman himself linked the external threat to insidious domestic subversion when he brought forward measures to scrutinise the loyalty of public officials just weeks after making the 'Containment' speech quoted previously. But anti-communism was not something that Truman had to invent. Godless communism had stimulated the fear and loathing of Christian true believers since 1917. Millions of the faithful and thousands of pulpits were ready to be mobilised. This was one reason why anti-communism had been a "hardy perennial in American politics before 1947."[63] The presidential campaign of 1944 had already provided a taste of its potential.

Fried suggests that the recurrence and potency of the Red Scare can only be explained in terms of its deep roots in "values shared by much of American society, a set of views antithetical to Communist doctrines and friendly to private property and political democracy (albeit sometimes oblivious to imperfections in the latter)."[64] As early as the 1880s, violence, anti-immigration prejudices and official repression were common features of responses to industrial conflicts in the US, as employers and politicians sought scapegoats, including foreign subversion, for the wave of discontent affecting the country. Much of the organised left was destroyed in the process.[65] Individual militants were often kept under surveillance in the mining and heavy industrial districts and towns and had to cope with the attentions of vigilantes, private security firms, far right organisations and zealous police forces. The First World War multiplied the agencies and amplified the fervour of patriotic conformism. The Red Scare of 1919–1920 which followed seems to have fed off a coincidence of panics related to the Bolshevik Revolution, opposition to mass immigration, political violence associated with leftists within the US and post-war economic problems. From this fusion of fears politicians, law enforcement agencies, newspaper proprietors and business leaders concerned about organised labour could engage in productive scare-mongering, often supported by the right-wing trade unionists of the American Federation of Labor (AFL). The violation of civil liberties was one of its features. Thousands of foreign-born activists were arrested and detained for deportation and communists were rounded up.

The enduring agencies of anti-communism in American civil society were easy to identify after the First World War, when they experienced a surge in recruitment. Organisations explicitly fighting for 'one hundred per cent Americanism' included the re-founded, reinvigorated Ku Klux Klan, which added anti-union and anti-communist activities to its repertoire in the 1920s.[66] The American Legion, founded in 1919, took a similar interest in fighting the left and both organisations used violence in the cause. The police were often zealously involved in the suppression of communist-led demonstrations too, though the presence of communists was inessential, since striking workers were often treated the same way, with 18,000 of them arrested between 1934 and 1936, according to one estimate.[67] Other methods for ensuring conformity included the efforts of the Catholic Church, J. Edgar Hoover's FBI, the loyalty oaths employed by many states and the lurid reports of the Hearst newspapers, which reliably conflated communism and militant trade unionism.

The FBI was ahead of the game. As its Director, Hoover had a heightened sense of the communist danger well before the Cold War began. He stepped up the FBI's surveillance of communists from 1936, at a time when the Hearst press was calling Roosevelt "the unofficial candidate of the Comintern" and the Republican vice-presidential candidate, Frank Knox, was accusing the President of "leading us towards Moscow" with his New Deal policies.[68] From 1939, and the creation of the Hatch Act, the FBI was engaged in the screening of Federal employees. But it had no shortage of support within civil society and by the end of the Second World War it was possible to identify an organised core within the "loosely structured, but surprisingly self-conscious, network of political activists who had been working for years to drive Communism out of American life."[69] Renegade communists, AFL trade unionists and individuals with a Trotskyist background – such as the New York intellectuals[70] – brought inside knowledge to bear on the problem in the 1940s. They could speak with authority about the communists' conspiratorial methods and their unquestioning devotion to the Soviet Union. The former Trotskyists in particular were informed by a dystopian view of the Soviet Union sometimes combined with a pessimistic sense of the world as destined to go the way of totalitarianism.[71]

What counted as 'communism' or 'socialism' in the US can be gauged from the opposition to Roosevelt's New Deal on the Republican, and even the Democrat, right-wing. The profound economic depression which afflicted the US in the early 1930s was the context for popular support for more state intervention, as embodied in the New Deal. From the beginning, opponents of this programme of reforms raised the communist or 'socialistic' bogey. This had strong resonance in the Republican grassroots, especially in the small-town, isolationist strongholds of the Midwest where the 'true' American values were to be found. It probably represented the larger part of Republican activism but, once the US entered the war, it was continuously frustrated by the north-eastern internationalist wing of its own party, as well as by Roosevelt's continuing popularity. Early victories against the New Deal were few and far between. One of the first opportunities for conservatives in Congress was presented when the efficacy of the New Deal was brought into question by the recession of 1937. The momentum of reform was broken. It was in this context that a Special House Committee on Un-American Activities (HUAC) was created in 1938 under the chairmanship of Texas Congressman Martin Dies. It was originally conceived as a device for opposing the New Deal but it soon discovered that anti-communist work generated more publicity. One of its first investigations was based on the idea that industrial conflict in California was the work of communists running the Congress of Industrial Organizations (CIO). Fried observes that:

> Americans shared Dies' distaste for Reds. In a 1939 poll, a majority of respondents thought the CPUSA took orders from Russia; only 9 per cent believed it operated independently. In June 1940, during the Nazi-Soviet Pact and the CP's antiwar phase, the public wanted drastic action against Communists. Some 26 per cent would deport them; 2 per cent backed capital punishment; 3 per cent would jail or intern them; 13 per cent would 'find some way of getting rid of them'.[72]

A strike wave in 1940, motivated by attempts to gain trade union recognition and pay rises for CIO-affiliated workers, was accompanied by fears of politically inspired sabotage of armaments production in California. With the communists having decided to denounce the war in Europe as an imperialist conflict, it was seemingly credible to see their hands in anything that stopped production. Talk of 'fifth columns' became common – the Roosevelt administration employed it often enough itself as we have seen – and Hoover was able to expand the FBI and its surveillance of domestic 'subversives' with the authority of the President behind him. Those who were already concerned with communist espionage activities and the loyalty of Federal government employees thus gained allies. By 1941 HUAC had found hundreds of civil servants whose loyalties it regarded as suspect. Names on the list already included the likes of Alger Hiss and Harry Dexter White. Nor was this growing suspicion of subversion confined to HUAC. Congress passed a succession of acts – including the Foreign Agents Registration Act (1938), the Voorhis Act (1940), the Hatch Act (1939) and the Smith Act (1940) – designed to monitor politically suspect groups and individuals.

The New Deal's forward momentum was halted as the anti-communist crusade gathered momentum. Elements associated with the Republican Party, bitter enemies of the New Deal, consciously used anti-communism as a tactic to discredit New Deal reforms and drag themselves back into political contention.[73] The 1944 Republican presidential campaign deployed rhetoric that sought to conflate the New Deal and the left-wing of the CIO, with propaganda identifying Roosevelt's administration as an environment conducive to left-wing extremism. As Ambrose tells it, middle-class Old Guard Republicans "were in a mood close to desperation" when Roosevelt won a fourth term for the Democrats: "They hated FDR, but had never been able to beat him, and now they were stuck with Harry Truman for three more years."[74] Truman even talked about extending the New Deal and the regulatory system that the Republicans opposed, while the unions got bigger and more hours were lost to strikes in 1946 than in any other year in American history. Republicans persuaded themselves that the country was heading for socialism.

> Republicans all across America felt in 1946 that if there ever was a time when the end justified the means, this was it. What they aimed to do, and to some extent managed to accomplish, was to recreate the Red Scare of 1919 . . . Republicans did not hesitate to charge, in 1946, that the New Deal Democrats, if not actually Communists themselves, were leading the country to socialism at home and surrender abroad."[75]

The chairman of the Republican party, Congressman B. Carroll Reece, announced just before the election that "the choice which confronts Americans this year is between Communism and Republicanism"; Senator Hugh Butler of Nebraska declared that: "If the New Deal is still in control of the Congress after the election, it will owe that control to the Communist Party in this country."[76] This was a national *motif* of the Republican midterm campaign which saw congressional victories for obsessive anti-communists of the future like Joe McCarthy, Bill Jenner, John Bricker, Harry Cain and James Ken. It was also evident in Richard Nixon's baptism as a Republican candidate; he followed the pattern, accusing his Democratic opponent, Jerry Voorhis, of being a communist sympathiser who drew upon communist support. A similar trick had been tried against Voorhis two years earlier but had failed to unseat him from the House of Representatives. Nixon's blatant lying succeeded, however, because the atmosphere had changed thanks to "a combination of the huge number of strikes in 1946 and Russian aggression in Eastern Europe" which together "made voters far more responsive to charges that Voorhis had communist support."[77] Of the 30 newspapers in Nixon's district, 26 backed Nixon, three were neutral and one supported the hapless Voorhis (author, ironically, of the Voorhis Act of 1940, requiring registration of communists) – a balance of forces that accurately reflected Nixon's greater backing from local businesses. Nixon alleged that communists were gaining positions in virtually every department of the Federal government; that it was evidence of a conspiracy to turn America communist and lead it to a foreign policy "depriving the people of smaller nations of their freedom."[78] His success against Voorhis – a strong supporter of New Deal initiatives who had held the seat since 1936 – showed that anti-communism worked. It later took Nixon to the vice-presidency.

Less than six months after these congressional elections, with Republicans solidly in control of both houses, Truman made his speech designed to scare the public into believing the Soviet Union was a global threat to America. Then, in the same month, he demanded loyalty tests for all Federal employees – a measure clearly informed by the Republican victories. The idea that the US was faced by a world-wide communist threat, centred upon Moscow, one that could only be contained under American leadership, was the view that some of Truman's advisers had also arrived at. It was not purely for public consumption. Such experts as George Kennan, for example, believed there could be "no permanent modus vivendi" with the fanatic Soviet state, with its "elaborate and far-reaching apparatus" for the subversion of other countries.[79] Kennan's 'Long Telegram' of February 1946 was required reading in Washington – circulated by Secretary of the Navy James Forrestal among others – and its successful reception within the political class suggests that its leading personnel were not merely inclined to support a tougher foreign policy stance, but were already persuaded, as Forrestal was, of the Soviet Union's ideologically driven behaviour.

Kennan argued that communist doctrine envisaged "no permanent peaceful coexistence" between the USSR and the capitalist West.[80] From this was deduced the lesson that Moscow ruthlessly pursued everything that could be done to strengthen the relative position of the USSR. Soviet methods and tactics had "sacrificed every single ethical value" in the name of Marxism. This dogma was all the more important in consequence of that sacrifice. According to Kennan it was the essential "fig leaf of their moral and intellectual respectability." Today Moscow tried to advance its power in northern Iran and Turkey, tomorrow it might be somewhere else, as opportunities arose:

> Toward colonial areas and backward or dependent peoples, Soviet policy, even on official plane, will be directed toward weakening of power and influence and contacts of advanced Western nations, on the theory that insofar as this policy is successful, there will be created a vacuum which will favour Communist-Soviet penetration.

In international economic matters the Soviets would pursue "autarchy" for both themselves and for Soviet-dominated adjacent areas. Foreign communist parties were run by an inner core closely co-ordinated "as an underground directorate of world communism, a concealed Comintern." The rank and file was thrust forward "as bona fide internal partisans of certain political tendencies genuinely innocent of conspiratorial connection with foreign states." Where the communists were weak and few in number, "they are used to penetrate, and to influence or dominate, as the case may be, other organisations less likely to be suspected of being tools of Soviet government." A wide variety of such organisations could be so deployed including "racial societies", religious groups, liberal magazines and publishing houses as well as the institutions of the labour movement. Governments and governing groups like Bulgaria, the North Persian regime and the Chinese communists put their policies, as well as their propaganda, at the disposal of Moscow. This "far-flung apparatus" would be used to disrupt, to exacerbate division and unrest, and "to stimulate all forms of disunity." A "particularly violent" effort would be made to "weaken the power and influence of Western powers over colonial, backward, or dependent peoples." Soviet puppets would be prepared to take over these countries once independence was achieved. In short, according to Kennan:

> we have here a political force committed fanatically to the belief that with the US there can be no permanent modus vivendi, that it is desirable and necessary that the internal harmony of our society be disrupted, our traditional way of life be destroyed, the international authority of our state be broken, if Soviet power is to be secure.

This was a versatile machine with global reach, "impervious to logic of reason" but "highly sensitive to [the] logic of force."

The fact that this was widely hailed as a lucid and cogent analysis speaks volumes about the pitch of anti-communism that had already been reached among Truman's leading colleagues by the beginning of 1946, let alone their Republican opponents. Kennan made no mention of the devastation of the Soviet Union in his 1946 despatches, the tens of millions of dead and maimed, the ruined cities and infrastructure, the return of hunger and overcrowding – or of the fear of Germany that obsessed the Soviet leaders and fixed their minds on Eastern Europe as a question of security, rather than the supposed ideological ambitions of communist theory. Kennan knew about the crippled state of the Soviet economy and also of the Kremlin's anxieties about national security. He made much of them in other contexts.[81] But he compounded the impression created by the Long Telegram by feeding Secretary of Defense James Forrestal – a visceral anti-Communist in any case – with more analyses of the same sort and then anonymously placed a new article with *Foreign Affairs* under the title 'The Sources of Soviet Conduct', where it was predictably interpreted as official US policy. A month after the Long Telegram, Frank Roberts of the British embassy in Moscow, and a friend of Kennan's, supplied three long despatches to the British Foreign Secretary Ernest Bevin pointing to the same conclusions but with the novel spin that the Soviets had special reasons to detest "a social democratic Britain." Roberts, like Kennan, also expressed more nuanced thoughts about future relations with the Soviet Union and accepted that it faced terrible problems of reconstruction. But, like Kennan, he kept such complications out of the advice tendered to policy-makers in the spring of 1946. Instead his despatches emphasised the Soviet threat. Both analysts were quick to deduce that any Soviet successes – in say Persian Azerbaijan – would have profound knock-on effects and lead to falling regimes across entire regions.

Versions of Kennan's argument later achieved prominence in mass circulation journals such as *Reader's Digest* (October 1947). The effect, to use his own words, was "sensational", a fact which he later ascribed to "the subjective state of readiness" of the Washington political elite, "influenced more by domestic-political moods and institutional interests than by any theoretical considerations of our international position."[82] The public, like the politicians, were exposed to theories of Moscow's quest for world domination. Greece, Turkey, Iran, Italy and France were named as its immediate targets when Dean Acheson spoke to congressional leaders on 27 February 1947 at the White

House, to prepare them for Truman's announcements on Greece and Turkey. He later recalled the gist of his talk:

> Like apples in a barrel infected by one rotten one, the corruption of Greece would infect Iran and all to the east. It would also carry infection to Africa through Asia Minor and Egypt, and to Europe through Italy and France . . . The Soviet Union was playing one of the greatest gambles in history at minimal cost . . . We and we alone were in a position to break up the play.[83]

Senator Vandenberg, by now Chairman of the Senate Foreign Relations Committee and a leading 'internationalist' within the Republican Party, assured Truman, "if you will say that to Congress and the country, I will support you and believe that most of its members will do the same."[84] Public support would require that Truman "scare hell out of the American people", Vandenberg advised.[85] And so he did. The talk in Washington was now of approaching war as the Russian juggernaut rolled westwards but there were already voices in Congress pointing to the East by sounding the alert in relation to civil war China. Criticism of Chiang Kai-shek was the work of communists and fellow-travellers inside America, according to Congressman Walter Judd, while the purpose of the Chinese communists was "to make Russia overwhelmingly the strongest power in Asia as well as Europe."[86] If Containment applied to Europe, why not to Asia too? This was a question Republicans made much of after October 1949.

The communist coup in Czechoslovakia in February 1948 was construed not as a defensive reaction to the Marshall Plan in a country with a mass communist party (and 38 per cent of the vote), but as confirmation of a pattern of unrepresentative groups seizing power under Soviet direction, as in Romania, Bulgaria and Poland. It was a presidential election year in the US and the connections continued to be made linking the domestic and international threats of communism to US national security. High profile trials of communists, alleged communists and communist spies assisted the process, so did prolonged industrial unrest, which was blamed on the Communist Party of the USA (CPUSA). If one's opponent could be depicted as insufficiently realistic, tough-minded and vigilant about the nature of this communist threat it was certainly to be used against him. Thus, Truman denounced Henry Wallace and the Progressive Party on all these counts in the presidential campaign of 1948. The public was invited to believe that with Western Europe on the brink of economic collapse, and Turkey and Greece imperilled by communist subversion, it was the US that had to defend democracy and freedom. Meanwhile communism was increasingly associated with criminality, conspiracy and deception, as well as the subversion of innocent countries. Republicans focused on the internal communist threat in 1948 to such an extent that China was rarely mentioned by campaigners. It was easier to score points this way. Doing something about China would cost a great deal of money and men and there was no sign that Republicans like Robert Taft were eager to spend them. But, confronted by Chiang's headlong retreat, even the *New York Times* (1 November 1948) took the view that: "Manchuria is being taken over by a Russian fifth column in a pattern of conquest which bears startling resemblance to Japan's own pattern."[87]

The Alger Hiss trial continued to stoke up fears of communist infiltration of the Federal government as 1948 came to an end. Chiang Kai-shek's position in China had already begun to look hopeless that year, before Dean Acheson took over from General George C. Marshall as Secretary of State in January 1949. Yet everyone had assumed that it was in America's gift to so manage China that it would conform to American requirements. This was still the view expressed in the *China White Paper* prepared at Acheson's request in the summer of 1949.[88] In September Truman announced that the Soviet Union possessed atomic bombs. By this time a communist victory was sealed in China. A ready explanation of Mao's ascent was now heard from all sides over the next five or six years – not only from Richard Nixon but also John F. Kennedy, not from just 'the primitives', but also from the man who had baptised them – the new Secretary of State, who advised that "Communism is the most subtle instrument of Soviet foreign policy that has ever been devised, and it is really the spearhead of Russian imperialism."[89] This was the line now repeated in Congress by 'the primitives', by the *New York Times*, *Collier's*, *Time*, *Life*, the Republican leader Thomas E. Dewey and many others. While Mao was merely the instrument of Stalin, according to this argument, his staunch opponent Chiang had been betrayed by the Truman administration which had withheld military aid at a crucial moment to facilitate the Truman-Marshall plan for reconciling Chiang with his communist enemies. Acheson, Kennan and the US Ambassador to the UN, Philip C. Jessup, all seemed to accept at least part of this argument because they all spoke of the communist revolution in China as an act of Soviet imperialism. They did this despite intelligence demonstrating that Stalin's support for Mao had been lukewarm at best.[90] Their view was soon to become the dominant view. For some Republican anti-communists the list of individuals who had sold out China included Generals Stilwell and Marshall, as well as State Department officials like John Paton Davies and John Stewart Service.

From October 1949, the communists under Mao Zedong formed the sole authoritative government of China, excluding Formosa, Hong Kong, Kowloon and Macao and Outer Mongolia. The British officially recognised this state of affairs diplomatically in January 1950. But in the US the great hue and cry that the Democrats had 'lost China' dominated public debate. Having lionised Chiang Kai-shek as a great leader and democrat, a true representative of China, a country destined to share in the policing of the post-war world, alongside the US, Britain and the Soviet Union, many Americans suddenly found that China had been taken out of the US orbit altogether and many were at a loss to explain why. Truman had tried to negotiate a deal between Chiang and the communists when General Marshall was sent to China in December 1945 and, as we mentioned, Marshall had recommended suspension of military aid to the Kuomintang to facilitate his 'honest broker' role. Even though Congress renewed such aid in February 1948 some Republicans blamed Chiang's defeat on Marshall. State Department officials who insisted that Mao's victory was related to his strength within large swathes of the Chinese peasantry were regarded as politically suspect in the same circles. All of this became evidence of a conspiracy to sell out China to the communists and those who had been saying this for some years – such as Alfred Kohlberg, a businessman with links to China – were now taken very seriously. Evidence of actual espionage – as supplied by the *Amerasia* affair, the Alger Hiss trial, the Judith Coplon case of 1949 and its 1950 sequel – was given massive publicity.[91]

The Soviet Union had thus entered public consciousness as a ruthless, ideologically driven, totalitarian aggressor, bent on world domination. Although all states in practice can invoke *raison d'état* and suspend ordinary moral precepts when it suits them, the Soviet state, on this reading, was uniquely evil. At its service was a monolithic and obedient communist movement, none the weaker for Stalin's decision to terminate the Communist International in 1943. This communist movement was often treated, as we have seen in relation to the CPUSA, as a fifth column – or series of fifth columns – devoid of real roots in the political cultures and histories of the countries concerned. It was rather an artificial implant owing its survival to external Soviet finance and instruction, an explanation of communism that perhaps derived credibility in America from the marginal state of the CPUSA. In some variants, slightly more sophisticated than the fifth column theory, as formulated in the early 1950s, communism was identified as a political religion, driven by chiliastic fervour to slaughter real people in a quest for human perfectibility. This at least recognised that the communists could have genuine mass support. Its roots could be found, on this reading, in the revolutionary tradition since Rousseau and the French Revolution of 1789.[92] In this analysis ideology itself was of course tainted and one of the claims of right-thinking intellectuals was about the wholesomeness of an anti-ideological disposition. Ideology was equated with closed doctrine imperviousness to evidence. Democratic politics in the West, fortunately, according to such thinkers, was becoming un-ideological.[93] Parties agreed on fundamentals such as the value of mixed economies, class antagonisms had softened and major divisions in society had been overcome or were in the process of disappearing. The values and methods worth celebrating, according to such arguments, were those of piecemeal reform, recognition of human fallibility, the limits of reason, the limitations of democracy and the inevitability of elites and interest groups – ideas strongly associated with conservatism, in fact, rather than liberalism, but now assimilated into what was becoming a Cold War liberalism. Thus, as America entered into ideological battle with communism, leading American ideologues declared that ideology was on the brink of extinction in mainstream American politics.

In reality, ideology was more important than ever. One aspect of this was emphasised by a report on American policy in South East Asia, which the National Security Council (NSC) received in March 1949. This recognised that "19th century imperialism is no longer a practicable system in SEA [South East Asia]."[94] People were becoming more politically sophisticated, more nationalistic, they would not acquiesce in the old arrangements. In South East Asia 'colonial imperialism' was up against militant nationalism:

> In such circumstances to attempt evasion of an obvious ideological issue is (1) objectively, to yield much of the field of conflict to our adversaries, and (2) subjectively, to subvert our own ideological integrity – that is, to deny consciously the heritage and philosophic concepts which are inner reasons that we are, for all our shortcomings, not only great but good, and therefore a dynamic force in the mind of the world.[95]

As the report concluded, "19th century imperialism is no antidote to Communism in revolutionary colonial areas. It is rather an ideal culture for the breeding of the Communist virus. The satisfaction of militant nationalism is the first essential requirement for resistance to Stalinism."[96] The authors might have added that the civil war in China was shaping up to illustrate the dangers, with the communists successfully emerging as bearers of national aspirations. But, as we have seen, the first instinct of leading politicians and their advisers was to deny that the communists were 'true' nationalists. When the communists took over it was politically impossible to extend diplomatic recognition. A Soviet fifth column had imposed itself on the country, according to the Truman administration and its Republican opponents, and the real nationalists had been pushed off the mainland into Formosa.

Only three months after Mao proclaimed the People's Republic of China, Truman commissioned a re-examination of US objectives in peace and war in the light of the probable fission bomb capability and possible thermo-nuclear bomb capability of the Soviet Union.

The report was delivered in April 1950 as NSC-68, drafted by Paul Nitze, Kennan's successor as Director of Policy Planning for the State Department and regarded by Acheson, his boss, as more of a hard-liner than Kennan and thus more in tune with the Secretary of State. It began by depicting the Soviet Union as a singular aspirant to "hegemony" animated by "a new fanatic faith, antithetical to our own", determined "to impose its absolute authority over the rest of the world."[97] Conflict was now "endemic" and being waged by the Soviet Union "by violent or non-violent methods" in accordance with what was expedient. Any substantial further extension of "the area under domination of the Kremlin" would run the risk of permanently strengthening its hand. What was at stake involved "the fulfilment or destruction not only of this Republic but of civilization itself."

Whereas the "fundamental purpose" of the US was to create conditions under which its free and democratic system could live and prosper, the fundamental design of the international communist movement was to retain and solidify the absolute power of those who controlled the Soviet Union. This latter design "calls for the complete subversion or forcible destruction of the machinery of government and structure of society in the countries of the non-Soviet world and their replacement by an apparatus and structure subservient to and controlled from the Kremlin. To that end Soviet efforts are now directed toward the domination of the Eurasian land mass."[98] The only peace the Soviet Union desired "is the peace of total conformity to Soviet policy." The assault on free institutions was world-wide and "a defeat of free institutions anywhere is a defeat everywhere." America had to "lead in building a successfully functioning political and economic system in the free world . . . by practical affirmation, abroad as well as at home, of our essential values":

> In a shrinking world . . . it is not an adequate objective merely to seek to check the Kremlin design, for the absence of order among nations is becoming less and less tolerable. This fact imposes on us, in our own interests, the responsibility of world leadership. It demands that we make the attempt, and accept the risks inherent in it, to bring about order and justice by means consistent with the principles of freedom and democracy . . . we must with our allies and former subject peoples seek to create a world society base on the principle of consent.[99]

There could be "no lasting abatement of the crisis unless and until a change occurs in the nature of the Soviet system." In the meantime, "at the ideological or psychological level, in the struggle for men's minds, the conflict is world-wide." Even military victory, though war might be necessary, was no adequate substitute for ideological struggle. The policy of Containment involved blocking further Soviet expansion, but also exposing "the falsities of Soviet pretensions", inducing "a retraction of the Kremlin's control and influence" and fostering "the seeds of destruction within the Soviet system" itself. A superior military strength was essential so that this policy was not seen as mere bluff and Nitze recommended "a more rapid build-up of political, economic, and military strength." He also argued that "dynamic steps" should be taken "to reduce the power and influence of the Kremlin inside the Soviet Union and other areas under its control." Such action would engage its attention, keep it off balance and "force an increased expenditure of Soviet resources in counteractions." The outlook Nitze presented was of a Soviet Union which in four or five years would be able to deliver a surprise atomic attack. He proposed an "affirmative program" beyond the solely defensive one of countering the Soviet threat but warned that: "The whole success of the proposed program hangs ultimately on recognition by this Government, the American people, and all free peoples, that the cold war is in fact a real war in which the survival of the free world is at stake."[100]

PROBLEMS OF ANALYSIS AND POLICY

NSC-68 was a defining document, one that framed the conflict as global "in almost purely ideological terms."[101] Even before the North Korean invasion of South Korea in June 1950 American thinking had arrived at certain conclusions which were difficult to turn into consistent policy. In the first place was the knowledge that the old imperialism had been weakened by the Second World War and had lost legitimacy even in the West. There was no doubt that a nationalist tide was sweeping across Asia and would soon affect even the most backward territories. Roosevelt had expressed this view many times. Decolonisation was to be supported and British withdrawal from India, Pakistan, Burma and Ceylon was on this reasoning to be applauded because it strengthened the West's case as the defender of progress against the darkness of communist totalitarianism. The Netherlands was pressurised by Washington into coming to terms with the nationalists in the Dutch East Indies (Indonesia) for the same reason. But America had acquired island bases of its own as a direct result of the war and the military leaders who were keen to retain those bases could also see that the restoration of European imperial control could act as a barrier to the spread of communism. The very fact of the Soviet domination of Eastern Europe was enough to identify a problem in the balance of power, to the Soviets' advantage. The emergence of mass communist parties in Europe and Asia held out the prospect of a further deterioration on top of that brought about by the success of Mao's armies in 1949. Mao's triumph was explained more in terms of betrayal, espionage and Soviet interference than anything that the Chinese might have wanted or done. It could not be admitted that communists held genuinely nationalist views or had the interests of the nation at heart or represented the nation in any way. But since communists often worked under cover and through the manipulation of 'useful idiots' and fellow-travellers, the way was clear to regarding non-communists in the same light, especially if they refused to regard communists as the main problem. The US was thus for self-determination and decolonisation but not if it left communists in charge – the danger in Malaya and Indochina – or forces working with communists, as in Greece, or even those indifferent to America's Cold War objectives, as in much of the Middle East, or actively seeking a policy of neutrality.

After the Prague Coup in February 1948 a Gallup poll had shown that 77 per cent of Americans were persuaded that the Soviet Union was seeking to be "the ruling power of the world."[102] This mood accurately reflected the publicly expressed concerns among the policy-making elite that the Soviets were working to a grand design, something like the one that most people thought Hitler had had. The authors of NSC-68 reflected and reinforced those convictions within the Washington elite. In doing so they credited Soviet foreign policy with a coherence, and even an idealism, which it never possessed. They also overestimated the Soviet Union's military capability to take over places like Western Europe and the Middle East and to deliver nuclear attacks in North America itself. NSC-68 intended to militarise the American response to this malevolent communist design and to provide such a persuasive rationale for rearmament that it would not only convince Truman but also enable him to convince Congress. It adopted a Manichean image of a struggle between good and evil, ignoring the divisions in the communist world and glossing over the reality of the 'free world' in which the ideal of liberal democracy was actually a rarity. Nitze admitted some of this many years later.[103] Events in Korea later made rearmament on the imagined scale possible, but NSC-68 provided the lens through which the North Korean offensive was interpreted as an item in a bigger global offensive for Soviet world domination. NSC-68 thus succeeded because it accurately summed up what was already the dominant way of looking at the Soviet problem in Washington. Thus, when communists came to power in China, well before NSC-68 was composed, many people who might have known better interpreted the event as an extension of the Soviet empire.

█ NOTES

1 See John Schwarzmantel, *The Age of Ideology: Political Ideologies from the American Revolution to Post-Modern Times* (London: Macmillan, 1998).
2 Karl Dietrich Bracher, *The Age of Ideologies: A History of Political Thought in the Twentieth Century* (London: Methuen, 1985), p.3.
3 Elie Kedourie, *Nationalism* (3rd ed. London: Hutchinson, 1966), p.50.
4 See Louis Hartz, *The Liberal Tradition in America* (New York: Harcourt, Brace, 1955).
5 See N. Gordon Levin, Jr., *Woodrow Wilson and World Politics: America's Response to War and Revolution* (Oxford: Oxford University Press, 1968).
6 See John Callaghan, *The Labour Party and Foreign Policy* (London: Routledge, 2007) and Massimo Salvadori, *Karl Kautsky and the Socialist Revolution, 1880–1938* (London: NLB, 1979), pp.181–218.
7 Thomas J. Knock, *To End All Wars: Woodrow Wilson and the Quest for a New World Order* (Princeton, NJ: Princeton University Press, 1992), pp.196–197.
8 Woodrow Wilson, Speech to Congress, 8 January 1918, in Richard Maidment and Michael Dawson (eds.), *The United States in the Twentieth Century: Key Documents* (London: Hodder and Stoughton, 1994), p.258.
9 Ibid.
10 Walter LaFeber, *Inevitable Revolutions: The United States in Central America* (2nd ed. New York: Norton, 1993), p.51.
11 This relies on Erez Manela, *The Wilsonian Moment: Self-Determination and the International Origins of Anticolonial Nationalism* (Oxford: Oxford University Press, 2007), p.21.
12 Arno J. Mayer, *Wilson versus Lenin: Political Origins of the New Diplomacy, 1917–1918* (New York: Vintage Books, 1970), pp.341–344.
13 Manela, *The Wilsonian Moment*, pp.45–52.
14 Ibid., pp.64, 77, 90, 91–2, 219.
15 Ibid., p.5.
16 Quoted in ibid., p.216.
17 See Michael D. Callahan, *Mandates and Empire: The League of Nations and Africa, 1914–1931* (Brighton: Sussex Academic Press, 2008) and *A Sacred Trust: The League of Nations and Africa, 1929–1946* (Brighton: Sussex Academic Press, 2004).
18 John Grafton (ed.), *Franklin Delano Roosevelt: Great Speeches* (New York: Dover Publications, 1999), pp.63–68.
19 Franklin Roosevelt, Speech in Charlottesville, 10 June 1940, in ibid., pp.72–77.
20 Ibid., pp.82–91.
21 Roosevelt, State of the Union Message, 6 January 1941, ibid., pp.92–100.
22 Ibid., p.104.
23 See on this, David Reynolds, 'The Origins of the "Second World War"' in his *From World War to Cold War: Churchill, Roosevelt and the International History of the 1940s* (Oxford: Oxford University Press, 2006), pp.9–23.
24 'The Atlantic Charter', in Maidment and Dawson (eds.), *Key Documents*, p.266.
25 See, Sarah Churchwell, *Behold, America: A History of America First and the American Dream* (London: Bloomsbury, 2018), Chs.12–13.

26 Roosevelt, Fireside Chat, 11 September 1941, ibid., pp.105–112.
27 http://millercenter.org/scripps/archive/speeches.
28 Roosevelt, Fireside Chat, 12 October 1942, ibid.
29 Roosevelt, Fireside Chat, 28 July 1943, ibid.
30 Lloyd Gardner, 'FDR and the Colonial Question', in David B. Woolmer, Warren F. Kimball and David Reynolds (eds.), *FDR's World: War, Peace, and Legacies* (New York: Palgrave, 2008), p.123.
31 Quoted in Clive Ponting, *Churchill*, (London: Sinclair-Stevenson, 1994), pp.535–536.
32 Norman Rose, *Churchill: An Unruly Life* (London: Simon & Schuster, 1994), p.288.
33 Quoted in Christopher G. Thorne, *Allies of a Kind: The United States, Britain and the War Against Japan, 1941–1945* (Oxford: Oxford University Press, 1978), p.209.
34 Gary Hess, *America Encounters India, 1941–1947* (Baltimore, MD: Johns Hopkins University Press, 1971), pp.18–19.
35 Ibid., p.23.
36 On this point see Frank Furedi, *Colonial Wars and the Politics of Third World Nationalism* (London: I. B. Tauris, 1994), pp. 72–73 and David Reynolds, 'Roosevelt, Churchill and the Wartime Anglo-American Alliance' in Wm. Roger Louis and Hedley Bull (eds.), *The Special Relationship: Anglo-American Relations since 1945* (Oxford: Clarendon Press, 1989), p.18.
37 Lloyd C. Gardner, *Economic Aspects of New Deal Diplomacy* (Madison, WI: University of Wisconsin Press, 1964), pp.177, 184.
38 Hess, *America Encounters India*, p.128; Thorne, *Allies of a Kind*, pp.242–243, argues that the peak of Roosevelt's pressure on Churchill over India was in the spring of 1942.
39 Warren F. Kimball, *Forged in War: Roosevelt, Churchill and the Second World War* (New York: Morrow, 1997), p.301.
40 Amos Perlmutter, *FDR and Stalin: A Not So Grand Alliance, 1943–1945* (Columbia, MO: University of Missouri Press, 1993), pp.90–91 and 231–246, where the full report can be found.
41 Warren F. Kimball, *The Juggler: Franklin Roosevelt as Wartime Statesman* (Princeton: NJ: Princeton University Press, 1991), p.127.
42 Ibid., p.144.
43 Wm. Roger Louis, *Imperialism at Bay, 1941–45* (Oxford: Oxford University Press, 1977), pp.212, 15–17, 464; Thorne, *Allies of a Kind*, pp.212–214.
44 Quoted in Hess, *America Encounters India*, p.155.
45 Cited in Colin Dueck, *Hard Line: The Republican Party and US Foreign Policy Since World War II* (Princeton, NJ: Princeton University Press, 2010), pp.59–60.
46 See Paul Kennedy, *The Parliament of Man: The United Nations and the Quest for World Government* (London: Allen Lane, 2006), p.32.
47 Hess, *America Encounters India*, pp.167–172.
48 Notably, William Appleman Williams, *The Tragedy of American Diplomacy* (New York: Norton, 1959); also Walter LaFeber, *The New Empire: Interpretation of American Expansion, 1860–1898* (Ithaca, NY: Cornell University Press, 1963); Lloyd C. Gardner, *Economic Aspects of New Deal Diplomacy*; and Marilyn Young, *The Rhetoric of Empire: American China Policy 1895–1901* (Cambridge, MA: Harvard University Press, 1969); Andrew Bacevich, *American Empire: The Realities and Consequences of US Diplomacy* (Cambridge, MA: Harvard University Press, 2002).
49 Quoted in Tony Smith, *America's Mission: The United States and the Worldwide Struggle for Democracy in the Twentieth Century* (Princeton, NJ: Princeton University Press, 1994), p.125.
50 See Irwin F. Gellman, *Secret Affairs: FDR, Cordell Hull and Sumner Welles* (New York: Enigma Books, 1995) for useful ideological portraits of Hull and his colleagues.
51 Michael A. Butler, *Cautious Visionary: Cordell Hull and Trade Reform, 1933–1937* (London: Kent State University Press, 1998), p.10.
52 Roy Harrod, *The Life of John Maynard Keynes* (London: Macmillan, 1951), pp.539, 558.
53 Robert Skidelsky, *John Maynard Keynes: Fighting for Britain, 1937–1946* (London: Macmillan, 2000), p.123.
54 Gardner, *Economic Aspects*, p.177.
55 Skidelsky, *John Maynard Keynes*, p.305, 322.
56 Harrod, *Life of John Maynard Keynes*, p.598.
57 Stephen Gill, *American Hegemony and the Trilateral Commission* (Cambridge: Cambridge University Press, 1990).

58 Perlmutter, *FDR and Stalin*.
59 President Harry Truman, 12 March 1947, in Maidment and Dawson (eds.), *Key Documents*, pp.269–272.
60 Ibid., p.271.
61 John Foster Dulles, *War, Peace and Change* (London: Macmillan, 1939), p.90.
62 Quoted in Lewis McCarroll Purifoy, *Harry Truman's China Policy: McCarthyism and the Diplomacy of Hysteria, 1947–1951* (New York: New Viewpoints, 1976), p.ix.
63 Richard M. Fried, *Nightmare in Red: The McCarthy Era in Perspective* (New York: Oxford University Press, 1990), p.vii.
64 Ibid., p.9. See also William Preston, *Aliens and Dissenters: Federal Suppression of Radicals, 1903–1933* (2nd ed. Chicago, IL: University of Illinois Press, 1994).
65 See Robert Justin Goldstein, *Political Repression in Modern America from 1870 to the Present* (Cambridge, MA: Schenkman, 1978).
66 Wyn Craig Wade, *The Fiery Cross: The Ku Klux Klan in America* (New York: Oxford University Press, 1987), Chs.4–7; David J. Chalmers, *Hooded Americanism: The History of the Ku Klux Klan* (3rd ed. Durham, NC: Duke University Press, 1987).
67 Goldstein, *Political Repression in Modern America*, p.66.
68 Ellen Schrecker, *Many are the Crimes: McCarthyism in America* (Princeton, NJ: Princeton University Press, 1998), p.90.
69 Ibid, p.xv.
70 Philip Rahv, William Phillips and others associated with the *Partisan Review*.
71 As in the writings of James Burnham.
72 Fried, *Nightmare in Red*, p.49.
73 Robert Griffith, *The Politics of Fear: Joseph R. McCarthy and the Senate* (Lexington, KY: University Press of Kentucky, 1970); Michael Rogin, *The Intellectuals and McCarthy: The Radical Specter* (Cambridge, MA: MIT Press, 1967).
74 Stephen Ambrose, *Nixon: The Education of a Politician, 1913–62* (London: Simon & Schuster, 1987), p.119.
75 Ibid., pp.128–129.
76 Quoted in David Halberstam, *The Coldest Winter: America and the Korean War* (London: Macmillan, 2008), p.174, 248.
77 Ambrose, *Nixon*, p.130.
78 Ibid., pp.136–137.
79 George F. Kennan, telegram, 22 February 1946, Part 5. This, the so-called 'Long Telegram' can be seen at www.gwu.edu/~nsarchiv/coldwar/documents/episode-1/kennan.htm.
80 George F. Kennan, Telegraphic Message of February 22nd 1946, Appendix C of George F. Kennan, *Memoirs, 1925–1950* (New York: Pantheon Books, 1967), pp.547–559.
81 Kennan, *Memoirs*, pp.393, 402; David Mayers, *George Kennan and the Dilemmas of US Foreign Policy* (Oxford: Oxford University Press, 1988), pp.105–106, 109–110, 120.
82 Kennan, *Memoirs*, p.295, 351, 403.
83 Dean Acheson, *Present at the Creation: My Years in the State Department* (New York: Norton, 1969), p.219.
84 Ibid.
85 Cited in Stephen E. Ambrose, *Rise to Globalism: American Foreign Policy Since 1938* (7th revised ed. London: Penguin, 1993), p.82.
86 Quoted in Purifoy, *Harry Truman's China Policy*, p.53.
87 Ibid., p.101.
88 US Department of State, *United States Relations with China with Special Reference to the Period 1944–1949*, introduction by Lyman P. Van Slyke (Stanford, CA: Stanford University Press, 1967).
89 State Department Bulletin, XXII, January 23 1950, p.114, quoted in Purifoy, pp.112–113. See also Acheson, *Present at the Creation*, p.356.
90 Purifoy, *Harry Truman's China Policy*, pp.134–139.
91 See Joseph Keeley, *The China Lobby Man: The Story of Alfred Kohlberg* (New York: Arlington House, 1969), p.91, 157.
92 Arendt, *The Origins of Totalitarianism*, pp.460–479. See also J. L. Talmon, *The Rise of Totalitarian Democracy* (New York: Beacon Press, 1952) and his *Utopianism and Politics* (London: Conservative Political Centre, 1957); Isiah Berlin, 'Russian Populism' (1960) in his *Russian Thinkers* (London: Penguin, 1994), p.217.

93 Edward Shils, 'The End of Ideology', *Encounter*, November 1955; Daniel Bell, *The End of Ideology* (London: Macmillan, 1960).
94 NSC-51, 'US Policy Towards Southeast Asia', 1 July 1949, cited in Odd Arne Westad, *The Global Cold War* (Cambridge: Cambridge University Press, 2005), pp.113–114.
95 Quoted in ibid., p.113.
96 Ibid., p.114.
97 National Security Council Paper 68, April 1950, in Maidment and Dawson (eds.), *Key Documents*, pp.279–298, 282.
98 Ibid., p.283.
99 Ibid., p.286.
100 Ibid., p.298.
101 Halberstam, *The Coldest Winter*, p.201.
102 Ernest R. May (ed.), *American Cold War Strategy: Interpreting NSC 68* (Boston, MA: Bedford Books, 1993), pp.2–3.
103 See his contribution to ibid., pp.104–105.

3 Anti-communism fixed

This chapter analyses the influence of anti-communism on the foreign policies of the Truman, Eisenhower and Kennedy administrations. Like many 'anti' ideologies, the anti-communism of this period lacked subtlety and nuance with a resultant negative impact on US foreign policy. 'Anti' ideologies generally exist as forms of out-and-out opposition. The climate of political fear that McCarthyism fuelled saw US anti-communism develop into a very rigid set of beliefs which endorsed 'hard-line' responses to most foreign policy dilemmas. Candidates and politicians sought to avoid any suggestion of being 'soft on communism', often at the cost of more measured and prudent foreign policy. Democrats were particularly vulnerable to such claims as they had already been blamed for the compromises of the Yalta summit, the 'loss' of Eastern Europe to the USSR and the 'loss' of China to the communist forces. With these accusations unsettling Democrats and with the anti-communist narrative gathering pace, Democrats tended to overcompensate. The results were increasingly bi-polar reactions to foreign conflicts: the US felt compelled to back a local protagonist in civil wars around the world, even when these protagonists regularly violated core American values that were being rhetorically promoted by Truman and Eisenhower. Such reactions reflect just how bold and simplistic the ideology of anti-communism was in the early Cold War era. The Kennedy administration was at its inception more aware than its predecessors that America was undermining its anti-colonial and freedom-promoting credentials in the Third World and promised to do more to alleviate poverty and hardship there; however, it was ultimately trapped by its own relationship with hard-line anti-communist rhetoric which it had stoked domestically for electoral purposes.

McCARTHY SHOWS THE WAY

Though the Truman administration had taken an aggressive stance against the Soviet Union since 1946 it was increasingly under attack from its domestic opponents in 1950 for being insufficiently anti-communist. Many of Truman's enemies were visceral opponents of the New Deal, which Truman talked about extending; they were unhappy about his military commitments to Western Europe and neglect of Asia; and, above all, they were deeply bitter that this 'accidental president' had extended the Democratic stranglehold on the White House. The charge that Truman was 'soft on communism' was one of the sticks with which to beat the administration and that fostered the perception that too many New Deal Democrats were themselves crypto-socialists. Dean Acheson offered a gift to this lobby when he refused to denounce Alger Hiss after the latter's conviction for perjury in January 1950. Just 15 days later the junior senator from Wisconsin, the Republican Joe McCarthy, picked out Acheson for attack. McCarthy provided much the most effective Republican demagogy, smearing the Truman administration and enjoying the support of most of his party, as long as the opinion polls supplied evidence of his popularity. He announced his discovery of anti-communism at Wheeling, West Virginia, by telling his audience that America was engaged in "the final, all-out battle between communistic atheism and Christianity."[1] The odds of victory, he said, had shifted in favour of the communists; "we see each day this country losing on every front", he asserted. It was the result of the "traitorous actions of those who have been treated so well by this Nation." He said this was "glaringly true in the State Department. There the bright young men who are born with silver spoons in their mouths have been worst." McCarthy picked out two for special mention: the diplomat John Service, who had allegedly backed the Chinese communists rather than Chiang Kai-shek, and Acheson, a "pompous diplomat in striped pants", who had protected Service and others accused of treason such as Hiss. The centrepiece of McCarthy's speech, was the claim that the senator had the names of 57 communists currently working in the US Foreign Service. Representative of these people was Hiss himself, whom Acheson had once vouched for, and whose conviction for perjury Truman had dismissed as a "red herring". Hiss, McCarthy told his audience, had played a leading role at Yalta drafting the conference report with senior Soviet diplomat Andrei Gromyko on such matters as Poland, Romania, Bulgaria and Hungary. The inference was clear.

These were the opening shots in a campaign that would only end when McCarthy's hunt for traitors extended to the army, and public opinion turned against him in the summer of 1954. In the meantime, McCarthy was one of those who made the running on anti-communism before congressional committees, in the press and to mass television audiences. The national mood became more receptive to McCarthy's basic case – which insisted that America had been weakened from within – when the Korean War began with the North Korean invasion of the South on 25 June 1950. It was now recalled, for example, that Acheson had made a speech in January of that year announcing that Korea was outside the "defensive perimeter" of the United States – thus giving the green light, it was said, for a communist takeover. Against the background of NSC-68 and the thinking that it now reflected in Washington, together with the furore generated by the 'loss' of China, the communist invasion of the Republic of Korea was seen as another example of Soviet expansionism and the denial of national self-determination, rather than evidence that self-determination could be violent and might involve civil war, as it had in the case of the US itself. In August 1950, for example, in the pages of the State Department *Bulletin* John Foster Dulles depicted the North Korean invasion of the South as the fruit of a Moscow-based plot.[2] Truman's decision to intervene – taken without reference to Congress – was justified as the logical extension of Containment, on the grounds that the Soviet Union had passed over to open forms of aggression. In Washington Korea was viewed through the lens of Munich. As Halberstam points out: "The immediate belief of the people gathering around the president in Washington was that the invasion was a direct Moscow move, ordered by Stalin and obeyed by his proxies in North Korea." That was not true, in fact, since the driving force was Kim Il-Sung. But "at that moment, the administration's Soviet experts considered North Korea simply a Soviet satellite." The suspicion was that the invasion was also a feint; an attack on Taiwan, Iran or Western Europe might come next, and might be the main prize. Recommendations of military aid programmes to the French in Indochina and the government of the Philippines – both engaged in wars against communist-led forces – were among the first responses to news of the invasion.[3] Truman's political enemies in Washington immediately linked the Korean problem with the 'loss' of China, with Senator Styles Bridges demanding to know of the Senate "will we continue appeasement?" Others linked the crisis to the Alger Hiss case in the same debate on 26 June 1950. On the 27th the US obtained a UN mandate for the use of American ground troops and on the 30th Truman approved their use.

Acheson explained that the US (and wider UN) response was all about upholding collective security and the ideals of the Four Freedoms, the Atlantic Charter and the United Nations – these "represented the ideas which our people felt in their hearts were worth fighting for." Korea had helped to seal the dubious but powerful idea of the communist world as a monolith ruled from Moscow; it also made the case for massive rearmament much better than NSC-68 could; and it poisoned domestic politics in the US, where politicians remained terrified long afterwards of being blamed for 'losing' a country to communism. It also functioned to consolidate Mao's control of China and reinforced all the foundation myths of the Maoist state, but most American politicians were either ignorant of this or indifferent to its consequences. As Purifoy says, American thinking about foreign affairs "had been completely ideologized by the McCarthyites", though this had been achieved with the essential assistance of the Truman administration. Even victims of communist smears, such as Owen Lattimore and Henry Wallace, joined in the rush to support the Korean intervention.[4] None of this restrained McCarthy, who continued to attack the 'Red Dean', Acheson, and all those who had sold out China. In fact, given what prominent members of the administration had told the public repeatedly about the relationship between China and the Soviet Union, hard-line critics could complain that it was irrational and insufficient to fight in Korea while ignoring the main threats – China and the Soviet Union themselves. North Korea was simply a tool of the Chinese communists who themselves were controlled from Moscow – as Truman explained to British Prime Minister Clement Attlee.[5]

Right-wingers – Democrat and Republican alike – argued that America had already lost much of what it had fought the war for, including the principles of the Atlantic Charter, the Four Freedoms, the independence of China and greater national and global security. They were further angered when Truman dismissed his insubordinate commander in Korea, General MacArthur, in April 1951. MacArthur had adorned the cover of *Life* magazine no fewer than seven times by July 1950. The right-wing of the Republican Party regarded him as one of their own. By January 1951 it seemed that MacArthur wanted a bigger war, telling British journalists that he was fighting for a "free Asia".[6] Only a failure of will stood in the way of a proper war with China that would bring lasting victory and break the stalemate. MacArthur's sacking brought a chorus of criticism on Truman from the usual sources – *Time*, Nixon and the Republican right-wing – seemingly backed by the huge crowds that greeted the General upon his return to the US. He addressed a joint session of Congress telling how he wanted to unleash Chiang's forces on Mao from Taiwan. But the MacArthur hearings, which began in May 1951, subjected the General's views to closer scrutiny, and exposed the weakness in his case. He turned out not to be the Republican saviour he was originally cast as.

The Senate Armed Services and Foreign Relations Committees devoted eight weeks to joint hearings investigating MacArthur's case. At the end of the hearings no official report was issued but a group of Republican members produced one of their own, accusing the State Department of losing China by withholding effective aid from the Kuomintang and of employing actively pro-communist elements in leading official and advisory positions. US aid to the Kuomintang, according to the same argument, had been relatively miserly, certainly compared to the help from America received by the Soviet Union during the war against the Nazis. It also came with strings attached – conditions not applied to Moscow, such as holding elections, combating corruption and increasing efficiency. In these accounts, Chiang Kai-shek, the long-suffering victim of such admonitions, was forced into the final humiliation in 1945 by being told to work with the communists in a future government. His refusal to do so had occasioned the aid embargo of August 1946 to May 1947 – the crucial period, it was now said, in which the communists seized the initiative. Meanwhile voices warning of the spread of Soviet influence in China – such as General Wedemeyer, who was sent to China in 1947 by Truman – were stifled or suppressed (in Wedemeyer's case by General George C. Marshall), the critics claimed. Truman made his own contribution to the communist success by issuing the executive order on 18 August 1946 which had the effect of preventing nationalists from acquiring US weapons.[7]

The fusing of fears about internal subversion and Soviet imperialism in the public mind – reflected in polls showing strong support for McCarthy – was not just the work of events. Sensational trials of communists and spies, the shocking news about China, the Soviet development of an atomic bomb and the communist invasion of South Korea – these were certainly all examples of raw material that could worked upon, but they had to be interpreted as evidence of a communist plot for world domination based in Moscow. The facts did not speak for themselves on this occasion more than they did on any other. The dominant interpretive theory of Soviet behaviour was, however, already treated as an established fact and reported as such in the news media. The Truman administration itself had given its authority to the theory of a worldwide communist conspiracy and instituted measures to contain it, while rooting out subversives at home under the Federal Employee Loyalty Program. It had established these positions as axioms of the political centre and left-of-centre. In so doing it had prepared public opinion, reinforcing those aspects of American political culture hostile to Federal government and all varieties of socialism. The fact that McCarthy could credibly attack Acheson, Truman, Ambassador Philip Jessup, General Marshall and other anti-communists as dupes of communism – "pied pipers of the Politburo" no less, in the case of Acheson and Jessup – is an indication of this. But if the Republican strategy was to turn anti-communism against their political rivals by focusing on its domestic dimensions inside the Truman administration, the Democrats were able to compete as paragons of anti-communism by stressing the global tentacles of the main threat – the Soviet Union. This, after all, was the argument that they had pioneered. Even before the Korean War and the advent of McCarthy, authoritative sources such as the *New York Times* ran articles predicting that the next places to fall to communism in the Far East would include the small countries of Indochina, where local leaders like Ho Chi Minh were merely agents of Moscow.[8] Within weeks of McCarthy's Wheeling speech, Acheson concocted the most simplistic account of how communism triumphed in China for the State Department *Bulletin*, according to which indoctrinated Chinese leaders returned from Moscow as agents of the Soviet regime.[9] Well before the Korean War the dictatorship of Syngman Rhee in South Korea had been transformed into a test case for the defence of democracy, as Acheson told the Senate Foreign Relations Committee on 7 March 1950. According to the same argument it was also imperative to bolster the countries of Indochina as communist-free zones, as Acheson raised the spectre of communist expansion throughout the region as far as Malaya and India.

McCarthy did not work alone and critics of the Truman administration were not confined to the Republican Party. The Senate Internal Security Subcommittee, known as the McCarran Committee, was created and chaired by one of the few congressional Democrats who completely opposed the New Deal, Senator Pat McCarran of Nevada. It concluded its investigations into the Institute for Pacific Relations (IPR) – an international NGO suspected of communist sympathies – in 1952 by arguing that: "The shaping of United States policy with respect to China was a factor in the success of Communism in that land, in the establishment of firm roots for Soviet influence in all Asia, and in the subsequent ordeal through which United States boys are being taken in Korea."[10] This report also found the IPR to be a largely lobbying and propaganda organisation, hiding behind a scholarly façade, disseminating its treasonous ideas to influential people and through the armed forces and the infant United Nations. At least since the 1930s, according to McCarran, "the net effect of the IPR activities on United States public opinion has been pro-Communist and pro-Soviet . . . such as to serve international Communist, Chinese Communist, and Soviet interests, and to subvert the interests of the United States'.[11] Owen Lattimore, a scholar of Central Asia, was said to have served these ends in his capacity as adviser to Chiang Kai-shek in 1941 and, on his return to Washington in February 1942, as special adviser to Roosevelt on Far Eastern affairs. But the anti-Kuomintang faction, according to this evidence, also included General Stilwell, John Davies and Vice-President Henry Wallace, as well as suspected communists such as Harry Dexter White, Alger Hiss and Lauchlin Currie. Truman, argued McCarran, adopted the fateful policies towards the Kuomintang in December 1945 because of arguments put by Lattimore and friends of his such as John Carter Vincent, the head of the Far Eastern Office of the State Department. It was in pursuance of that policy that General Marshall was sent to China in the same month and, according to McCarran, the initiative that was held by the nationalists was lost. Chiang's failure to comply with US demands led to the withholding of military assistance, while the Russians armed their communist allies to the teeth. Not content, the State Department and Truman were poised to recognise Red China, and disown the nationalists on Formosa, according to their critics, when the Korean War broke out and discredited the whole policy.[12] Eisenhower's victory in the presidential election of 1952 meant, according to conservative supporters of this analysis, like William F. Buckley, that Acheson was "chased out of public life . . . as the symbol of a futile, epicene anti-Communism, to make way, we were assured, for a vigorous, purposive, clearheaded anti-Communism."[13]

Republican activists were making the most of their opportunities to undermine the New Deal Democrats by attacking them where they were vulnerable. Some of McCarthy's supporters within the political elite of the Republican Party calculated that he offered "a way back to national power after twenty years in the political wilderness."[14] Others – like Eisenhower – feared that to attack McCarthy would endanger the unity of the party. While these motives persisted, McCarthyism functioned also as an attack by one section of the political elite – primarily its Republican section – against another, the Democrats, rather than as a populist revolt against the entire political class. McCarthy's power derived from fears about communism, Korea and the Cold War. But polling evidence from the early 1950s showed that fear of communism was "generally more salient among those who already voted conservative" and "far more salient to the conservative elite – from precinct workers to national politicians – than to the mass of voters." It was this elite which structured otherwise disorganised attitudes among the voters to produce the ideology associated with McCarthy – composed of authoritarianism, isolationism, ethnocentrism, political intolerance and a 'get-tough' foreign policy.[15] For the voters in the 1952 presidential election it was foreign policy – not domestic subversion – that was the salient issue concerning communism; the more concerned the voter was about foreign policy the more likely they were to support the Republicans. The stress of McCarthy and his most prominent supporters on internal subversion had little popular resonance at this point. It was the Korean War that now mattered to the public. But the political elite only turned against McCarthy when he began to attack a Republican administration and such bastions of the establishment as the army, the Senate and General George Marshall. By this time popular fears over foreign policy had been allayed by the truce in Korea.

When the elite turned against McCarthy he was effectively finished.[16] But 'McCarthyism' survived the Senator's demise in important ways. Much of the radical left had been demobilised, dispersed and demoralised by the anti-communist campaigns of the decade after 1944, its organisations wound up and its campaigning issues discredited or forgotten.[17] The anti-communist flood had assisted the passage and acceptance of the Taft-Hartley Act of 1947, which permanently weakened the unions. Anti-communism strengthened the defenders of the racial status quo in the South in the 1950s and helped to preserve the region from labour organisations.[18] The left was destroyed and fear also silenced liberal critics of the anti-communist consensus. The State Department was purged of many of its East Asia experts. Those who survived the witch-hunt tended to conform to the Cold War consensus rather than question it. Conformism required its adherents to fight communism, rather than muddy the waters with analyses of the peoples, cultures and histories of the countries in which it had gained popular support. Understanding the revolutionary processes that were often involved in Asia was superfluous to requirements.[19] Officials who departed from the anti-communist mission could have their reports suppressed before they came to the attention of decision-makers, while politicians were only too aware of the political consequences of appearing to be 'soft' on communism.[20]

'Moderate' Republicans take over

The Korean War turned NSC-68 into unquestioned truth and realised its demands for a massive increase in military expenditure. While Truman had capped defence spending at US$13.5 billion as late as May 1950, it reached US$48.4 billion in 1951 and US$50.4 billion in 1953. Few questioned its reasoning and assumptions. George Kennan, however, now opposed the military build-up logic of NSC-68 on the grounds that it misread Soviet intentions, presented the communist world as a monolith controlled by Moscow, would lead to militarisation of American foreign policy and begin an arms race. In his heavily revised view, traditional Russian fears guided Moscow's policy, not global ambitions. There would be no Soviet invasion of Western Europe or lasting unity between Moscow and Peking – national rivalries would see to that. But Kennan had not said these things in the Long Telegram or in his anonymous 'The Sources of Soviet Conduct' article. He was frozen out as a policy adviser by 1948, as his second thoughts became more insistent; he was wordy and contradictory and now stood for an approach that had become politically impossible in the febrile atmosphere he himself had helped to generate.[21]

The issue of China in particular "would hang over . . . the Democratic Party for the next two political generations."[22] China provided the lens through which Korea was viewed and the Republicans had used China as dazzling proof of internal subversion.

China had been sentimentalised and romanticised to such an extent during the Second World War that a large domestic constituency had invested emotionally in the idea of a free democratic China under Chiang. Immense amounts of American aid had been spent on the nationalists. Half a million nationalist troops had been airlifted from south-western China in 1945 to assist Chiang in directing the Japanese surrender, before the communists could do it in his place. Acheson's China White Paper told the documentary history of this aid so well that Mao himself invoked it as evidence of America's enduring enmity to his regime. Henry Luce, publisher of *Life* and *Time* magazines, the most important publisher of the period, puffed up Chiang and China throughout the war. The loss of China, according to General MacArthur, whose views were also broadcast by *Life*, imperilled America itself. Someone had to be blamed for this disaster and the Republicans blamed the Democrats

The Republican Party chose the popular Eisenhower, rather than Robert Taft, to fight the 1952 presidential election. Eisenhower's campaign formula – K1C2 – referred to the Korean War, plus corruption in government, and communism. He said he would go to Korea, and the voters understood this to mean he would end the war. His rival for the Republican nomination, Taft, lacked tact and 'personality' and had none of Eisenhower's ability to radiate warmth and honesty and to generate trust among the voters. Eisenhower came across as an honest man and of course he carried great prestige because of his war record. Many thought of him as being above politics because of his military background. Yet the General had carefully prepared for the presidency while routinely denying he had any interest in it. He cultivated big business and leading companies nurtured him. One series of stag parties for 'Ike' organised by New York investment banker Edward Bermingham involved a list of companies that "read like excerpts from lists of *Fortune*'s annual 500".[23] Morris argues that Eisenhower's "shadow promoters were to be historically important not only in sculpting his views – increasingly conservative and orthodox in domestic affairs alongside a Russophobic internationalism – but also to reinforce the conviction he carried into the ring" as a candidate for the nomination.[24] Like Taft he called the New Deal 'socialistic'. He came out as an enemy of waste, inflation, excessive spending and taxation, of big government, corruption and dishonesty. He spoke portentously about self-avowed liberals who in fact worked "unceasingly" for ideas that would take America "one more step toward total socialism, just beyond which lies dictatorship."[25] One of his biographers, Stephen Ambrose, says that "his emphasis on Yalta and China was exactly what the uncommitted . . . wanted to hear . . . [and] set the tone for the campaign that followed."[26] Eisenhower denounced Yalta and blamed Truman for losing China and being soft on domestic corruption. Once he won the nomination he moved quickly to further accommodate the Republican Old Guard. One of his devices for doing this was to select Richard Nixon as his vice-presidential running mate

He first met Nixon in Paris in May 1951 shortly after the latter had given a widely reported speech boasting of MacArthur's "personal victory" over Truman, despite the recent dismissal of the General. Nixon and Eisenhower found themselves in agreement about the need not only for military preponderance at home and abroad but also to commit huge amounts of additional money and resources to combating the Soviet threat. Nixon went home from that meeting telling everyone that the 1952 election was the last chance for power for the Republicans and that the election would be won only by a programme that emphasised "winning the ideological war with communism" on a scale hitherto unimagined.[27]

Nixon's credentials as a running mate included the fact that he was from the West, had congressional experience (in both the House and the Senate), spoke effectively and complemented Eisenhower's age with his youth. He supported NATO and the Marshall Plan, which suited Eisenhower, but was also popular with the Republican right-wing because of the way he had conducted his anti-communism. Nixon's central message was repeated scores of times. He blamed Truman for the loss of 100 million people a year to communism over the previous seven years and claimed that it was immaterial if the cause was incompetence or the "questionable loyalty" of policy-makers.[28] Nixon still wanted all-out war in Korea, which meant taking the war into China and unleashing Chiang's forces from Taiwan. He said stalemate was unacceptable, while an armistice could only mean "appeasement" – a word that now meant rotten compromise with sworn enemies. Eisenhower introduced Nixon to the Republican National Convention as "a man who has a very special talent and ability to ferret out any kind of subversive influence wherever it may be found and the strength and persistence to get rid of it."[29] He used that talent during the campaign, labelling Democrat candidate Adlai Stevenson a "PhD graduate of Dean Acheson's cowardly college of Communist containment."

Eisenhower also reassured the militant faithful by accepting the party platform, much of it written by John Foster Dulles. It was, as Ambrose says "an extreme right-wing document".[30] It said that the Democrats had shielded traitors to the nation in high places. It wanted to repudiate all commitments contained in secret understandings such as those of Yalta, which allegedly aided the communist enslavement of Eastern Europe. It denounced Containment as "negative, futile and immoral" on the grounds that it abandoned countless human beings to a "despotism and godless terrorism". And it held out the prospect of genuine independence for the "captive people". In his acceptance of the Republican nomination Eisenhower affirmed his intention to lead the "crusade" that was needed to achieve these objectives. Nevertheless, he liked to see himself as being above the demagoguery of McCarthyism. But then he not only had Nixon to keep up this end of things, he had John Foster Dulles too, a man he leaned upon not only for shaping foreign and military policies, but also for communicating them to the world – despite the fact that privately he thought Dulles lacked the capacity to understand how his words and manner affected other people.[31]

Dulles, who became Eisenhower's Secretary of State, had been virtually born into foreign policy. His grandfather, John Watson Foster, Secretary of State under Benjamin Harrison, took him to the second Hague Conference in May 1907 and gave him a job as secretary to the Chinese delegation. He was taught by Woodrow Wilson at Princeton and went to Versailles in 1919 as legal counsel to the American delegation, drafting parts of the reparations document. After Wilson's retirement Dulles turned to making money, which he combined with a continuous interest in global financial and diplomatic issues. His firm – Sullivan and Cromwell – assumed that a close relationship existed between these matters, as was illustrated in the Dawes (1924) and Young Plans (1929) for the rescheduling of German reparations payments, which Dulles had a hand in formulating. He was active in the Council on Foreign Relations too, contributed to *Foreign Affairs* and even developed his own theory of international relations in *War, Peace and Change* (1937). Dulles believed in God and the free market. God supplied a moral framework for the respect of individual life and social order. Missionary work could spread these virtues abroad and provide the basis for a United Nations of the future. America represented the model economy that the rest of the world aspired to and would need to adopt if it was to keep up with the pace of progress. *War, Peace, and Change* also recognised the inevitable conflict of selfish desires between the satisfied and dissatisfied parts of the international system. International relations were all about the clash between forces content with their material and status position and those that were not. These forces – respectively static and dynamic – periodically went to war with one another. Global economic expansion, in Dulles' view, could help to keep war at bay by increasing the size of the material wealth that was to be shared out. Free markets promoted this objective of wealth-making better than any economic alternative.[32] But Dulles also believed that Christianity could supply the moral foundations of enduring peace. The "six pillars of peace" which he outlined in *War, Peace and Change* followed Wilsonian principles and included multilateral free trade, flexible treaties that could adapt to changing conditions, guarantees for the self-determination of subject peoples, the regulation and control of arms and military establishments, and recognition of the right of all people to religious and intellectual freedom.

As an unabashed nationalist and moralist Dulles was fond of invoking Manifest Destiny, the 'American Dream' and the equation of American self-interest with the rights of mankind as a whole, something that he believed earned for America "the good-will of people everywhere". His speeches in the 1940s were littered with these sentiments. In 1944 Dulles drafted a statement on foreign policy, at Senator Vandenberg's request, which was designed to appeal to both wings of the Republican Party. It stressed America's global responsibilities while defending sovereign rights and self-government.[33] It attacked Roosevelt's foreign policy for promoting "the rankest form of imperialism" by seeking to "subject the nations of the world, great and small, permanently to the coercive power of the four nations holding the [Dumbarton Oaks] conference."[34] Dulles was appointed adviser to the US delegation at the UN in San Francisco in April 1945, evidence of his appeal to both party elites, despite the inflated 'anti-imperialist' rhetoric of the previous year. During the Truman administration he served as special adviser to the Secretary of State and Ambassador-at-Large and attended ten conferences of foreign ministers and UN General Assemblies.[35] As the Cold War unfolded it was inevitable that he would draw the contrast between the moral mission of the US to promote liberty and justice in the world (while not deviating from its true national self-interest) and the Godless pandemonium spreading out from Moscow. There could be no genuine reconciliation of "our faith with that now held by the Soviet leadership", he told *Life* in 1946.[36] His nationalism became increasingly strident and was of course calculated to appeal to the biases of the American political culture in which he was deeply rooted. Only the United States could save the world from evil while relentlessly pursuing its self-interest and those who could not or would not see this were moral inferiors, when not mischievous and wicked enemies of the light.[37]

By February 1946 Dulles was publicly attributing Soviet behaviour to its ideologically driven hostility to the West. He agreed with the Containment policies of Kennan and Truman and did all he could to persuade the Republican Party of the need for Marshall Aid and NATO. In 1948 he talked about the Soviets' lack of moral restraint and their fanaticism. By 1950 he was publicly criticising Truman's foreign policy for inattention to the Third World, and Asia in particular, thus chiming in with the Republican right-wing. Defence of the status quo was no longer enough. A *jihad* was necessary. His inter-war theory, after all, said that the most dynamic must prevail. The Soviets posed as champions of freedom, national self-determination and progress, while the West was tarred with colonialism.[38] Here was an obvious liability. The Korean War was evidence for Dulles of "a single pattern of violence planned and plotted for twenty-five years and finally brought to a consummation of fighting and disorder" throughout Asia, as he told Dean Acheson and Senator Taft at the end of November 1950.[39] In the same memorandum he talked about a counteroffensive using subversion and paramilitary interventions. As Hoopes points out, Dulles' thinking "reflected an inflated estimate of Chinese and Russian power in Asia and of Chinese-Russian policy coordination, and gave too little weight to the thrust of dynamic local forces determined to change the status quo in the name of anti-colonialism, self-determination, or a better economic deal."[40] But these errors were dominant themes of anti-communist rhetoric in the US, as we have seen, and remained so for the next 20 years, whether we look at the press, the political class or the public. Nor was Dulles alone in wanting an active fight-back, a sentiment that was rooted, he believed, in a "national impulse" that was magnified by General McArthur's defiance of Truman's relative restraint in the conduct of the Korean War.

Containment required patience and commitment to the long-run, with the implication of high costs and, in the light of NSC-68 and Korea, global fronts and possible over-extension of American resources. The Korean conflict had given credibility to the alarmists – not only McCarthy but anti-communist intellectuals like James Burnham who had been warning of relentless communist expansionism for ten years. MacArthur had used the publicity generated by his own dismissal to reinforce the view that the enemy was 'communism' – an ideology that had to be stamped out wherever it raised its head. Dulles opportunely joined this chorus to emerge in 1952 as one of the champions of the anti-communist crusade. Truman's approval rating at 23 per cent was the lowest on record when Eisenhower announced his candidacy for the presidency. In May 1952 Dulles published 'A Policy of Boldness' in *Life* – an early draft of which had already been sent to Eisenhower. Soviet Russia's "long-term strategy of encirclement and strangulation" had prompted, according to the article, the current costly response that threatened to warp the American way of life. A "dozen people in the Kremlin were already attempting to rule 800 million people" while plotting to conquer more. Defence against their multi-million armies, along a 20,000 mile front was only possible using nuclear weapons. Dulles advocated a policy of instant, massive retaliation using nuclear weapons to respond to aggression by "Red Armies". He also asserted "three truths". First, "the dynamic prevails over the static; the active over the passive". Second, "nonmaterial forces are more powerful than those that are merely material. Our dynamism has always been moral and intellectual rather than military or material." Third,

> there is a moral or natural law not made by man which determines right and wrong and in the long run only those who conform to that law will escape disaster. This law has been trampled by the Soviet rulers, and for that violation they can and should be made to pay. This will happen when we ourselves keep faith with that law in our practical decisions of policy.

In a classic use of ideological precepts to present the Cold War as a struggle between Americanism and Soviet communism, Dulles argued that:

> we should let these truths work in and through us. We should be *dynamic*, we should use *ideas* as weapons; and these ideas should conform to *moral* principles. That we do this is right, for it is the inevitable expression of a faith . . . But it is also expedient in defending ourselves against an aggressive, imperialistic despotism. For even the present lines will not hold unless our purpose goes beyond confining Soviet Communism within its present orbit.[41]

Dulles claimed that the 20-odd non-Western nations sharing borders with the "Soviet world" were "close to despair because the United States, the historic leader of the forces of freedom, seemed dedicated to the negative policy of 'containment' and 'stalemate'". He acknowledged that in reality good work was being done by the Truman administration to "promote liberation" but had to be kept secret. This "liberation from the yoke of Moscow" would take time but:

> courage in neighboring lands will not be sustained, *unless the United States makes it publicly known that it wants and expects liberation to occur* (original emphasis). The mere statement of that wish and expectation would change, in an electrifying way, the mood of the captive peoples. It would put heavy new burdens on the jailers and create new opportunities for liberation.[42]

Dulles believed that the President and the Congress should declare that such liberation was US policy "and that we will not be a party to any 'deal' confirming the rule of Soviet despotism over the alien people which it now dominates." He favoured "the creation in the free world of political 'task forces' to develop a freedom program for each of the captive nations" composed of "proved patriots, who have practical resourcefulness and who command confidence and respect at home and abroad." He wanted "to stimulate the escape from behind the Iron Curtain of those who can help to develop these programs." He thought Voice of America and Radio Free Europe could be "coordinated with these freedom programs", as could "our economic, commercial and cultural relations". The US "could end diplomatic relations with present governments which are in fact only puppets of Moscow" and "could seek to bring other free nations to unite with us in proclaiming, in a great new Declaration of Independence, our policies toward the captive nations." Dulles thought "there can be peaceful separation from Moscow, as Tito showed [in 1948], and enslavement can be made so unprofitable that the master will let go his grip." He said he did not want bloody uprisings and reprisals. But he believed that "within two, five or 10 years substantial parts of the present captive world can peacefully regain national independence" and "mark the beginning of the end of Soviet despotism's attempt at world conquest." His alternative to Containment was thus a reaffirmation of the US moral commitment to bring independence to the nations of Asia and Europe, now dominated by Moscow. This policy of liberation was self-determination, as preached by his old mentor Woodrow Wilson, in a new context. It became the Republican foreign policy platform in the 1952 presidential election, an election dominated by foreign policy, and one in which the Republicans stressed the immoral, costly and futile policy of Containment and the repudiation of all commitments and secret understandings that may have given the Soviets the belief that the US endorsed their sphere of influence.

Dulles was clearly pandering to the anti-Yalta rhetoric that had surged in Republican circles since the 'loss' of China. He ministered to those who accused Roosevelt of having negotiated secret deals with Stalin that had enabled the Soviet empire to spread and consolidate itself in Eastern Europe. Truman's Containment was depicted as being of a piece with this treachery in "abandoning" the peoples concerned to Soviet tyranny. The context was one in which Acheson and Truman had been denounced as principals of the "College of Cowardly Communist Containment". Eisenhower went along with this approach partly out of conviction, partly for reasons of political opportunism. But it was Dulles who most alarmed many of America's allies with his hectoring style, self-righteous, moralistic and apocalyptic talk of Good versus Evil and his rhetoric of 'roll-back the Communists or die'. This served to strengthen and deepen prevailing prejudices and helped to maintain the public in that "sense of peril from abroad" that Dulles himself identified as a prerequisite needing to be "created" to sustain public interest in a "vigorous" foreign policy.[43]

The tone of emergency that he adopted reinforced the McCarthyite mood and helped to keep the public and America's allies in a state of battle readiness. Meanwhile, by taking away the remaining protections against unfair dismissal of federal employees accused of disloyalty, the Eisenhower administration vindicated McCarthy. Eisenhower privately justified these draconian measures, speaking to Dulles, on the grounds that the top ranks of the State Department were riddled with subversives devoted to the "socialistic doctrine . . . practiced over the past two decades."[44] Five hundred employees were gone in less than a year, including men whose only crime was to have warned that the nationalists were losing in China by virtue of their own incompetence. Eisenhower validated McCarthyism in another way too, by inflating the danger of subversion by explaining his refusal of clemency for the Rosenbergs, executed in June 1953 after being convicted of passing on atomic secrets to the Soviet Union, because their work had "immeasurably" increased the chances of atomic warfare. At the end of 1953 Gallup Polls showed that almost two-thirds of the public supported McCarthy.

In reality, a consensus had emerged within the political class. Truman's 1950 decisions to send US forces to Korea received the support even of Republicans like Taft. And when the military campaign in Korea reached stalemate there was Republican support for a campaign of rollback against the communist countries which erstwhile 'isolationists' like Taft actually championed. By the presidential campaign of 1952 the Republicans wanted both 'rollback' and less public spending on defence. Behind the, often incoherent, oppositional talk both Republicans and Democrats accepted a global role for the US pitched against the communist enemy, involving everything from the NATO alliance to the use of foreign aid and direct military intervention. Both parties were dominated by people who shared the perception that the 'free world' – defined as the world outside the communist bloc – had to be safeguarded for international commerce – 'free trade' – against communist encroachments. Arguments would continue over the management and tactics of the operation. Would nuclear weapons save money? Was covert action useful inside the communist bloc? Was economic aid useful politically in this or that country? How much money would have to be spent on defence? But the lines of continuity with the Truman administration were clear to see and the Democrats had no coherent alternative to Eisenhower's approach for most of the 1950s.

The Dulles-Eisenhower rhetoric of 1952–1953 was intended to strengthen American leadership and Western unity, justify a global policy of anti-communism and appease the fanatics at home. Though Eisenhower's speeches and public appearances as President often suggested confusion and amateurishness, behind the scenes he was in charge of policy and effective in managing his team.[45] He made full use of the inflated powers of the presidency as bequeathed by his two Democrat predecessors and fought off Republican attempts, such as the Bricker Amendment, to curb executive agreements. Soon after taking office, however, with the 1953 Soviet suppression of riots in East Germany, it was apparent that the US would do nothing to liberate people from communist Eastern Europe. The death of Stalin in March 1953 produced signs of a new, more conciliatory approach in Moscow which Washington ignored. Stalin's demise was used by his successors to stress Moscow's belief that the 'peaceful coexistence' of communism and capitalism was both possible and desirable. Dulles professed to see only deception and business as usual in these developments. On 16 April Eisenhower's first public speech in response to Soviet overtures, 'A Chance for Peace', delivered to the American Society of Newspaper Editors, demanded to see evidence of Soviet sincerity, with progress towards an honourable armistice in Korea and Soviet withdrawal from Austria constituting proof; these came in 1953 and 1955 respectively.

The discredited old regime, as represented by Acheson and Truman, allegedly too soft on communism for the taste of the Republicans, privately fretted about the post-Stalin question, if Acheson's correspondence to Truman is anything to go by. For while Acheson admitted in July 1953 that he could see that:

> What Stalin did to the Russia of Lenin was to impose upon it a personal, oriental, despotism, in which the whims, fears, and ideas of one man and a small coterie greatly enlarged the field for intrigue and the uncertainty of life for everybody from the highest officials to the man in the street [and that] . . . there was an almost audible sigh of relief when Uncle Joe died . . .

He now worried that Stalin's departure could make the Russians want "a period of relaxation in foreign affairs" as they "make greater concessions to the Soviet and satellite peoples". Acheson feared that this could lead to peace proposals in Germany, Korea and Indochina that would undermine the allied will to maintain the Cold War effort and tempt people to think that the problem had changed. But, as Truman knew, Acheson continued, "it isn't merely the imminent threat of aggression from the Soviet movement which causes instability and the danger of war, but the capacity for successful aggression whenever the mood or the desire to engage in it exists."[46] In the same letter, Acheson also expressed concern that the "White House must discredit the demagogic isolationist wing of the Republican Party which wishes to insulate and separate us from our allies." No one would guess from Acheson's anxieties that American power was expanding into every corner of the globe outside the communist states. Dulles facilitated the process by his popularisation of the 'New Look' and the creation of defence pacts in parts of the world which did not already have them, such as the Middle East and South East Asia. In January 1954 he told the Council on Foreign Relations that US defence policy would rely on instant nuclear retaliation – the idea that frightened America's allies as much as it frightened the Kremlin. The Democratic candidate in the 1956 presidential election, Adlai Stevenson, took the Republican administration to task for its recklessness and belligerence but at the same time criticised it for allowing the consolidation of communist ascendancy in Eastern Europe and North Vietnam.

THIRD WORLD INTERVENTIONS

No place was too small to be insignificant in the global contest, no conflict too irrelevant to anti-communism, as the US military intervention in Lebanon attested in 1958, as did the fluctuating perceptions of local conflicts such as that between India and Pakistan.[47] The CIA occasionally worried, as it did in 1947, that Moscow could "undermine the strength of European states" by subverting former colonial countries.[48] Dangerous power vacuums had arisen because of Britain's withdrawal, according to the State-Army-Navy-Air Force Coordinating Committee (SANACC), in October of the same year, in areas where political instability and economic distress increased susceptibility to "Communist penetration".[49] Newly independent countries might align with Moscow, depriving the US of access to military bases and raw materials. The Chinese communist revolution and the insurgencies in Indochina and Indonesia provided dramatic support for such analyses. Under these circumstances policy-makers saw everything in Cold War terms including the Indo-Pakistan dispute over Kashmir. They "wound up exaggerating the importance of the subcontinent to the United States and overestimating their ability to convert two impoverished, developing societies into strategic Cold War partners." They also consistently overrated their ability to resolve the Kashmir dispute and other conflicts between India and Pakistan.[50] Petitioners for aid understood all of this and accordingly played up the Cold War dimensions of their local concerns.

Like Roosevelt, Eisenhower reflected on the rise of Third World nationalism and how out of touch the British were on this vital matter – a thought prompted anew by Churchill's visit to Washington just before Eisenhower's inauguration.[51] But, unlike Roosevelt, Eisenhower lived in a world where the dominant worry was that the nationalists would be manipulated and exploited by the communists. "Nationalism is on the march", he wrote, "and world communism is taking advantage of that spirit of nationalism." In this situation, it was vital that Britain and America did "not appear before the world as a combination of forces to compel adherence to the status quo."[52] Yet this unattractive prospect was realised by decisions taken by Eisenhower himself. A case in point was the administration's response to the nationalist leader Mohammad Mossadegh in Iran. Eisenhower was persuaded by "friends in the oil industry", among others, that the example of Iranian nationalisation of the British-owned oil refinery at Abadan might encourage copycat behaviour elsewhere in the developing world and thus endanger corporate interests.[53] Mossadegh threatened "chaos" in Iran and the unseating of a staunch anti-communist ally in the person of the Shah, according to Ambassador Loy Henderson. Eisenhower soon concluded that Mossadegh was either a communist or one of Moscow's stooges. He was overthrown in August 1953 in an Anglo-US operation and in 1955 Iran was incorporated into the anti-Soviet Baghdad Pact.

The new anti-communist ideological consensus, however, did not stop American politicians worrying about British imperialism, or prevent them from imagining that US policy in the Third World (to use the Cold War name) stood for something completely different. There was, however, an obvious dilemma in that British imperialism, this unsavoury thing, was an asset in the fight against communism, in so far as it provided governance and order in places that the communists might otherwise move into, as in Malaysia where a communist insurgency was taking place from 1948 and would last throughout the 1950s. Unfortunately, British imperialism was widely hated by nationalists. Too close an association with British rule would tar the US with the same brush, as Eisenhower and Dulles recognised. Yet in Asia the British had been ahead of the Americans in realising that the government of China embodied "the national revolt of China" and Mao's regime was not to be confused with the externally imposed 'People's Democracies' of Eastern Europe. In 1954, in the context of the Geneva Accords on Indochina, the former Prime Minister, Clement Attlee, admitted that the same spirit that had swept China was now evident in Indochina.[54]

The British had also backed the Colombo Plan in 1950 to facilitate economic development and were officially committed to the view that there was an urgent need to redistribute resources to the colonial and post-colonial world. In 1953 the Labour Party's *Challenge to Britain* referred to a "world uprising against the old imperialism" especially in Asia. But the US simultaneously allowed anti-communism to dominate its thinking on Asia while posing as a nuisance in British eyes on colonial matters in Africa and the

Middle East. Nationalism was regrettably encouraged by America's general anti-colonialism, according to the Permanent Under-Secretary in the British Foreign Office in 1952.[55] Even British trade union leaders such as Victor Tewson (Trades Union Congress General Secretary 1946–1960), who was involved in the project of establishing 'responsible' trade unionism in the African and West Indian colonies, objected that American anti-colonial rhetoric was doing untold harm. Tewson complained bitterly of AFL-CIO critics of colonialism who argued that colonial repression in places such as Cyprus and Algeria was handing gratuitous propaganda to the communists. Tewson lamented the fact that:

> it is widely assumed that the territorial enemy is the [British] Government and this assumption is fostered both by the ICFTU [International Confederation of Free Trade Unions] and by the Americans in their constant reiteration of the terms 'anti-imperialism' and 'anti-colonialism' . . . In theory, practice and experience we know more about the sound development of African trade unions than either the ICFTU or the Americans.[56]

Lord Perth, the Minister for the Colonies from 1956 to 1962, expressed a similar point to the prime minister in February 1957, referring to "persistent misinterpretation by the Americans of our colonial policy and record" and to the "apparently ineradicable American distrust of so-called British 'Colonialism'."[57] The French were equally bitter about America's attitude to Indochina, a region in which Washington wanted resistance to the communists and paid the French to supply it, but then explained the lack of progress in terms of French colonialism. Some conservatives could see that American imperialism – absurdly, irresponsibly preaching universal values and rights – was pushing the old empires under.[58]

Lord Perth thought this same 'anti-imperialist' pose coloured the American attitude to "such vital matters as the Suez problem and the Baghdad Pact, and has encouraged a spirit of neutralism on these and other issues (eg. Cyprus)." It was necessary to point out, he thought,

> that what we are doing in our colonial territories has no relation to their out-of-date conception of 'Colonialism' but is, on the contrary, a constructive job of *nation-building* which is of the utmost importance to the free world and which they have a duty as well as an interest to support.[59]

The root of American thinking on this subject, according to Perth, was the implicit assumption that "there is something inherently wrong with the colonial relationship". This had practical effects. While the US could see the folly of premature withdrawal from colonies, this insight only engendered "a sense of painful dilemma" in US positions, most clearly seen at the UN "where the Americans tend to sponsor compromise resolutions which can only have the effect of undermining the authority of the Administering Powers." The US had "taken the lead" in advocating immediate target dates for self-government in Trust territories; it had elaborated proposals for a UN study of the concept of self-determination, which Perth thought "would go far, if put into effect", to undermine the political authority of the Administering Powers throughout the colonial world. With the advent of some 20 new members the situation in the UN was now dangerous because "the United States have come to realise that they cannot successfully pursue their foreign policy unless they conciliate the so-called Afro-Asian bloc." What was required of the Americans, Perth argued, was the abandonment of the notion "that all our international policies are suspect because of the taint of colonialism"; that they must consult with Britain before attempting to mediate between Britain and the anti-colonialists and they should be guided by British views; and if they believed Britain was doing a good job they should say so publicly, especially at the UN where there was a tendency "of extending the field of United Nations interference" that had to be stopped.[60]

But even the British could see that in the Middle East the country was tainted as an imperial power and one that had aided Zionism. Thus, nationalism in the Middle East "usually means violent hatred of Britain", said one Labour Party document.[61] The US saw an opportunity. In Egypt it tried to be the friend of the nationalists, recognising the depth of anti-British feeling among its people. Nasser was recognised initially as an anticommunist, opposed to Islamic fundamentalism and pro-American – partly because the US was not an old imperialist power in the region.[62] He was to be nurtured. The British military position in Egypt, on the other hand, could not be wholeheartedly supported by Washington – but nor could it be publicly damned. Dulles, who had "an instinctive reluctance to support even residual forms of colonialism",[63] complained to Eden that while the US was keen to "sponsor" nationalism as a way of beating the Soviets at their own game, and also in accordance with America's "historic tradition", he was "often restrained from doing so by a desire to cooperate with Britain and France in Asia, in North Africa and in the Near and Middle East."[64] Open US support for Britain, he thought, would align the US with imperialism. The trouble was that because they were on the same side in the Cold War and both supported Israel, Middle Eastern perceptions of the Anglo-American relationship often missed the nuances Dulles wanted to make visible. In a 1953 memorandum he saw that the British position was beyond repair and that the "Israeli factor" combined with the Arab tendency to link the US with the old imperial powers were "millstones around our neck".[65]

For the Eisenhower administration the Suez Crisis illustrated all the faults of imperialism. At the height of the crisis, on 1 November 1956, Dulles told the NSC that:

> the United States has been walking on a tightrope between the effort to maintain our old and valued relations with our British and French allies on the one hand, and on the other trying to assure ourselves of the friendship and understanding of the newly independent countries who have escaped from colonialism . . . Unless we now assert and maintain . . . leadership, all of these newly independent countries will turn from us to the USSR. We will be looked upon as forever tied to British and French colonialist policies . . . In short the United States would survive or go down on the basis of the fate of colonialism if the United States supports the French and the British on the colonial issues. Win or lose, we will share the fate of Britain and France.[66]

Ironically, Prime Minister Sir Anthony Eden's belief that he could get rid of Nasser was probably influenced by the fact that the overthrow of Mohammad Mossadegh was regarded in Washington and London as a great success that could be repeated elsewhere. Another paradox of the abortive attempt to overthrow Nasser in 1956 was the conviction in Washington that the US would have to become more involved in the Middle East because of the 'vacuum' created by Britain's retreat after the Suez Crisis and the emergence of Nasser as a supposed 'puppet' of the Soviets, as Eisenhower privately confided in July 1958.[67] For all its awareness of the ideological problem posed by the old imperialist powers in the region, the US nevertheless continued to assist and encourage the maintenance of the remnants of British power in the Middle East as part of the battle against communism.[68] Britain was able to remain in the region until the early 1970s with US approval.[69]Anti-communism, meanwhile, meant promoting reactionary versions of Islam (Saudi Arabia), supporting feudal states opposed to progressive modernity (Oman), engineering regime change by successive coups (for example in Syria), supporting the Western military presence in the region and openly intervening to maintain the status quo. It therefore pitched the US against a wide span of Arab publics as well as those pan-Arabists like Nasser who denounced the reactionary Arab regimes, Western imperialism and Zionism. Critics of the administration could see these problems at the time.

In the 1956 presidential campaign John F. Kennedy, in support of Adlai Stevenson, complained of Republican indecision in the face of communist advances in Indochina, the Middle East and North Africa, observing that the US had fallen "silent on colonialism". He told the Senate in July 1957 that freedom was suppressed by both Soviet and Western imperialism and that "the single most important test of American foreign policy . . . is how we meet the challenge of imperialism."[70] On this would the "uncommitted millions in Asia and Africa" finally judge the US and so far it was failing the test. The French war in Algeria was an example, said Kennedy, and America's equivocal remarks at the UN on that crisis had damaged its prestige in that body, undermined American relations with the North African states and weakened the US position in the Middle East. Kennedy argued that the record of the US under Eisenhower and Dulles had been one of "retreat from the principles of independence and anti-colonialism" on which America had once stood proud. He returned to this theme in March 1958, warning of the folly of regarding neutrals as dupes of communism, as American policy was wont to do. Non-involvement in the great international controversies of the day – a position the infant United States had adopted after 1776 – was the only way emergent nations could find the political balance and social stability which were the true defence against communist penetration.[71] Congressional Democrats like Kennedy, however, wanted it both ways; Eisenhower's Third World policy was blind to the social and economic roots of anti-colonialism, but the administration was not spending enough on defence.

South East Asia was, by this time, an increasingly pressing problem in Washington's view. Here the US laboured under an interconnected system of false reasoning familiar from our discussion of its reaction to the Chinese revolution. US leaders did not accept the indigenous roots of communism in Vietnam and its capture of the main nationalist sentiment in the country; they did not understand that they had already lost the political battle for hearts and minds. They were also wrong in believing that their anti-communist policies were working and that their local allies were committed to democracy and reform. They sometimes laboured under, and always promoted, the illusion that monolithic communism, directed by Moscow, was working through its global agencies – of which the Chinese Communist Party was locally the most relevant – to install its agents in Vietnam, led by Ho Chi Minh. Ho's nationalist credentials were publicly dismissed. The US had praised the Elysee Agreements of 1949 between France and Bao Dai, the former emperor now returning as head of state of Vietnam, who it commended for "making sincere efforts to unite all truly nationalist elements within Vietnam." Dean Acheson publicly identified "genuine nationalism" as a solution to the Indochina problem in 1950 and asserted that the US government was convinced that "neither national independence nor democratic evolution exist in any area dominated by Soviet imperialism."[72]When the State

Department recommended military aid to the French in 1950 it identified the communist threat in South East Asia as external to the region by saying that:

> The USSR will endeavour to bring about the fall of Southeast Asian governments which are opposed to Communism by using all devices short of war, making use of Communist China and indigenous communists in this endeavour . . . The United States should furnish military aid in support of the anti-Communist nationalist governments of Indochina.[73]

The NSC was confidently informed that "the threat of communist aggression against Indochina is only one phase of anticipated communist plans to seize all of Southeast Asia", even though it acknowledged that Ho Chi Minh had "seized" a large segment of the nationalist movement in 1945 and had non-communist as well as communist support.[74] It was told that French success in containing Ho's forces was "doubtful". This was at a time when the French had 140,000 soldiers in the field. It went on to observe that the US had advised France since the Japanese surrender that "a return to pre-war colonial rule is not possible" and that it was necessary to establish governments in Indochina capable of attracting the non-communist nationalists. The governments of Vietnam, Laos and Cambodia were recognised by the US and the UK in February 1950 as a step in this direction, while the USSR and China recognised Ho Chi Minh as head of the legal government of Vietnam. Communist success in Indochina, NSC-64 maintained, would lead to the fall of Thailand and Burma.

In 1954, with the French struggling to hold out militarily at the Battle of Dien Bien Phu, Eisenhower wrote to Churchill to express his "fear that the French cannot see the thing through."[75] He predicted the spread of communism to Thailand, Burma and Indonesia, and to Malaya, Australia and New Zealand, if Indochina fell. There was no secure negotiated solution that he could imagine of benefit to the West, short of "a Communist retirement." He wanted Britain to join in an alliance prepared to take military action. Likewise, for Dulles and his colleagues "Indochina was less a deplorable colonial problem than a crucial link in the chain of global resistance to international communism. Still judging the Mao regime to be basically the agent of a unified, compulsively expansionist movement controlled by the Kremlin, the Eisenhower administration thought a breaching of the chain in South East Asia would set off a whole series of communist insurrections throughout Asia."[76] The communists in Indochina were a fifth column that had to be defeated and Dulles played a prominent part in maintaining that if such a vital asset as Vietnam should fall the rest of the region would follow. This had been a recurring theme since 1946, but it was Eisenhower who popularised the image of falling dominoes at a press conference in April 1954. But the President and Congress would support no military intervention in Indochina in the 1950s without allied support. This was not forthcoming from the British, who favoured a diplomatic settlement and, under Eden's leadership, sought to negotiate one at the Geneva Conference in May 1954. With the French defeat at Dien Bien Phu public support for France's continued war in South East Asia collapsed and the conference opened with Ho Chi Minh's forces in the ascendancy. The Geneva Accords nevertheless partitioned Vietnam, produced a ceasefire and delayed national unification elections – elections that Ho was certain to win – for two years. The US refused to be bound by these agreements. We shall return to the situation bequeathed by the Geneva Accords in the next chapter.

Far less obvious than overt US involvement in the question of Vietnam's future was the 'subversion as foreign policy' that was practised by America throughout the Third World in the 1950s.[77] Domestic ignorance of this type of military intervention – the supply of weapons, logistical support and deployment of CIA forces – was not confined to events in faraway Indochina or Indonesia. It was practised in the US 'backyard' too, in Latin America, and of course ran counter to Article 15 of the Charter of the Organisation of American States of 1948 which said that "no State or group of States has the right to intervene, directly or indirectly, for any reason whatever, in the internal or external affairs of any other State." But even when these words were written the problem of instability in the region was already linked to communism, though in truth the greater cause was the massive inequality which prevailed in the countries concerned, based as they were on avaricious dictatorships (in 13 of the 20 Latin American nations by 1954) and monopolies of land ownership and business concentrations such as United Fruit. Politicians promising reforms of this system were often viewed in Washington as communist dupes, such as José Figueres in Costa Rica in the late 1940s and early 1950s. Only months after taking over the presidency Eisenhower approved NSC-144/1 which spelled out US objectives in Latin America where there was seen to be a grave and dangerous drift toward "radical and nationalistic regimes" which had to be stopped by a combination of measures, including military aid, to bolster reactionaries in government. Dulles told Congress in January 1953 that "the conditions in Latin America were somewhat comparable to conditions as they were in China in the mid-thirties when the Communist movement was getting started."[78] The instrument of the *coup d'etat* – having been so successful in Iran – was bound to be used again to solve this problem. In June 1954 it was employed in Guatemala to remove Jacobo Árbenz, another nationalist leader thought to be under communist direction and at the time embarked on a programme of land reform that involved nationalising uncultivated land owned by United Fruit and offering compensation based on the value of the land as declared by the US company for tax purposes. Dulles and Nixon were quick to praise the "popular uprising" as they described it, against Árbenz that they said had saved the country from despotism. Dulles told an American television audience that Guatemala's problems had nothing to do with United Fruit and everything to do with "communist infiltration"; if United Fruit "gave a gold piece for every banana, the problem would remain just as it is today", he confidently asserted.[79] After Árbenz was overthrown Dulles congratulated "the people of Guatemala", whose urban and peasant unions were destroyed in the years that followed, thus eliminating in Guatemala the 'tyranny of the weak' which Dulles feared in the Third World.[80] The CIA, led by the Secretary of State's brother, Allen Dulles, orchestrated the arrival of Castillo Armas to replace Árbenz. Both Dulles brothers had a professional relationship with United Fruit through the legal firm Foster & Allen and reportedly also had shares in the company, raising the question of how far in this particular case their diagnosis of a communist threat was genuinely held and how far it was self-serving.[81] Nevertheless, what is clear is that the ideological framework was provided by NSC-144/1 which interpreted the question of inter-American relations in globalist Cold War terms. The guiding principle was anti-communism, which left little room for consideration of democracy, self-determination or human rights. In this context, regardless of the Dulles brothers' business interests, Árbenz had failed what the US Ambassador to Guatemala had in 1950 described as his 'duck test': "A duck wore no label identifying it as a duck. But . . . if the bird quacked and swam like a duck, it was probably a duck."[82]

OVER TO KENNEDY

By the late 1950s it was increasingly felt by critics of the administration that military solutions could not deal with the chronic economic problems of Latin America and that economic progress in the communist bloc and the victory of Fidel Castro's forces in Cuba at the beginning of 1959 could tempt the poor to pursue alternative developmental paths. President Kennedy's Alliance for Progress programme, first mentioned in 1960, was informed by the need to offer a positive vision of the future that presented an alternative to the Cuban model and was particularly necessary in the wake of the failure to overthrow Castro by armed invasion in April 1961. Neat surgical removal of governments was not as easy, it turned out, as the CIA had imagined in the 1950s. Funds were to be found for economic development in Latin America – US$100 billion during the next decade – while an economic blockade was imposed on Cuba. However, much of this money was eventually spent on military aid. Nine Latin American governments were overthrown by their own militaries between 1961 and 1966. Most of the American aid that did not go to the military went to US-owned firms and local oligarchs. State socialism in Cuba was perceived as a dangerous precedent. Any perceived success of this system threatened to "have an extensive impact on statist trends elsewhere in the area."[83] Kennedy's policies thus ended up reproducing the pattern of Eisenhower's (as they did also in the Middle East).[84] Before the end of his first year as president he explained to Prime Minister Nehru of India that while the foreign policy of the United States was to support countries with democratic systems, it even more basically sought to support national sovereignty. Sometimes this meant, unhappily, that the US-backed governments were "not fully supported" by their own people. And, alas, it was not always easy to withdraw from such places if "we believe . . . communism might take over by subversion. This is the problem that faces us." He added, inaccurately, that this logic did not apply when communists take over by electoral means; Cheddi Jagan's election victory in British Guiana in 1953 prompted British military intervention, with American support.[85]

Kennedy was certainly aware of the pattern of US involvement in Latin America under Eisenhower and his Alliance for Progress rhetoric signalled at the least a fresh propaganda offensive in the region. While stressing that the independence of the Western Hemisphere was "menaced from abroad", his campaign speeches in 1960 made much of the distrust, suspicion and disillusion felt in Latin America towards the US. In announcing the Alliance for Progress, allegedly designed to strengthen democracy and economic advance, he made much of Republican failures. Goodwill had been dissipated by the Eisenhower administration, as demonstrated by the mobs that attacked Nixon on his vice-presidential tour of Venezuela in 1958, the riots in Mexico City and the anti-Americanism displayed in demonstrations in Brazil and Panama. This was because, Kennedy said, America had failed to identify itself with "the rising tide of freedom". On the contrary, it was seen as the supporter of dictatorships, even giving medals to the dictators of Peru, Venezuela and Paraguay, while "dumping" hundreds of millions of dollars worth of arms in the region "to strengthen the hand of dictatorships". America was seen as the defender of stable regimes rather than free governments, more interested in fighting communism and securing investments than in defending liberty. Economic aid had been neglected and the communists were reaping the benefits.[86]

The 1960 presidential campaign was fought at a time of recession and when Soviet economic and technological advances gave concern, not only about a 'missile gap', but about the greater attractive power of the Soviet economic model in the Third World. Khrushchev was making much of movements for Third World self-determination in Soviet propaganda, aligning Moscow with the tide of anti-colonialism. The Cuban Revolution was a local case in point and Nixon, the Republican candidate, aware of Eisenhower's plans to overthrow Castro, privately "pushed as hard for action as he dared".[87] Nixon was convinced that focusing on foreign policy was the best way to beat Kennedy and chose Henry Cabot Lodge as his running-mate because he was "nationally known for tearing into the Communists in the UN."[88] Nixon stood for a tougher line with the communists and talked about a "strategy for victory for the free world", while Kennedy complained about the failures of the Eisenhower years, which had weakened America's relative position in the great struggle. There would be continuity on both anti-communism and executive direction of foreign policy whoever won the election. But Kennedy's campaign rhetoric also insisted that the 'free world' needed more than the arms race and the Cold War.[89] It needed a national strategy embracing aims that got to the social and economic roots of conditions that the communists exploited. Kennedy stressed the civil and economic rights that were denied in the Third World, because of poverty and hunger, as well as the political rights denied in the communist bloc. He argued that the advance of communism fastened on such deprivation in Asia and the Middle East. America had to prove that it could compete with "the single-minded advance of the Communist system".[90] In his first televised debate with Nixon during the 1960 election campaign, Kennedy explained that the "Communist offensive" was based on the "productive power of the Soviet Union" (a waste economy in reality), its greater production of scientists and engineers, the danger that it would produce more energy than the US by 1975, and serve as a model of economic development in Latin America, Africa and Asia. Under Eisenhower, he argued, there had been stagnation (the US economy actually grew by 37 per cent in the 1950s and by the end of it the median family had 30 per cent more purchasing power). On other occasions, Kennedy returned to this theme arguing that America needed to be stronger militarily, economically, scientifically and educationally so that it could launch an attack on world poverty, as the communists were doing for their own purposes. "There are a billion more people crowding our globe . . . the white race is in a minority, the free-enterprise system is in a minority", the question was whether freedom would endure, let alone prevail.[91] The 'failings' Kennedy drew attention to were the failings of an administration, rather than fundamental weaknesses of the US. The Kennedy administration remained convinced that it had the ability to achieve desired results around the globe. If anything, it was more convinced of its powers of overseas social engineering than any administration that had preceded it.

In his 1961 Inaugural Address the new President asserted that America would "pay any price, bear any burden, meet any hardship, support any friend, oppose any foe, to assure the survival and success of liberty". Kennedy made special reference to states that had just thrown off colonialism and promised to help Latin America in particular to overcome poverty, while warning that the US would "oppose aggression or subversion anywhere in the Americas".[92] But he was also careful, before and after he became president, to acknowledge the communist objective of world domination, a spectre given shape by the crises in Indochina, the Cuban Revolution, events in Berlin and the Cuban Missile Crisis. Three times between 1961 and 1963, Kennedy later observed, America had been on "the verge of direct military confrontation" with the Soviet Union – in Laos, Berlin and Cuba. The Cubans were a "captive people" led by "puppets and agents of an international conspiracy".[93] There was no place for local agency in this world-view. Kennedy's address in May 1961 to a Joint Session of Congress referred to the relentless pressures of the Chinese communists menacing the whole of Asia from the borders of India to the jungles of Laos. "Communist agents" endangered Latin America too and the Middle East. He told Congress that:

> The great battleground for the defense and expansion of freedom today is the whole southern half of the globe – Asia, Latin America, Africa and the Middle East – the lands of the rising peoples. Their revolution is the greatest in human history. They seek an end to injustice, tyranny, and exploitation . . . the adversaries of freedom did not create the revolution; nor did they create the conditions which compel it. But they are seeking to ride the crest of its wave – to capture it for themselves.[94]

Their techniques for doing so were arms, agitators, aid, technicians and propaganda. Low intensity, or guerrilla, warfare had been "the most active and constant threat to Free World security" since 1945. Nibbling away at the periphery were "forces of subversion, infiltration, intimidation, indirect or non-overt aggression, internal revolution, diplomatic blackmail" – such were the communist methods.[95] America stood for a peaceful world community of free and independent – but interdependent – states and Kennedy occasionally saw clearly that this meant diversity, self-determination and partnership. These were strengths that a conformist communist model did not and could not have. The world was against the monolithic, the single dogmatic creed and system. The communists were also disadvantaged by the reality of the internal divisions beneath the monolithic façade – their peoples disaffected, their economies very far from efficient.

Kennedy's public utterances alluding to the communist world-plan, implying a monolithic, carefully co-ordinated and successful strategy, with local conflicts merely its particular expressions, was mirrored in the private discussions he had with his civilian and military advisers. This logic survived all evidence to the contrary, including the President's own sceptical contributions to the various discussions. It was a logic that accepted the validity of the domino theory, over-estimated Soviet and Chinese power and influence in Vietnam, would not accept that the communist campaign in the South of Vietnam was largely indigenous, did not appreciate the extent to which communism and nationalism were identified with one another, and always believed that a military solution was just around the corner.[96] Unwelcome information nevertheless occasionally filtered through to the President and the tone of his comments in discussion was sometimes sceptical. He was told on becoming president that discontent with the government of Ngo Dinh Diem in South Vietnam was widespread and existed at all levels of society.[97] Confronted by demands for an increase in the size of the South Vietnamese army, which the US would have to finance, Kennedy wondered why this was necessary, given that the problem Diem faced was allegedly only 10,000 'guerrillas'. Was the situation not one of "politics and morale", rather than military force?[98] Representatives of the Diem government answered his doubts in his own currency of "subversion, infiltration, intimidation". The problem, they explained, stemmed from indoctrination of the peasantry by the communists during the French period, coupled with ongoing blackmail and intimidation.[99] Then there were the consequences of 'failure'. General Bonesteel was only one of the many voices arguing that failure to stop the communists in Vietnam would lead to damaging consequences "in all other areas of the world" and specifically the Near East and Latin America.[100] Vice-President Johnson returned from a trip to Asia in May 1961 reporting a picture of tremendous social and economic, even political, progress in South Vietnam under Diem, and of the ordinary peoples' desire for better housing, schools and hospitals. But this effort was "frustrated and disrupted by the agents of terrorism" – the communists.[101] Though the British and French were opposed to armed intervention, and the Indian government repeatedly advised against it, by November 1961 this was precisely what was being recommended by the advocates of the domino theory – the Secretary of State, the Secretary of Defense and the Joint Chiefs of Staff – even as they continued to define the problem in Vietnam as "a nation of twenty million . . . intimidated by an active force of fifteen to twenty thousand Vietcong".[102]

Notwithstanding the very public nature of the Sino-Soviet split, CIA Director Allen Dulles was one of those unable to liberate himself from the old monolithic view of communism, warning at a National Security Council meeting in November 1961 that the Soviets and Chinese would act together against any nation "which threatened Communist interests".[103] At the same meeting Kennedy said he could make a rather persuasive case against military intervention in a situation, thousand of miles away, where millions of dollars and a native army of 200,000 had been unable to succeed against 16,000 guerrillas. CIA intelligence also showed as late as January 1963, that this force, now estimated at 22–24,000, was often armed with old French equipment or "crude homemade rifles and pistols" – not exactly evidence of enthusiastic Soviet support.[104] Chester Bowles, demoted to the rank of a 'special adviser' to the President, to ease him out of the State Department, was one of the few who put the proposition to Kennedy, in March 1963, that anti-communist efforts in Vietnam amounted to a "striving in defiance of powerful indigenous political and military forces, to insure the survival of an unpopular Vietnamese regime with inadequate roots among the people". And yet, he added, as in 1954, before the French defeat at Dien Bien Phu, "many able U.S. military authorities are convinced that the situation is moving in our favor and that victory can be foreseen within two to three years."[105]

Kennedy had plenty of opportunities to get tough with the communists and some of those opportunities also constituted the most dramatic incidents of the Cold War. But none of this seemed to satisfy the Republican grassroots. Republicans had criticised Eisenhower for negotiating with the communists when he should have been doing something to overthrow them or prevent them from coming to power in the first place, as in Cuba. They were not likely to warm to Kennedy. Such right-wing activists were equally unhappy that the New Deal had not been dismantled during the eight years of Eisenhower's presidency. None of this compromise, as they saw it, had done anything to promote the Republican Party in Congress, or in the states. Barry Goldwater led the critics in Congress from 1957, championing smaller government at home and a foreign policy of 'defeating communism'. In this view summit talks, economic aid programmes and the UN were all useless, whereas tactical nuclear weapons, military offensives by the nationalist (Taiwanbased) Chinese or active support for insurgency within the communist bloc could be useful. Goldwater saw Kennedy as a failure in Berlin, South East Asia and Cuba and called for firmer military action in the last two. Kennedy was aware of such criticisms, from what he called the "extreme right", and also of the "sharp rise in pro-Republican sentiment in the Middle West" by the summer of 1962.[106]

Domestic issues were undoubtedly to the fore in the minds of such right-wing activists and none more so than liberal reforms that smacked of 'socialism'. Civil Rights for black Americans had been of growing salience since the Supreme Court ruling of 1954 in the case of Brown versus the Board of Education of Topeka, Kansas, against segregation in schools. Both presidential candidates had taken a stand on the issue in the campaign of 1960, but the enforcement of court orders was something Kennedy had to deal with as president. His championing of Civil Rights culminated in a bill being sent to Congress in June 1963 to outlaw discrimination in all public and private facilities and services. Opinion polls in 1963 showed that 50 per cent of Americans thought he was pushing integration too fast.[107] Racism and post-McCarthy anti-communism continued to provide unifying points of departure for right-wing activists. Grouped in scores of organisations across the South and West of the United States in particular in the early 1960s, right-wing activism was stimulated as Cuba, the rise of the Civil Rights movement, Democrat political victories, "political collectivism, social decadence and effeminacy" combined to spread alarm.[108] This was predominantly an activist, middle-class movement, backed by business, local media and the churches, which stood, in effect, for a "free economy and a strong state". Convinced that the New Deal was still to be defeated, that welfare sapped individual initiative, that taxes were too high and that the state was heading for some form of socialism, these activists saw themselves as anti-statists opposed to corruption and conspiracy in Washington. But they were also enthusiasts for the armed forces and defence spending, advocates of law and order and religious moralities that would ban many manifestations of liberal secularism, if they had the chance. Communism, for many of these people, was present in the schools, and the universities – indeed wherever liberal ideas surfaced.[109] "Anti-communist Red-baiting became a cloaked means of attacking [trade] unionists and the labor movement along with other progressive causes, such as civil rights and civil liberties, as well as a vehicle through which ambitious politicians launched their careers."[110] A visceral racism was endemic in these circles, of course, but the broader ideology they stood for was carefully fashioned by business groups, evangelicals, intellectuals and the journals they published. The fact that a social movement took shape from such elements, backing Goldwater in 1964 (and Reagan in 1980), suggests that the values and arguments they advanced resonated with an older right-wing tradition with roots deep in the political culture of the South and West, regions of growing demographic, electoral and cultural significance.[111] McCarthyism had been an earlier expression of it. The anti-communist consensus in foreign policy did nothing to challenge its prejudices.

NOTES

1 Joseph McCarthy, Speech at Wheeling, full text at http://us.history.wisc.edu/hist102/pdocs/mccarthy_wheeling.pdf.
2 State Department *Bulletin*, XXIII, 7 August 1950, p.207.
3 Halberstam, *The Coldest Winter*, pp.90, 92–93, 153.
4 Quoted in Purifoy, *Harry Truman's China Policy*, p.196, 201, 207. See also James Peck, *Washington's China: The National Security World, the Cold War, and the Origins of Globalism* (Amherst and Boston: University of Massachusetts Press, 2006), pp.49–62.
5 Harry S. Truman, *Memoirs – Volume 2: Years of Trial and Hope* (New York: Doubleday, 1956), p.399.
6 Ibid., p.592.
7 Keeley, *The China Lobby Man*, p.157.
8 Article by South East Asia expert Foster Hailey in *New York Times*, 12 February 1950, cited in Purifoy, *Harry Truman's China Policy*, pp.168–170.
9 State Department *Bulletin*, 20 March 1950, p.428, quoted in ibid., p.176.
10 Quoted in ibid., p.169.
11 Quoted in ibid., p.175.

12 Ibid., p.187.
13 William F. Buckley Jr., 'Introduction' in Keeley, *The China Lobby Man*, p.xiii.
14 Keeley, *The China Lobby Man*, p.216.
15 Ibid., pp.224–225, 227–228.
16 Ibid., pp.242–243.
17 Schrecker, *Many are the Crimes*, pp.359–415. See also Ted Morgan, *Reds: McCarthyism in Twentieth-Century America* (New York: Random House, 2004), pp.514–547.
18 Robert Cook, *Sweet Land of Liberty? The African-American Struggle for Civil Rights in the Twentieth Century* (London: Longman, 1998), pp.92–98.
19 See David Halberstam, *The Best and the Brightest* (New York: Ballantine Books edition, 1992), pp.462–465.
20 Robert S. McNamara, *In Retrospect: The Tragedy and Lessons of Vietnam* (New York: Times Books, 1995), p.33.
21 Halberstam, *The Coldest Winter*, pp.194–198.
22 Ibid., p.171.
23 Roger Morris, *Richard Milhous Nixon: The Rise of An American Politician* (New York: Henry Holt, 1990), p.663.
24 Ibid.
25 Kevin McCann, *Man from Abilene* (New York: Doubleday, 1952), pp.179–180.
26 Stephen Ambrose, *Eisenhower: Soldier and President* (New York: Pocket Books, 2003), pp.275–276.
27 Morris, *Richard Milhous Nixon*, p.667.
28 Ambrose, *Nixon: The Education of a Politician*, p.251.
29 Quoted in Rick Perlstein, *Nixonland: The Rise of a President and the Fracturing of America* (New York: Scribner, 2008), p.36.
30 Ambrose, *Eisenhower*, p.280.
31 Chester J. Pach, Jr. and Elmo Richardson, *The Presidency of Dwight D. Eisenhower* (revised ed. Lawrence, KS: University Press of Kansas, 1991), p.85.
32 Stephen W. Twing, *Myths, Models and US Foreign Policy: The Cultural Shaping of Three Cold Warriors* (Boulder, CO: Lynne Rienner, 1998), pp.55–60.
33 Richard H. Immerman, *John Foster Dulles: Piety, Pragmatism and Power in US Foreign Policy* (Wilmington, DE: Scholarly Resources Inc., 1999), p.24.
34 Ibid.
35 Ibid., p.25.
36 Quoted in Twing, *Myths*, pp.65–66.
37 Immerman, *John Foster Dulles*, p.26.
38 John Foster Dulles, *War or Peace* (London: Macmillan, 1939), pp.162–163.
39 Townsend Hoopes, *The Devil and John Foster Dulles* (New York: Andre Deutsch, 1974), p.115.
40 Ibid.
41 John Foster Dulles, 'New Policy of Boldness', *Life*, May 1952 and http://teachingamerican-history.org/library/index.asp?document=1615.
42 Ibid.
43 Dulles, *War, Peace and Change*, p.90.
44 Pach and Richardson, *The Presidency of Dwight D. Eisenhower*, p.64.
45 On this issue see, Fred I. Greenstein, *The Hidden-Hand Presidency: Eisenhower as Leader* (Baltimore, MD: Johns Hopkins University Press, 1994).
46 David S. McLellan and David C. Acheson (eds.), *Among Friends: Personal Letters of Dean Acheson* (New York: Dodd, Mead and Company, 1980), pp.86–87.
47 Robert J. McMahon, *The Cold War on the Periphery: The United States, India and Pakistan* (New York: Columbia University Press, 1994), p.4.
48 CIA, 'Review of the World Situation as it Relates to the Security of the United States', September 12 1947, cited in ibid., pp.14, 352.
49 Ibid., p.15.
50 Ibid., p.6.
51 Robert H. Ferrell (ed.), *The Eisenhower Diaries* (New York: Norton, 1981), p.223.
52 Ibid.
53 Pach and Richardson, *The Presidency of Dwight D. Eisenhower*, p.88.

54 See Callaghan, *The Labour Party and Foreign Policy*, pp.204–208.

55 Letter from Strang to Lloyd, 21 June 1952 in David Goldsworthy (ed.), *The Conservative Government and the End of Empire, 1951–57* (London: HMSO, 1995), p.17.

56 Victor Tewson, 'TUC: Reassessment of the Situation in Africa', TUC Colonial Advisory Committee, 4 February 1959, MSS 292/932.9/4 (Modern Records Centre, University of Warwick).

57 PREM 11/3239, PM(57)9, 'Colonialism': Minute by Lord Perth (CO) to Mr. Macmillan, 23 February 1957 in R. Hyam and Wm Roger Louis (eds.), *The Conservative Government and the End of Empire, 1957–1964*, Part 2 Economics, International Relations and the Commonwealth (London: The Stationery Office, 2000), pp.224–228.

58 A well-documented example is Enoch Powell. See Camilla Schofield, *Enoch Powell and the Making of Postcolonial Britain* (London: Cambridge University Press, 2013), pp.31, 50, 73.

59 See footnote 57, p.224.

60 Ibid., p.226.

61 'Problems of Foreign Policy', NECISC, n.d. (1952), pp.12–13.

62 Said K. Aburish, *Nasser: The Last Arab* (London: Duckworth, 2005), pp.38–39, 43.

63 Hoopes, *The Devil and John Foster Dulles*, p.318.

64 Quoted in John Charmley, *Churchill's Grand Alliance: The Anglo-American Special Relationship 1940–57* (London: Hodder & Stoughton, 1995), pp.282–283.

65 Hoopes, *The Devil and John Foster Dulles*, p.183.

66 Wm. R. Louis, 'American Anti-Colonialism, Suez and the Special Relationship', in his *Ends of British Imperialism: The Scramble for Empire, Suez and Decolonization* (London: IB Tauris, 2006), p.601.

67 Salim Yaqub, *Containing Arab Nationalism: The Eisenhower Doctrine and the Middle East* (Chapel Hill, NC: University of North Carolina Press, 2004), p.1.

68 Ibid., p.4.

69 Ibid., p.7.

70 John F. Kennedy, *"Let the Word Go Forth": The Speeches, Statements, and Writings of John F. Kennedy, 1947–1963*, selected with an introduction by Theodore C. Sorenson (New York: Delacorte Press, 1988), pp.331–337.

71 Ibid. pp.338–340.

72 Robert J. McMahon (ed.), *Major Problems in the History of the Vietnam War: Documents and Essays* (Boston, MA: Houghton Mifflin, 2003), p.59.

73 Ibid., pp.55–56.

74 National Security Council Paper, Number 64, 1950, in ibid., p.57.

75 Eisenhower to Churchill, 1954, in ibid., p.88.

76 Hoopes, *The Devil and John Foster Dulles*, pp.204–205.

77 On Indonesia, for example, see Audrey R. Kahin and George McT. Kahin, *Subversion as Foreign Policy: The Secret Eisenhower and Dulles Debacle in Indonesia* (Seattle, WA: University of Washington Press, 1995).

78 LaFeber, *Inevitable Revolutions*, pp.110–111.

79 Quoted in ibid., p.121.

80 Ibid., p.141.

81 See, for example, Stephen Kinzer, *The Brothers: John Foster Dulles, Allen Dulles, and Their Secret World* (New York: St. Martin's Press, 2013), Ch.6.

82 Stephen G. Rabe, *The Killing Zone: The United States Wages Cold War in Latin America* (2nd ed. New York: Oxford University Press, 2016), p.39.

83 Quoted in LaFeber, *Inevitable Revolutions*, p.159.

84 See Roby C. Barrett, *The Greater Middle East and the Cold War: US Foreign Policy Under Eisenhower and Kennedy* (New York: IB Tauris, 2007), pp. 6–7, 174–190, 314–328.

85 Memorandum of a Conversation, 7 November 1961, *Foreign Relations of the United States (FRUS), 1961–63, Volume 1: Vietnam 1961*, doc.218. Jagan was first forcibly removed from power, even though he was elected, by the British, with American support, in 1953. See Colin A. Palmer, *Cheddi Jagan and the Politics of Power* (Chapel Hill, NC: University of North Carolina Press, 2010) and Stephen J. Rabe, *US Intervention in British Guiana* (Chapel Hill, NC: University of North Carolina Press, 2005).

86 Kennedy, *"Let the Word Go Forth"*, Campaign Speech, Tampa, 18 October 1960, pp.109–117.

87 Ambrose, *Nixon: The Education of a Politician*, p.550.

88 Ibid., pp.553–555.
89 Arthur M. Schlesinger, Jr. *The Imperial Presidency* (New York: Houghton Mifflin, 1973 and Mariner Books, 2004), pp.168–169, 177.
90 Kennedy, *"Let the Word Go Forth"*, Acceptance of Presidential Nomination, 15 July 1960, p.102.
91 Al Smith Memorial Dinner, New York, 19 October 1960, ibid., pp.137–140.
92 Inaugural Address, ibid., pp.12–13
93 Televised Address, 22 October 1962, ibid., p.277.
94 Special Address to Congress, 25 May 1961, ibid., p.226.
95 Special Message to Congress, 28 March 1961, ibid., pp.239–240, 252.
96 Lawrence Freedman, *Kennedy's Wars: Berlin, Cuba, Laos and Vietnam* (New York: Oxford University Press, 2000), p.372, 376, 410, 419.
97 Visit of General Lansdale to Vietnam, 2–14 January 1961, *Foreign Relations of the United States 1961–63, Volume 1: Vietnam 1961*.
98 Ibid., doc.3.
99 Ibid., doc.21.
100 Ibid., doc.43.
101 Ibid., doc.59.
102 Ibid., docs 222 and 228.
103 Ibid., doc.254, Notes on the National Security Council Meeting, 15 November 1961. The 'assumption of a unified enemy' also seems to have nullified evidence of age-old hostilities between the Vietnamese and China, evidence that Kennedy was occasionally reminded of. See Bruce Kuklick, *Blind Oracles: Intellectuals and War from Kennan to Kissinger* (Princeton, NJ: Princeton University Press, 2006), p.128. Through 1961–1963 evidence of the Sino-Soviet split was treated with caution and scepticism. See Freedman, *Kennedy's Wars*, pp.255–260.
104 Current Intelligence Memorandum, 11 January 1963, *Foreign Relations of the United States, Volume 3: Vietnam 1963*, doc.11.
105 Ibid., doc.52, Memorandum to Kennedy from Bowles, 7 March 1963.
106 Ibid., p.73.
107 Ibid., p.203.
108 Lisa McGirr, *Suburban Warriors: The Origins of the New American Right* (Princeton, NJ: Princeton University Press, 2001), pp.5, 63, 67. See also Kirkpatrick Sale, *Power Shift: The Rise of the Southern Rim and Its Challenges to the Eastern Establishment* (New York: Vintage Books, 1976).
109 McGirr, *Suburban Warriors*, pp.54–56.
110 Ibid., pp.36, 45, 95–103.
111 See, John Micklethwait and Adrian Wooldridge, *The Right Nation: Why America is Different* (London: Penguin Books, 2005), pp. 40–93; Lieven, *America Right or Wrong*.

4 The Johnson administration and the defence of freedom in Vietnam

This chapter focuses on the thinking of the Johnson administration in relation to the 'problem of Vietnam' and, in particular, the way in which one powerful idea – that of the domino theory – limited the range of options held to be available in dealing with the problem. The Cold War anti-communist consensus in Washington was at its height when Johnson became president in November 1963, following the assassination of John F. Kennedy. A year later Johnson defeated the Republican candidate, Barry Goldwater, to become president in his own right. Goldwater had talked about "the advisability of invading Cuba, making Social Security voluntary, establishing a 'national right-to-work' law, giving control of nuclear weapons to battlefield commanders, and pulling the United States out of the United Nations if Red China were admitted."[1] He voted against the Civil Rights Act of 1964. He wanted to roll back the communists and voiced the anger of supporters who believed that Dulles and Eisenhower had failed in their promises of 1952 in this crucial respect. His followers were attracted by what they took to be "his moral and existential authority."[2] Johnson was the moderate in this context. He presided over a swollen Cold War empire with only token oversight from Congress and a largely supine press. Americans had never been richer and had rarely been more complacent about their national superiority. Much of the world had been tied in to American military priorities. Intimate relations were enjoyed with military establishments across the free world. Neutralists like Nasser, Nehru and Sukarno had been anathematised and the meaning of 'communist' had been distended to embrace any popular movements proposing social and economic reform or opposing dictatorships sponsored by the US. On this evidently satisfactory landscape 'the problem of Vietnam' came to represent an ugly blot.

As president, Johnson portrayed his own commitment to Vietnam as part of a "solemn private vow" made on board *Air Force One* while returning from Dallas to Washington on 22 November 1963 to achieve the goals Kennedy had set for himself but not lived to realise.[3] In fact his administration's commitment emerged from the currents of the broader American political culture and drew upon the consensus concerning the necessity of containing international communism. Analysing the ways in which the dominant anti-communist ideology impacted on the decisions that deepened US involvement in Vietnam is necessary to fully understand the situation outlined by Michael Howard in his classic account of *War and the Liberal Conscience*, in which the US military commitment to Vietnam, revealed what a hideous gap separated rhetoric from reality . . . And the appalling suspicion began to grow among liberals in the United States that the United States, the very embodiment of democratic and peaceful values, might, as it approached the end of its second century, be waging a murderously oppressive war against a small people struggling to be free.[4]

During the Second World War, Japanese occupation of Vietnam had displaced French colonialism. In the brief power vacuum created by the Japanese surrender Ho Chi Minh had proclaimed Vietnam's independence on 2 September 1945. As we saw in chapter two, in so doing Ho consciously invoked the US Declaration of the Independence, condemned French colonial rule and ended with a plea couched in the US anti-colonial tradition: "We are convinced that Allies . . . cannot fail to recognize the right of the Vietnamese people to independence. A people who have courageously opposed French enslavement for more than eighty years, a people who have resolutely sided with the Allies against the Fascists during these last years, such a people must be free, such a people must be independent."[5] His conviction was misplaced, and instead the US acquiesced in the British-assisted return of French colonial administration in Vietnam, while the Truman administration provided direct credit to France to help reassert its rule. A cycle of individual acts of resistance, repression and reaction soon escalated into a war of independence.[6] As a result, Vietnam registered as another among a growing number of post-Second World War problem areas dotted across the US State Department's map of the world. In Asia these included the ongoing civil war in China and unrest in Korea, elsewhere they included even more acute problems in Greece, Turkey and Iran. International communism was held to be the common denominator in each of these cases, leading to State Department efforts to assess just 'how Communist' Ho Chi Minh was. These drew a blank in terms of identifying a link with Moscow, but the absence of evidence could not shift the firm belief of Secretary of State Dean Acheson, conveyed in a May 1949 telegram, that:

> In light Ho's known background, no other assumption possible but that he outright Commie so long as (1) he fails unequivocally repudiate Moscow connections and Commie doctrine and (2) remains personally singled out for praise by internatl Commie press and receives its support. Moreover, US not impressed by nationalist character red flag with yellow stars. Question whether Ho as much nationalist as Commie is irrelevant. All Stalinists in colonial areas are nationalists. With achievement natl aims (i.e., independence) their objective necessarily becomes subordination state to Commie purposes and ruthless extermination not only opposition groups but all elements suspected even slightest deviation.[7]

The logical extension of this thinking was that communists could not be 'real' nationalists, merely international communist wolves in nationalist sheep's clothing. The nationalists, by definition, were the non-communists. Therefore, support for Vietnamese nationalism involved resisting the communists who threatened genuine independence. This led the US down an ideologically constructed blind alley. Though no non-communist nationalist movement existed in Vietnam, its absence did not demonstrate the unity of the two causes under the leadership of Ho Chi Minh. Communism and nationalism were separate causes; all that was required was the identification of appropriate non-communist nationalists who could direct the genuine nationalist aspirations of the country. This was a formula that allowed the US to reconcile its anti-colonial ideology with the emerging Cold War policy of Containment of communism, which rested on the imagery of disease and infection. As Marilyn Young has argued, in this context it was understood that:

> The task of the United States was to stand by those governments attempting to 'root it out', as well as to pose a credible military threat to the main sources of contamination – China and the Soviet Union. Communism could be contained. When it was frozen within its borders, Communism could be prevented from attacking healthy organisms.[8]

As we saw in chapter two, this logic was formalised as US policy via NSC-68, drafted in April 1950.[9] This analysed recent and profound changes to the international system: the collapse of the Ottoman, Austro-Hungarian, German, Italian and Japanese empires; the rapid weakening of the British and French imperial systems; the Russian and Chinese revolutions and the emergence of the US and Soviet Union as the two dominant world powers. The characterisation of the USSR contained in NSC-68 was unflaggingly bleak. Conflict with the Soviet Union was actual, occurring and endemic; the only variation would come in the form it took with the ever-present possibility that, if mishandled, it could escalate to atomic war and annihilation. What the document called the "fundamental design of the Kremlin" called for the "complete subversion or forcible destruction of the machinery of government and structure of society in the countries of the non-Soviet world and their replacement by an apparatus and structure subservient to and controlled from the Kremlin."

The document, which it is important to remember was not for public consumption or itself part of a public information campaign,[10] is a key source for understanding the meaning of 'freedom' as a Cold War concept. This was understood in NSC-68 to be in conflict with its antonym, "the idea of slavery under the grim oligarchy of the Kremlin." Unlike the situation under communism, the essence of the free society was to be found in the way in which it "values the individual as an end in himself, requiring of him only that measure of self discipline and self restraint which make the rights of each individual compatible with the rights of every other individual." This inherently more attractive ideology represented a "permanent and continuous threat to the foundation of the slave society" which as a consequence regarded as "intolerable the long continued existence of freedom in the world."

This then was a battle of ideas, but a battle of ideas complicated by the fact that the attractiveness of the free society lay not simply in the principle of freedom, but in the success of the free society of the US, which in turn rested on its material environment. It therefore followed that the "objectives of the free society are determined by its fundamental values and by the necessity for maintaining the material environment in which they flourish", and the Kremlin's war on the free society was a war to undermine this material environment. The corollary of this was that the US had an interest in building a "successfully functioning political and economic system in the free world." However, NSC-68 noted, current trends favoured the Soviet Union and its satellites. It was "imperative that this trend be reversed by a much more rapid and concerted build-up of the actual strength of both the United States and the other nations of the free world." Any further 'loss' to the Soviet Union would exacerbate the unfavourable trend as well as erode the environment necessary to securing the material strength of the free world. The intersection of what was understood to be the relentless logic of communist expansion at the expense of freedom, and anxiety about the impact of any potential 'loss' on perceptions of what NSC-68 called "the integrity and vitality of our system" spawned the domino theory.

This line of thinking was already evident in NSC-64 of February 1950, which warned of the importance to US "security interests that all practicable measures be taken to prevent further communist expansion in Southeast Asia." The document advised that Indochina, "is a key area of Southeast Asia and is under immediate threat. The neighboring countries of Thailand and Burma could be expected to fall under Communist domination if Indochina were controlled by a Communist-dominated government. The balance of Southeast Asia would then be in grave hazard."[11] Four years later, asked to comment on the strategic importance of Indochina, President Eisenhower responded by outlining what he called the "falling domino principle": "You have a row of dominos set up, you knock over the first one, and what will happen to the last one is the certainty that it will go over very quickly. So you could have a beginning of a disintegration that would have the most profound influences." The 'loss' of Indochina could be followed by the loss of Burma, Thailand and of the entire peninsula. From there, via Japan, Formosa and the Philippines "it moves in to threaten Australia and New Zealand" meaning that the "possible consequences of the loss are just incalculable to the free world."[12]

This compelling anti-communist ideological framing provides the context for understanding US reactions to the 1954 French military defeat at Dien Bien Phu, which marked the end of the French colonial project in Indochina. The US, France, Britain, the Soviet Union and China were already holding a conference in Geneva to discuss Cold War issues when Dien Bien Phu fell. Each of these five powers had their own interest over Vietnam and none sought, or attached a high priority to, a unitary Vietnamese state. This state of affairs helps explain the compromise solution agreed at Geneva – the temporary division of Vietnam along the 17th parallel with elections supervised by the International Control Commission scheduled for two years' time, in July 1956, leading to unification. The Final Declaration, which was endorsed by all participants except the US, noted "the clauses in the agreement on the cessation of hostilities in Viet-Nam prohibiting the introduction into Viet Nam of foreign troops and military personnel as well as of all kinds of arms and munitions" and those "on the cessation of hostilities in Viet-Nam to the effect that no military base at the disposition of a foreign state may be established in the regrouping zones of the two parties."[13]

Hence, the Geneva Accords established two separate Vietnamese entities, the Democratic Republic of Vietnam north of the 17th parallel and the State of Vietnam to the south. Given that the North remained committed to the unification of the country and the logic of the South was that it could never be any more than a state that ended at the 17th parallel, the artificiality of the South as a state was arguably greater than that of the North. Indeed, the state in the south was one lacking many of the characteristics of statehood. The US moved quickly to supply a number of these,[14] including an apparently credible nationalist leader in the form of the Catholic Ngo Dinh Diem and a regional security pact, the Southeast Asia Treaty Organisation (SEATO) concluded in 1955, modeled on NATO and offering quasi-legal cover to US intervention in the name of countering communist aggression.[15] The creation of SEATO also pre-dated the elections scheduled under the terms of the Geneva Accords and so existed in tension with their stated aim of producing a single Vietnamese state. Concurrently, there was a growing awareness in the US that if the scheduled elections were held in the closely supervised way agreed at Geneva, the outcome was likely to favour the North. As a State Department intelligence report from 1955 noted: "Almost any type of election would . . . give the Communists a very significant if not a decisive advantage" with the added problem that the Geneva conditions of "maximum freedom and the maximum degree of international supervision might well operate to Communist advantage and allow considerable Communist strength in the South to manifest itself at the polls."[16] Diem understood this too and with US support declined to hold the elections agreed at Geneva. Instead, voters in the South were offered a referendum, held in October 1955, through which they could confirm the *de facto* partition of Vietnam by endorsing Diem as president, which they did with 98.2 per cent of the vote, achieved via widespread manipulation and fraud.[17] By the time the date set at Geneva for the elections leading to unification – July 1956 – passed by, Diem was president of a separate state, the Republic of Vietnam, which could not have been created without the close involvement of the Eisenhower administration. Anti-communist ideology, rooted in the US historical experience, played a role in obscuring the depth of the problems this would entail. As Marilyn Young has written:

> The United States had created itself and it could help other nations to do the same. The United States declared South Vietnam a new nation . . . and did not take seriously the evidence that this new nation was really half of an old one, whose long struggle for independence against outside invaders informed the social and personal imagination of every Vietnamese.[18]

In May 1957 the reality of the South's statehood was confirmed when Diem paid a state visit to Washington, accompanied by flattering US press coverage. By this time a pro-Diem US lobby group, the American Friends of Vietnam, had been in existence for over a year, and was attracting national political figures to its meetings.[19] At one of these meetings, in August 1956, Senator John F. Kennedy explained that the "fundamental tenets of this nation's foreign policy . . . depend in considerable measure upon a strong and free Vietnamese nation." More accurately, he went on to note that the Republic of Vietnam "is our offspring."[20] The challenges facing this offspring were heightened with the December 1960 formation of the National Front for the Liberation of South Vietnam (NLF) which organised the People's Liberation Armed Forces (PLAF), routinely referred to as the 'Viet Cong' by the US and Saigon governments.

By the time American Friend of Vietnam John F. Kennedy became president, PLAF strength was growing and would continue to do so throughout his presidency; from an estimated 17,000 in late 1961 to 25,000 in 1962. Increasingly, the authority of Diem's government was confined to Saigon and the provincial capitals, its forces liable to successful ambush beyond these. For Kennedy, guerrilla warfare was a signature communist tactic, something on which officials like Deputy Special Assistant for National Security Affairs Walt W. Rostow and Director of the State Department's Bureau of Intelligence and Research Roger Hilsman were in agreement. For Hilsman, guerrilla war represented "a new kind of aggression in which one country sponsors internal war within another."[21] This ruled out nationalism as a cause of the conflict and led to the activities of the NLF and PLAF being understood by US policy-makers as externally directed and therefore alien to the political culture of Vietnam. Indeed, 'Viet Cong' and 'Vietnamese' quickly came to be accepted as being two separate things.[22]

As dissatisfaction with Diem increased within the new Republic of Vietnam, and within the American Friends of Vietnam, so frustration in Washington grew. The repression of Buddhists led to negative press coverage in the US, much heightened following the self-immolation of Buddhist monk Thich Quang Duc in June 1963. As part of the US response, Ambassador Frederick Nolting, now considered too close to Diem, was replaced by Henry Cabot Lodge. Nolting returned to Washington in late August 1963, where a letter awaited him from President Kennedy noting his "significant contribution to strengthening relations between the Governments and peoples of the United States and Viet-Nam . . . your actions have embodied the determination of the United States and other free nations to assist Viet-Nam in maintaining its freedom."[23] Nevertheless, the Kennedy administration was already involved in coup plotting against Diem with key figures – prominent among them Ambassador Lodge – convinced that Diem was more part of the problem than the solution, and that the fortunes of the Republic of Vietnam could be improved by changing its leadership. This analysis was flawed and either ignored or downplayed the structural causes of the challenges it faced. To what extent the US sponsored the coup of 1 November 1963 and to what extent it simply did nothing to prevent it remains keenly debated,[24] but the outcome was clear; on 2 November Diem was murdered. Three weeks later so was Kennedy.

JOHNSON: BACKGROUND, FOREIGN POLICY BELIEFS AND INHERITANCE

A month after his elevation to the presidency, Lyndon Johnson was already asking a question that he would repeat with only slight variation but increasing exasperation to a range of confidants, advisers and Cabinet appointees: "Now what are we going to do about Vietnam?"[25] Johnson had been in Congress as the Cold War had developed. From the House of Representatives he had fully supported the proclamation of the Truman Doctrine with its implication of a more interventionist future for US foreign policy, explaining that "we have fought two world wars because of our failure to take a position in time."[26] The lessons of the Second World War were clear, when "the siren songs of appeasers convinced us it was none of our business what happened in Europe or the world."[27] They were also transferable because, Johnson explained, whether "Communist or Fascist, the one thing a bully understands is force, and the one thing he fears is courage."[28] On this basis he dismissed concerns that the new approach to foreign policy outlined by Truman might lead to war with the Soviet Union, arguing instead that if:

> Russia is not willing to stop with the land she has taken away from Poland, Finland, and Czechoslovakia; is not willing to get out of Austria, but insists on a foothold in the Mediterranean . . . then now is the time for us to decide whether we will meet her there and meet her now. When democracy lays down before any other ideology, there is no more democracy.[29]

A freshman Senator at the time of the 1950 North Korean invasion of the South, he called Truman's commitment of US forces "courageous and essential", adding that: "The world has expected the United States to lead the free nations unafraid and unbullied. Now we are showing that we mean what we say."[30] By the time of the French military defeat at Dien Bien Phu, Johnson was Senate Minority Leader and sought to make party political capital out of the crisis, asking at its height: "What is American policy in Indo-China? It is apparent only that American foreign policy has never in all its history suffered such a stunning reversal . . . Our friends and allies are frightened and wondering, as we do, where are we headed. We stand in clear danger of being left naked and alone in a hostile world."[31] In using such hyperbole Johnson also contributed to an exaggerated sense of Vietnam's importance to US security, something that would severely constrain what he understood to be his options as president a decade later.

But no one took this process further then President Eisenhower himself who, as we have seen, articulated the "falling domino" principle in the same year. His Secretary of State, John Foster Dulles, and Vice-President, Richard Nixon, spoke similarly. In part, their statements may have reflected domestic political concerns and electoral calculations, but they also reflected a genuine belief in an expansive international communism. The domino metaphor was a powerful simplifying device, but at the same time one that was unlikely to withstand sustained scrutiny – after all, the fall of China in 1949 had yet to precipitate the fall of other countries in the region. However, the domestic political context of the 1950s was not one that was tolerant of what could be construed as apologias on behalf of international communism. In this context, asserted repeatedly for a range of reasons but seldom seriously challenged, the domino theory quickly assumed the place of established orthodoxy in the framing of Cold War US foreign policy.

Moreover, the apocalyptic language of the domino theory favoured by Eisenhower not only tied US security to the future of South Vietnam (as Johnson administration principals usually referred to the Republic), it also left his successors with limited room for manoeuvre unless they were to publicly distance themselves from his analysis – something that the anti-communist drumbeat of conservative groups in the US made too risky to warrant seriously considering.[32] Take, for example, the warning Eisenhower delivered in a speech at Gettysburg College, Pennsylvania in April 1959, and which is quoted by Lyndon Johnson in his memoirs:

> Strategically South Vietnam's capture by the Communists would bring their power several hundred miles into a hitherto free region. The remaining countries in Southeast Asia would be menaced by a great flanking movement. The freedom of twelve million people would be lost immediately and that of one hundred fifty million others in adjacent lands would be seriously endangered. The loss of South Vietnam would set in motion a crumbling process that could, as it progressed, have grave consequences for us and for freedom.[33]

To accept that the domino idea had a domestic political utility, which it clearly did, is not to say that it was simply deployed cynically. It is not clear how far any of its advocates understood it to be a mechanistic process,[34] but Johnson's belief in some form of it can be seen from a paper he drafted as vice-president on his return from a May 1961 tour of Asia that took in South Vietnam and a meeting with President Diem. In this he warned of how:

> The price of the failure to make the sacrifices now in Viet Nam will be paid for later in the increased jeopardy to the United States and other free nations. The failure to act vigorously to stop the killing now in Viet Nam may well be paid for later with the lives of Americans all over Asia.[35]

More arrestingly, he told Kennedy that: "We must decide whether to help these countries to the best of our ability or throw in the towel in the area and pull back our defenses to San Francisco and a 'Fortress America' concept."[36]

Also significant was the sense he gained from this trip that South Vietnam's leaders simply did not understand what needed to be done to promote democracy and establish bonds with civil society. Johnson's own experience of politics in Texas had taught him how to reach out to the public, and he sought to demonstrate how it was done on his arrival in Saigon, having his motorcade from the airport to the city centre stopped repeatedly so that he could shake hands with locals and disburse cheap gifts and, improbable as it sounds, free passes to the US Senate gallery.[37] Robert Dallek has argued that there is a sense in which through this behaviour Johnson was trying to sell the virtues of American politics to both mass and elite in South Vietnam, and that "like Woodrow Wilson and other evangels of democracy", Johnson was "a crusader for the American dream, an exponent of the idea that inside of every impoverished African and Asian there was an American waiting to emerge."[38] There is undoubtedly an element of truth to this and, as the war progressed, Johnson came to understand well the link between success and the promotion of political stability in the South. At the outset of his administration, however, there were limits to his ambition for engaging in social reform in South Vietnam. Two days into his presidency, he told a meeting that:

> he wanted to make it abundantly clear that he did not think we had to reform every Asian into our own image. He said that he felt all too often when we engaged in the affairs of a foreign country we wanted to immediately transform that country into our image and this, in his opinion, was a mistake. He was anxious to get along, win the war—he didn't want as much effort placed on so-called social reforms.[39]

Nevertheless, it was to be to the constant frustration of Johnson and the principals in his administration that the South Vietnamese so stubbornly refused to release their inner American. This inability to accept that another country and society could forego the benefits of an exported American political culture was rooted in ignorance of Vietnamese history and culture. Further, it left the Johnson administration serially over-optimistic about the possibilities for political development in the South, with a tendency to over-sell the significance of any indication that governmental or societal developments were at last moving in their preferred direction.

THINKING ABOUT US AIMS AND OPTIONS IN VIETNAM: IDEOLOGY AS CONSTRAINT

As president, Johnson's leadership style was very different to that of Kennedy and called for uniformity in advice emanating from Vietnam. At a meeting on his second full day as president, he warned that he "wanted no more divisions of opinion, no more bickering and any person that did not conform to policy should be removed" from Vietnam.[40] Nevertheless, from his earliest days in office Johnson received advice on alternatives to a deepening US military commitment to South Vietnam. As with Johnson's own understanding, this advice also drew on analogies to explain possible outcomes. For example, responding to Johnson's argument that he didn't want 'another China', in early January 1964 Senate Majority Leader Mike Mansfield drew on one of the most powerful and regularly deployed analogies to tell him:

> Neither do we want another Korea. It would seem that a key (but often overlooked) factor in both situations was a tendency to bite off more than we were prepared in the end to chew. We tended to talk ourselves out on a limb with overstatements of our purpose and commitment only to discover in the end that there were not sufficient

American interests to support with blood and treasure a desperate final plunge. Then, the questions followed invariably: 'Who got us into this mess?' 'Who lost China?' etc.[41]

Instead of a deepening of the US commitment to the unstable South Vietnam, Mansfield recommended a lowering of the rhetorical temperature, a greater focus on finding a peaceful settlement (which would inevitably mean some compromise on understandings of what could be achieved in terms of South Vietnamese independence) and a greater emphasis on the role of the Vietnamese themselves as the responsible agents in this process. However, viewing Vietnam through the prism of anti-communist ideology, and specifically the domino theory, suggested that what was at stake was not simply South Vietnam itself. This was precisely the view of the advisers Johnson inherited from the Kennedy administration – 'the Harvards', the self-consciously intellectual group of policy advisers whose academic backgrounds contrasted with his own at San Marcos College in Southwest Texas.

It was the Harvards who extracted and explained the lessons of China and Korea for US foreign policy. For example, National Security Adviser McGeorge Bundy warned Johnson, in terms he would be highly receptive to, that:

> The political damage to Truman and Acheson from the fall of China arose because most Americans came to believe that we could and should have done more than we did to prevent it. This is exactly what would happen now if we should seem to be the first to quit in Saigon.[42]

Defense Secretary Robert McNamara's analysis of the consequences of a communist-dominated South Vietnam drew on images of a monolithic international communism to create one of the starkest statements of belief in the domino theory ever laid out by a senior US Cabinet member:

> In Southeast Asia, Laos would almost certainly come under North Vietnamese domination, Cambodia might exhibit a facade of neutrality but would in fact accept Communist Chinese domination. Thailand would become very shaky, and Malaysia, already beset by Indonesia, the same; even Burma would see the developments as a clear sign that the whole of the area now had to accommodate completely to Communism (with serious consequences for the security of India as well) . . .
>
> In the eyes of the rest of Asia and of key areas threatened by Communism in other areas as well, South Vietnam is both a test of U.S. firmness and specifically a test of U.S. capacity to deal with 'wars of national liberation.' Within Asia, there is evidence – for example, from Japan – that U.S. disengagement and the acceptance of Communist domination would have a serious effect on confidence. More broadly, there can be little doubt that any country threatened in the future by Communist subversion would have reason to doubt whether we would really see the thing through. This would apply even in such theoretically remote areas as Latin America.[43]

Hence, Johnson was trapped by anti-communist ideology which held that much more than the fate of South Vietnam was at stake. Even as he looked for alternatives, a shared belief in the domino theory ruled them out and pointed inexorably in a single direction.[44] This affected the administration's ability to offer answers to critical questions, such as

how to square the circle of recognition that the situation was essentially a Vietnamese responsibility with the evidence that the South Vietnamese state was not capable
of assuming it without drawing the US in ever deeper. For one of the few who openly
accepted this reality, Chairman of the State Department's Policy Planning Council Walt
W. Rostow, the logical response was not negotiation over the future of South Vietnam,
but escalation to "a direct political-military showdown with Hanoi over the question of
its direct operation of the war in South Vietnam including infiltration of men and supplies",[45] an option he had first advocated to Secretary of State Dean Rusk as early as
November 1962.

By January 1964 the Joint Chiefs of Staff were on the same page as Rostow, advocating
bombing key targets in North Vietnam. This reflected their own attachment to domino
theory principles, which meant that: "in Viet-Nam we must demonstrate to both the
Communist and the non-Communist worlds that the 'wars of national liberation' formula
now being pushed so actively by the Communists will not succeed."[46]

The coup by General Nguyen Khanh on 30 January 1964 left Johnson again asking what was to be done, this time of McNamara. In a telephone call to Dean Rusk,
McNamara explained that "his only suggestion was to step up South Vietnamese operations" which Rusk thought "a very good idea."[47] The absence of a politico-military
strategy capable of delivering 'victory' was becoming evident. In preparation for a 10
February 1964 meeting with opponent of the deepening US commitment Mike Mansfield,
McGeorge Bundy advised Johnson to say,

> that for the present any weakening of our support of anti-Communist forces in South
> Vietnam would give the signal for a wholesale collapse of anti-Communism all over
> Southeast Asia. Khanh's government may be our last best chance, and we simply can-
> not afford to be the ones who seem to pull the plug on him.[48]

But Johnson did not dismiss Mansfield's alternative to escalation – the 'neutralisation'
of North and South Vietnam – out of hand, and asked Maxwell Taylor, Chairman of the
Joint Chiefs, to "initiate a State/DOD/CIA/COMUSMACV examination of the realism
of Senator Mansfield's plan."[49] Johnson's own uncertainty in part reflected the fact that
he did not feel he had a mandate for escalation before being elected president in his own
right, telling McGeorge Bundy in a March 1964 phone conversation that "I'm a trustee"
and repeating what he had told the Joint Chiefs; that "we haven't got any Congress that
will go with us, and we haven't got any mothers that will go with us in a war."[50] In this
context, Johnson felt he was navigating a middle course until the November 1964 elections, but this still constituted a deepening of the US commitment to South Vietnam.

This sense of drift without decision was, for some, a fundamental component of the
problem the US faced in South East Asia. On leaving his post as Assistant Secretary of
State for Far Eastern Affairs, Roger Hilsman offered Dean Rusk an analysis that located
it in "the gnawing doubts of both the Southeast Asians and the Communists as to our
ultimate intentions in the region" which had existed ever since the fall of Dien Bien Phu in
1954, since when "all Asians have wondered about our determination to fight in Southeast Asia, should fighting become necessary."[51] The solution, Hilsman advised, lay in a
clear demonstration of a US commitment to escalate the conflict as far as necessary:

> If we can successfully convince our friends and allies as well as the Communists and
> those, such as De Gaulle and Sihanouk, who tend to serve the Communists' purposes,

that we are determined to take whatever measures are necessary in Southeast Asia to protect those who oppose the Communists and to maintain our power and influence in the area, we will have established an atmosphere in which our problems in Laos, Viet-Nam and Cambodia may be amenable to solution. In such an atmosphere, the Communist side must inevitably be more cautious as it contemplates the possibility that we might escalate hostility to a level unacceptable to them. It is not necessary that they be certain of what we will do; but we must give them reason to assume that we are prepared to go as far as necessary to defeat their plans and achieve our objectives.[52]

Hence, 'neutralisers' such as De Gaulle – who in August 1963 had offered to mediate over Vietnam on the basis of a US troop withdrawal, the neutralisation of South Vietnam, and renewed North-South relations – were portrayed within the administration as serving the purposes of 'the communists'. This reflected the strong belief that 'neutralisation' was a kind of communist Trojan Horse. In January 1964 Rostow referred to it as something "which might well produce the greatest setback to US interests on the world scene in many years."[53]

This was not too different from the perspective of General Khanh, at this point Prime Minister of South Vietnam. As reported by General Minh, Chief of State of South Vietnam, during a May 1964 meeting with Ambassador Lodge and General Taylor in Saigon, whereas "Diem used to see communists everywhere; now Khanh sees neutralists everywhere." Minh provided further evidence, were it needed, of the problems South Vietnamese governments faced in generating legitimacy. Khanh was unpopular, he reported, and "government has lost the confidence of the people." This was recognised as constituting a problem, although Taylor offered the view that, "it was difficult to be popular in time of civil war", and that "there were times when Lincoln's popularity was very low in the United States during our civil war."[54]

The problems the US faced in shoring up the South Vietnamese state were by this time clearly understood, as were the consequences of failing in this task. However, they were understood in the apocalyptic terms of the domino theory, as set out by McNamara (once again) in a memorandum for Johnson in March 1964:

Unless we can achieve this objective in South Vietnam, almost all of Southeast Asia will probably fall under Communist dominance (all of Vietnam, Laos, and Cambodia), accommodate to Communism so as to remove effective U.S. and anti-Communist influence (Burma), or fall under the domination of forces not now explicitly Communist but likely then to become so (Indonesia taking over Malaysia). Thailand might hold for a period with our help, but would be under grave pressure. Even the Philippines would become shaky, and the threat to India to the west, Australia and New Zealand to the south, and Taiwan, Korea, and Japan to the north and east would be greatly increased.[55]

In May 1964 McNamara was dispatched to Saigon on a fact-finding mission. His assessment provided no fresh grounds for optimism: the Viet Cong held the initiative, the number of villages held by the government in the South continued to fall, desertion rates were high and the strength of military forces inadequate and falling.[56] The implication was clear but unstated: if the US government was to achieve its aim of maintaining an independent South Vietnam, the present combination of South Vietnamese military force and US military advisers was inadequate; direct US military intervention would be required. A memorandum from the CIA's Directorate of Intelligence contained an even bleaker outlook. Indeed, this had been drafted as something of a corrective because DCI John McCone felt the situation was even more serious than McNamara's analysis suggested. This made it clear that, "if the tide of deterioration has not been arrested by the end of the year, the anti-Communist position in South Vietnam is likely to become untenable."[57]

This was the background to a 24 May 1964 National Security Council meeting, in which the pressure for an additional military commitment, and clear demonstration of US political commitment to South Vietnam, was strong. McNamara warned that, "where our proposals are being carried out now, the situation is still going to hell. We are continuing to lose. Nothing we are doing will win."[58] Together with Rusk and Bundy, McNamara recommended that Johnson

> make a presidential decision that the US will use selected and carefully graduated military force against North Vietnam . . . after appropriate diplomatic and political warning and preparation and . . . unless such warning and preparation – in combination with other efforts – should produce a sufficient improvement of non-Communist prospects in South Vietnam and in Laos to make military action against North Vietnam unnecessary.[59]

Still, Johnson sought alternatives. In a telephone conversation with Adlai Stevenson, he explained that he was "just sitting here at the desk thinking about the alternatives and how horrible they are", only to be told by Stevenson how he had, "been shuddering on this thing for three years and I'm afraid that we're in a position now where you *don't* have any alternatives."[60] In a call to his old political friend Richard Russell immediately afterwards, Johnson asked "How important is it to us?" Russell's reply was that: "It isn't important a damn bit, with all these new missile systems."[61] And yet it was in terms of US credibility and the inexorable logic of the domino theory. As Johnson explained to Russell:

> I spend all my days with Rusk and McNamara and Bundy and Harriman and Vance and all those folks that are dealing with it and I would say that it pretty well adds up to them now that we've got to show some power and some force, that they do not believe – they're kinda like MacArthur in Korea – they don't believe that the Chinese Communists will come into this thing. But they don't know and nobody can really be sure. But their feeling is that they won't. And in any event, that we haven't got much choice, that we are treaty-bound, that we are there, that this will be a domino that will kick off a whole list of others, that we've just got to prepare for the worst.[62]

Russell had no doubt that US escalation would mean that, "the Chinese will be in there and we'd be fighting a danged conventional war against our secondary potential threat and it'd be a Korea on a much bigger scale and a worse scale."[63] What about the Soviet Union, asked Russell, was there "any truth in their theory that they are really at odds with China?" Johnson replied: "They are, but they'd go with them as soon as the fight started. They wouldn't forsake that Communist philosophy."[64]

Immediately following this conversation, Johnson phoned McGeorge Bundy to test out Russell's argument that Vietnam was not important to the US "a damn bit." "What the hell is Vietnam worth to me?" Johnson asked Bundy: "No, we've got a treaty but, hell, everybody else's got a treaty out there and they're not doing anything about it." Reflecting his own deep ambivalence, Johnson then invoked the domino theory to undermine his initial proposition, telling Bundy: "Of course if you start running from the Communists, they may just chase you right into your kitchen." Bundy agreed: "Yeah, that's the trouble. And that is what the rest of that half of the world is going to think if this thing comes apart on us. That's the dilemma."[65] With Bundy offering up no alternatives, Johnson asked him if he could think of anyone else who might offer a new approach. No, he could not, Bundy replied.

Given that the domino assumption was so clearly the obstacle, constituting the framework within which Johnson could identify no alternatives, it was only natural that he should seek a CIA assessment of its validity. The CIA response to Johnson's request for this assessment, drafted by Sherman Kent, provided a clear indication that the domino theory had only limited utility as an explanatory device. Kent defined the domino effect in the following terms:

> when one nation falls to communism the impact is such as to weaken the resistance of other countries and facilitate, if not cause, their fall to communism. Most literally taken, it would imply the successive and speedy collapse of neighboring countries, as a row of dominoes falls when the first is toppled—we presume that this degree of literalness is not essential to the concept. Most specifically it means that the loss of South Vietnam and Laos would lead almost inevitably to the communization of other states in the area, and perhaps beyond the area.[66]

However, the CIA did "not believe that the loss of South Vietnam and Laos would be followed by the rapid, successive communization" of the region. On the contrary, "a continuation of the spread of communism in the area would not be inexorable and any spread which did occur would take time—time in which the total situation might change in any of a number of ways unfavorable to the Communist cause."[67] In terms, then, of its implication of sequential and rapid change, the CIA did not subscribe to the domino theory. It did, however, believe in the demonstration effect, noting the effect the 'loss' of South Vietnam and Laos would have on China, "both in boosting its already remarkable self-confidence and in raising its prestige as a leader of World Communism", which would "tend to encourage and strengthen the more activist revolutionary movements in various parts of the underdeveloped world."[68]

This was the setting against which Congress passed the Gulf of Tonkin Resolution on 10 August 1964 in support of South Vietnam's "defence of its freedom." But that 'freedom' had not translated into stable or effective government and by most qualitative measures, democracy in South Vietnam was highly limited. Key Johnson administration figures were only too aware of this, but the reality on the ground was conceptually separate from the protection of 'freedom', which was an aspiration that the administration saw itself as laying the ground for. This teleological approach to South Vietnam may well have generated wishful thinking about the capacity of the South Vietnamese state to survive in some quarters, but Ambassador Maxwell Taylor was unaffected. Less than a month after the Gulf of Tonkin Resolution sailed through Congress Taylor was telling Dean Rusk that the latest political crisis in South Vietnam, in the form of demonstrations in opposition to a proposed new constitution, was not totally unexpected, and that the "very nature of the social, political and ethnic confusion in this country makes governmental turbulence of this type a factor which we will always have with us." He went on to advise that:

> What has emerged from these recent events is a definition within fairly broad limits of the degree to which perfectability in government can be pushed . . . We now have a better feel for the quality of our ally and for what we can expect from him in terms of ability to govern. Only the emergence of an exceptional leader could improve the situation and no George Washington is in sight. Consequently we can and must anticipate for the future an instrument of government which will have definite limits of performance.[69]

One of Taylor's key concerns was that this situation could result in a search for "a broadened consensus involving and attempting to encompass all or most of the minority elements with political aspirations until it approaches a sort of popular front." While such behaviour might be considered a logical and even desirable outcome for a democratic polity, in the context of South Vietnam this could "become susceptible to an accommodation with the Liberation Front, which might eventually lead to a collapse of all political energy behind the pacification effort", and so was highly undesirable.[70] Here, the tension between the rhetoric of freedom and democracy and the actual implications on the ground was laid bare. The South Vietnamese political process could not be allowed to result in any kind of popular front that included a communist element as "this may in due course require the U.S. to leave Vietnam in failure." Instead, given that "the consequences of this defeat in the rest of Asia, Africa and Latin America would be disastrous" the US had no option, in Taylor's view, but to assume increased responsibility for the outcome. He warned that, "we see no quick and sure way to discharge our obligations honorably in this part of the world." While he accepted that his forecast was "fairly grim", he warned that "the alternatives are more repugnant."[71] However, this was only on the basis that the assumptions underpinning the domino theory (with which, as we have seen, there was clear dissent within the CIA) held true.

There was still no clear answer to Johnson's question of "what are we going to do about Vietnam?" In the face of a crisis of morale in South Vietnam, chronic political instability, evidence of war-weariness and anti-American sentiment, and the corresponding risk of a rise in neutralist sentiment,[72] the only option he was being offered was the one that McGeorge Bundy presented to Johnson as the view of "nearly all of us"; that at some point either the US would need to increase the pressure on North Vietnam by military means or watch the inevitable break-up of the South.[73] At a 9 September 1964 White House meeting involving his most senior advisers – Rusk, McNamara, McCone, Wheeler, Taylor and McGeorge and William Bundy – Johnson again asked for confirmation that Vietnam was of such importance to justify the implications of the analysis; was Vietnam "worth all this effort"?:

> Ambassador Taylor replied that we could not afford to let Hanoi win, in terms of our overall position in the area and in the world. General Wheeler supported him most forcefully, reporting the unanimous view of the Joint Chiefs that if we should lose in South Vietnam, we would lose Southeast Asia. Country after country on the periphery would give way and look toward Communist China as the rising power of the area. Mr. McCone expressed his concurrence and so did the Secretary of State, with considerable force.[74]

The domino theory held powerful sway, with even McCone in agreement despite his own Agency's more nuanced analysis, and the participants offered no alternative perspectives. However, a contrasting view did emerge from within the administration the following month, in the form of a 67-page paper from George Ball in the State Department. This noted the deteriorating situation in South Vietnam, observed that there was no serious prospect of a government that could "provide a solid center around which the broad support of the Vietnamese people" could develop and rejected as misleading the frequent drawing of parallels between Vietnam and Korea. Having set out four options he felt were available to the US – to continue along current lines; to take over responsibility for the war from the South; mount an air offensive against the North; or seek to bring about a political settlement – and rejected the first three as paths to disaster, Ball advocated consideration of the fourth.[75] Ball recalled sending his paper to McNamara, Rusk and McGeorge Bundy and that, "McNamara in particular seemed shocked that anyone would challenge the verities in such an abrupt and unvarnished manner."[76] When the four met in November 1964 to discuss the paper, Ball recalled he was regarded with "benign tolerance" and his paper seen as "merely an idiosyncratic diversion from the only relevant problem: how to win the war."[77] It was a missed opportunity, as McNamara would subsequently concede.[78]

At the same time, the deteriorating political situation in South Vietnam made the initial policy of shoring up the legitimacy of the Khanh regime (so as to improve morale in the South before any major escalation of the war to the North) seem unrealistic. In January 1965 McGeorge Bundy informed Johnson that both he and McNamara now believed that, "the worst course of action is to continue in this essentially passive role which can only lead to eventual defeat and an invitation to get out in humiliating circumstances."[79] The urgency of the case was reinforced by an attack on a US military base at Pleiku the following month.

At an 8 February 1965 White House meeting to discuss US policy in light of this attack and the US reprisal bombing of North Vietnam, Senate Minority Leader Everett M. Dirksen asked what the effect would be if the US pulled out of South Vietnam. McGeorge Bundy explained that:

> there would be a strong feeling in the nations of Southeast Asia that we had failed to carry out our policy of assisting the Vietnamese to continue as an independent state. The consequences in Southeast Asia of our pull-out would be very large. In other parts of the world, the effect would also be very serious, even to the extent of affecting the morale in Berlin.[80]

McCone noted a shift on the part of the principals from supporting specific reprisal attacks against the North to his own position and that of Bundy, where reprisal was understood as involving sustained action against the North. However, there was also a shift in the rationale offered for the attacks, which were now being framed by Bundy in terms of their positive impact on the South's morale, a rationale with which the intelligence community essentially disagreed.[81] Johnson concluded the meeting by saying that it "was incumbent upon him as President to conduct our activities in South Vietnam in order to stop aggression and to destroy the aggressor if necessary but in any event to take such actions as might be required in support of the free peoples of South Vietnam."[82] This was less a statement of democracy promotion than of Containment of communism.

The flaw in this logic was pointed out by Senator Mike Mansfield in a memorandum he sent to Johnson immediately after the meeting. He reminded the President that

> we have approximately 42 mutual security agreements of one kind or another with countries or groups of countries scattered over the face of the globe. Short of nuclear war, we have not got the resources or the power to honor those agreements if the demand-payments on them multiply. We are stretched too thin as it is and even with total mobilization there would be little hope of fulfilling simultaneously any large proportion of these commitments.[83]

This was the problem with application of the Containment logic; because it did not offer a basis for distinguishing between the relative importance of different cases, it did not offer any guide to the question of the price worth paying (in essence, Johnson's repeated question over Vietnam) in any particular instance. Nevertheless, this logic paved the way for the Operation Rolling Thunder bombing campaign of the North, which began on 2 March 1965, by which time Johnson had agreed to the despatch of some 3,500 US marines to protect the US air base at Da Nang. They arrived six days after Operation Rolling Thunder began.

DEEPENING COMMITMENT

However, Operation Rolling Thunder did not have quite the impact predicted by McGeorge Bundy in February, when he told the President that: "It seems very clear that if the United States and the Government of Vietnam join in a policy of reprisal, there will be a sharp immediate increase in optimism in the South, among nearly all articulate groups."[84] The CIA thought there had been some improvement in morale as a result of Rolling Thunder, but that this had been off-set by "divisive sparring among political cliques in Saigon" and the dispiriting ability of the Viet Cong to "to dominate large areas of the country previously under Saigon's control."[85] Hence, rather than leading to an improvement in the situation in the South, by 20 March the Joint Chiefs of Staff were warning of the prospect of South Vietnam being "lost", and that "such a loss would be a US defeat, which we cannot afford and which would be recognized world-wide as such."[86] The debate was no longer whether to undertake reprisal attacks against the North, nor whether they should be isolated or sustained, but whether air power alone was sufficient. The Joint Chiefs of Staff, in March 1965, advocated a US ground war as the only means of sustaining South Vietnam in its current form.

With a US ground war by now inevitable, Johnson delivered a speech at Johns Hopkins University on 7 April to prepare the US public. This speech highlighted the extent to which ideologically informed understandings of the situation in Vietnam had had a distorting effect. The commitment that Johnson outlined rested on the flawed assumption that the role of the North in the South represented a simple case of external aggression by one state on another state in pursuit of "total conquest." This denied the context of Vietnamese history, omitted the context of the Geneva Accords, and left the administration unable to account for the force of Vietnamese nationalism. Moreover, it denied Vietnamese nationalism any sense of agency by framing the conflict in terms of an international communism orchestrated from China, with the

> rulers in Hanoi . . . urged on by Peking . . . a regime which has destroyed freedom in Tibet, which has attacked India and has been condemned by the United Nations for

aggression in Korea. It is a nation which is helping the forces of violence in almost every continent. The contest in Vietnam is part of a wider pattern of aggressive purposes.[87]

With the administration facing criticism that the US position in Vietnam in 1965 was similar to that confronting the French in 1954, and destined for a similar outcome, McGeorge Bundy drafted a memorandum for Johnson reassuring him that "despite superficial similarities", the two situations were "not fundamentally analogous."[88] For one thing, opposition to the war in France had left it "deeply divided" whereas the US public, despite some vocal critics, was in essence supportive. More significantly, Bundy pointed out, France in 1954 was "a colonial power seeking to re-impose its overseas rule, out of tune with Vietnamese nationalism." In contrast, the US was "responding to the call of a people under Communist assault, a people undergoing a non-Communist national revolution."[89] This was delusional stuff.

In the event, the commitment of US ground forces was quickly followed by requests for additional forces. George Ball recognised that this "transforms our whole relation to the war" and that "the world reaction will be very difficult." He argued that the US was "losing the propaganda war", although McNamara "contradicted this view by stating that he thought we were winning public opinion and that criticism appearing here and there did not amount to much."[90] In the course of debate over the following weeks about whether to accede to the request from General William Westmoreland, the commander of US forces in Vietnam, for an increase in ground force levels to over 150,000, the domino theory was again to the fore. William Bundy produced a record of a meeting on 23 June at which George Ball argued that, "we should stop at 100,000 and then think hard – even about plans for cutting our losses and shifting our focus of action in Southeast Asia to Thailand." Rusk and McNamara objected: "Thailand, they thought, could not be held if SVN had given up. Rather, Rusk said, we would end up with the only secure areas Australia, New Zealand, the Philippines, and NATO, with even India falling to the Communist Chinese."[91]

With McNamara and Ball offering conflicting advice on the question of ground force deployments, Johnson asked them to prepare studies on what the US should do next. Dean Rusk and William Bundy also produced papers. In his paper, Rusk restated the logic of Containment:

> The integrity of the U.S. commitment is the principal pillar of peace throughout the world. If that commitment becomes unreliable, the communist world would draw conclusions that would lead to our ruin and almost certainly to a catastrophic war. So long as the South Vietnamese are prepared to fight for themselves, we cannot abandon them without disaster to peace and to our interests throughout the world.[92]

McNamara advocated meeting Westmoreland's troop requests and intensifying the bombing campaign alongside a global diplomatic offensive. He calculated that: "Even though casualties will increase and the war will continue for some time, the United States public will support this course of action because it is a combined military-political program designed and likely to bring about a favorable solution to the Vietnam problem."[93]

Writing in the mid-1990s, McNamara conceded that from a post-Cold War perspective, it may have seemed "incomprehensible that Dean [Rusk] foresaw such dire consequences from the fall of South Vietnam." He sought to explain this to a new generation of readers by reference to the experiences of their generation:

We had lived through appeasement at Munich; years of military service during World War II fighting aggression in Europe and Asia; the Soviet takeover of Eastern Europe; repeated threats to Berlin, including that of August 1961; the Cuban Missile Crisis of 1962; and, most recently, Communist Chinese statements that the South Vietnam conflict typified 'wars of liberation,' which they saw spreading across the globe.[94]

William Bundy made a similar point, looking back from the mid-1980s to reflect on how:

There's one thing that I don't think any historian has put in writing . . . that of the decision-making group, Johnson, Rusk, McNamara, my brother, Walt Rostow, myself, all of those of us who were of age in 1940–41 were interventionists in the isolationist-interventionist debate . . . it doesn't show that they all believed in Munich, but they all believed that you have to stand up to aggression of some sort.[95]

In contrast to the analyses of Rusk and McNamara, in the paper he prepared Ball warned clearly against escalation:

No one can assure you that we can beat the Viet Cong or even force them to the conference table on our terms no matter how many hundred thousand white foreign (US) troops we deploy. No one has demonstrated that a white ground force of whatever size can win a guerrilla war—which is at the same time a civil war between Asians—in jungle terrain in the midst of a population that refuses cooperation to the white forces (and the SVN) and thus provides a great intelligence advantage to the other side.[96]

Ball advocated a troop freeze and a direct approach to Hanoi. McGeorge Bundy forwarded the four papers to Johnson, together with his hunch that "you will want to listen hard to George Ball and then reject his proposal. Discussion could then move to the narrower choice between my brother's course and McNamara's."[97] It has been suggested that subsequent meetings were merely window-dressing, for the record, and that Johnson had decided he had no alternative but to support the McNamara option. Nevertheless, Johnson clearly agonised over the key Vietnam decisions and was ill-served in terms of options presented by his closest advisers before George Ball emerged as a devil's advocate, only for his devil's advocacy to be rejected, as devil's advocacy often is. The issue was less the 'freedom' of South Vietnam in the sense of the promotion of liberal democratic values, and more, as former President Eisenhower put it during a February 1965 meeting in the White House, "denying Southeast Asia to the Communists."[98] Ultimately, for Johnson, in early to mid-1965 the compromises Ball suggested carried too great a risk that they would result in South Vietnam falling to the communists by invitation.

Hence, the February 1965 coup that ultimately brought to power Air Vice-Marshal Nguyen Cao Ky and General Nguyen Van Thieu as Prime Minister and titular head of state respectively, was welcomed as a stabilising development rather than deplored as anti-democratic. As Dean Rusk explained in the midst of the confusion of February 1965: "The highest possible priority must be given by us and the South Vietnamese to the establishment of a government and leadership which not only is stable but looks stable. Without the elementary platform, other efforts in the military and political field are likely to prove fruitless."[99] On this basis, by April 1966 'preserving' Ky had become one of Johnson's key Vietnam aims, despite the major compromises this involved in relation to any notion of democratic governance.[100]

Nevertheless, the formal appearance of democracy was of great symbolic importance, and a new South Vietnamese constitution was unveiled in April 1967, modelled on that of the United States and paving the way for elections in September designed to legitimise the government of South Vietnam. Johnson asked McNamara to personally tell Thieu and Ky that: "It is absolutely essential to my ability to continue to back the struggle for South Vietnamese independence and self-determination that the election be conducted with complete honesty and fairness, and that this honesty and fairness be apparent to all."[101] McNamara duly conveyed the message, but the glaringly fraudulent process of electing Thieu and Ky did nothing to enhance either man's reputation, nor that of the Johnson administration's commitment to democracy in South Vietnam.[102] Nevertheless, Johnson clung to any indicator of democratic consolidation available to him, up to and well beyond the point of self-delusion. For example, in November 1967 in a telephone conversation with former President Eisenhower, he told of how:

> we took us from 1776 to 1789 to get a Constitution in this country, and we had all that Anglo-Saxon heritage and background and freedom. Now these people in 13 months have had 5 elections and . . . the fact is that they had a higher percentage of their total people voting than we have and they've had five elections and they have ratified a Constitution and they've elected a House and a Senate and a President and Vice President and I think that is pretty encouraging.[103]

Since 1966 evidence of democratic legitimacy in the South had become increasingly important as the deteriorating military situation created more advocates of some form of coalition government, including communist representation, as an essential first step to a plausible exit strategy. Most irritatingly for Johnson, Robert Kennedy, having already criticised the administration's bombing policy at a press conference (on 21 February 1966), stated that inviting "discontented elements in South Vietnam" – including the National Liberation Front – "to a share of power and responsibility is at the heart of the hope for a negotiated settlement."[104] In a conversation the following morning with Dean Rusk, Johnson could see himself having to respond to the Kennedy initiative:

President: Well, they'll just say "do you agree with Senator Kennedy that we ought [to] appoint some Viet Cong ahead of time?" I'm inclined to say – I may be wrong on this – but I'm inclined to say that we have made it abundantly clear that we're for free elections, that we're willing to let the United Nations supervise them or anybody else that'll give us an honest free election and we're not in the business, that's just not our occupation of the moment, going around appointing Communist governments.

Rusk: That's right. That's right.

President: And we believe in self determination and we don't believe in trading with the Communists and appointing them. Now, what's wrong with that?

Rusk: I think that's right.

President: OK.[105]

While Kennedy's intervention would have been irritating to Johnson, the fact that McNamara was moving to the same conclusion should have been alarming. Johnson discussed McNamara's doubts in his conversation with Rusk immediately after the Kennedy press conference. By May 1966, McNamara was confiding in Averell Harriman his belief that: "we should get in touch direct with the NLF, also the North Vietnamese, but particularly the NLF, and begin to try to work up a deal for a coalition government."[106] By this time, McNamara no longer enjoyed the confidence of the President to the same extent as previously. Johnson, he complained, "was surrounded by Rostow, Clark Clifford and others who seemed to think that victory was around the corner", a view with which he did not agree (in February 1966 Johnson had shared with Rusk his reaction when McNamara "said the other day that we only have one chance out of three of winning, it just shocked me and furthermore it shocked everybody at the table."[107]), while McNamara despaired that Dean Rusk "expected a VC surrender."[108] How and where McNamara's Damascene conversion took place remains debateable, but by 1966 his behaviour was clearly perplexing those he confided in.[109]

By this time, McNamara's earlier role as the trusted adviser advocating an offensive military route to a settlement had been assumed by Walt Rostow. Unlike the 'Harvards' he inherited from Kennedy, Rostow was, Johnson would explain: "my intellectual. He's not your intellectual. He's not Bundy's intellectual. He's not Galbraith's intellectual. He's not Schlesinger's intellectual. He's going to be my goddamn intellectual and I'm going to have him by the short hairs."[110] Rostow was a hardliner, optimist and anti-communist ideologue. Arthur M. Schlesinger, Jr. captured his style and method well in a mid-1966 journal entry, noting how:

> Walt Rostow has suddenly emerged from a long eclipse and is now established as the Pangloss of the White House, telling the President with great authoritativeness all the things the President wants to hear. Everything, according to Walt, is getting better and better; and I can see him when the bombs begin to fall on Washington, assuring LBJ that the deep-running historic tendencies are on our side, that we are turning the corner in Zambia and Tasmania, and that all is for the best in the best of all possible worlds.[111]

That McNamara no longer believed in the approach he had previously advocated was made clear in a 1 November 1967 memorandum to the President – in effect a letter of resignation as Defense Secretary (his resignation was formally announced on 29 November). Johnson arranged for McNamara's memorandum to be sent to a group dubbed the 'Wise Men'. They were asked five questions, a detailed version of the "Now what are we going to do about Vietnam?" question to which Johnson still sought a silver bullet solution, including "should we get out of Vietnam?" None of the Wise Men thought they should. Neither were they, collectively, all that keen on negotiations. One of the Wise Men, former Secretary of State Dean Acheson, believed that negotiation was not the answer, and clung instead to the relevance of the Korea analogy:

> When these fellows decide they can't defeat the South, then they will give up. This is the way it was in Korea. This is the way the Communists operate . . . I would not talk about negotiations any more. You have made it clear where you stand. This isn't the Communist method. If they can't win they just quit after a while.[112]

Just under three months later, with the launch of the Tet Offensive, the redundancy of this thinking became clear. However, it would take Tet to shift some of the President's closest advisers from their inflexibility over Vietnam. During February 1968, the US military suffered its highest casualty figures for a single week in the entire conflict, and that year would prove the single most costly in terms of US lives lost, with approximately 16,500 US troops killed. By this time, while the US had been spared the "divisive and destructive debate" Johnson had anticipated should South Vietnam be 'lost', US politics was increasingly polarised with the Americanisation of the war mirrored by a growing anti-war movement and a radicalising effect on parts of the Civil Rights movement.[113] In this context, Johnson chose not to contest the 1968 presidential election and face the humiliating prospect of defeat; not just of defeat to the Republican candidate, but of losing his own party's nomination to "that grandstanding little runt" Robert Kennedy.[114]

IN RETROSPECT

Some 30 years later McNamara would produce the clearest statement of how the dominant anti-communist ideology influenced and constrained policy-making over Vietnam in the 1960s. In his account of the "tragedy" of Vietnam, *In Retrospect*, published in 1995, McNamara identified 11 "major causes of our disaster." These included: that the US misjudged the geopolitical intentions of its adversaries and "exaggerated the dangers" they posed to the US; that "we viewed the people and leaders of South Vietnam in terms of our own experience. We saw in them a thirst for – and a determination to fight for – freedom and democracy. We totally misjudged the political forces within the country"; that "we underestimated the power of nationalism to motivate a people"; and that

> we did not recognize that neither our people nor our leaders are omniscient. Where our own security is not directly at stake, our judgment of what is in another people's or country's best interest should be put to the test of open discussion in international forums. We do not have the God-given right to shape every nation in our own image or as we choose.[115]

Although readers of his book could be forgiven for assuming that the passage of time and Cold War were necessary to arriving at these judgements, the reality is that such arguments were being made during the war and were dismissed by McNamara and his colleagues at the time. For example, McNamara's 1995 analysis seems to borrow from George Ball's 1964 paper, which at the time, Ball recalled, McNamara was "dead set against."[116] In April 1966 Arthur M. Schlesinger, Jr. wrote to Vice-President Hubert Humphrey, highlighting how; "we have consistently underestimated the power of nationalism in Asia . . . we have consistently construed Asia too much in terms of western ideas, models, structures and issues. We have not known enough about Asia, nor have we tried to understand the problems of Asia in Asian terms."[117] Cogent argument in opposition to the war could be found amongst the statements and writings of diplomats, academics, journalists and clergy throughout the period of escalation. For example, author of the Containment strategy George Kennan had dismissed the Johnson administration's insistence on the global significance of taking a stand in South Vietnam in his 1966 appearance before the Fulbright congressional hearings into the war.[118] Some Protestant, Catholic and Jewish clergy provided a source of moral critique throughout.[119] The eminent Realist scholar Hans J. Morgenthau was a vocal critic, warning in *Foreign Affairs*, the house journal of the US foreign policy establishment, that:

> we tend to intervene against all radical revolutionary movements because we are afraid lest they be taken over by communists, and conversely we tend to intervene on behalf of all governments and movements which are opposed to radical revolution, because they are also opposed to communism. Such a policy of intervention is unsound on intellectual grounds . . . it is also bound to fail in practice.[120]

There were, then, alternative analyses available at the time that challenged the ideological orthodoxy applied to Vietnam by the Johnson administration principals via the domino theory. But this orthodoxy invited an understanding of the costs of failure in Vietnam as being so high as to make any deviation from it far too risky to contemplate prior to the Tet Offensive.

However, the passage of time did not lead all participants in Vietnam decision-making to concede that the bases of their commitment had been flawed. Walt Rostow, applying his characteristic *longue durée* approach to political analysis, continued to insist on the necessity of the commitment and the success of the outcome. Responding to the publication of *In Retrospect*, he argued that while the communists had succeeded in Vietnam, they had, because of the US stand there, failed to conquer the rest of South East Asia, thus paving the way for the success of ASEAN. He quoted approvingly a 1981 speech by the Malaysian Foreign Minister, who looked back on the early years of ASEAN's development between 1968 and the mid-1970s and argued that these were:

> very useful years to further bind the member countries together . . . In 1975 North Vietnamese tanks rolled past Danang, Cam Ranh Bay, and Ton Son Nut into Saigon. The United States withdrew their last soldiers from Vietnam, and the worst of ASEAN's fears which underscored the Bangkok Declaration of 1967 came to pass. But ASEAN by then had seven solid years of living in neighbourly cooperation. Call it foresight, or what you will, the fact remains that with ASEAN solidarity there were no falling dominoes in Southeast Asia following the fall of Saigon to the Communists, and the United States withdrawal from Southeast Asia.[121]

Lest further evidence was required, Rostow pointed out that Vietnam itself joined ASEAN in 1995. Untroubled by the need to identify a causative link in any of this, Rostow concluded a review of *In Retrospect* by saying that:

> No one has promised that American independence itself, or America's role as a bastion for those who believe deeply in democracy, could be achieved without pain or loss or controversy. The pain, loss, and controversy resulting from Vietnam were accepted for ten years by the American people. That acceptance held the line so that a free Asia could survive and grow; for, in the end, the war and the treaty which led to it were about who would control the balance of power in Asia.[122]

The ideological struggle over Vietnam, then, continued long after the physical conflict ended, reunification had been achieved and US-Vietnamese relations normalised. Vietnam represents the case study *par excellence* of how anti-communist ideological framings and assumptions could serve to constrain choice in US foreign policy decision-making, with disastrous consequences. The war was Johnson's war, in that the key escalatory decisions were ultimately his. In a wider sense, though, as Michael Hunt has observed, it was a war deeply rooted in a Cold War consensus "amounting almost to a religion among the nation's best and brightest."[123] As we have seen, Robert McNamara came to see that the US had misunderstood the nature of a conflict that was rooted in resistance to colonialism. But the Vietnam War became both an anti-colonial conflict *and* a Cold War conflict. It was the understanding of the world held by the US foreign policy elite during the 1950s and 1960s and applied inflexibly in the case of Vietnam that led to this; there was nothing inevitable about it.

NOTES

1 Geoffrey Kabaservice, *Rule and Ruin: The Downfall of Moderation and the Destruction of the Republican Party from Eisenhower to the Tea Party* (New York: Oxford University Press, 2012), p.79.
2 Ibid., p.115.
3 Lyndon Baines Johnson, *The Vantage Point: Perspectives of the Presidency 1963–1969* (New York: Holt, Rhinehart and Winston, 1971), p.42.
4 Michael Howard, *War and the Liberal Conscience* (Oxford: Oxford University Press, 1981), p.129.
5 Declaration of Independence, 2 September 1945, in Michael Hunt (ed.), *A Vietnam War Reader: American and Vietnamese Perspectives* (London: Penguin, 2010), p.14. On the geopolitical context in which the Declaration was made, see David G. Marr, *Vietnam, 1945: The Quest for Power* (Berkeley, CA: University of California Press, 1997).
6 For overviews, see for example, Stanley Karnow, *Vietnam: A History* (London: Century Hutchinson, 1983), Ch.4 and Christopher Goscha, *The Penguin History of Vietnam* (London: Allen Lane, 2016), Ch.8.
7 Telegram, Secretary of State to the Consulate at Hanoi, May 20 1949, *Foreign Relations of the United States, 1949*, Vol.VII, Part 1, *The Far East and Australasia*, doc.28, https://history.state.gov/historicaldocuments/frus1949v07p1/d28.
8 Marilyn B. Young, *The Vietnam Wars 1945–1990* (New York: HarperCollins, 1991), pp.24–25.
9 The original NSC-68 document is available at www.trumanlibrary.org/whistlestop/study_collections/coldwar/documents/pdf/10-1.pdf.
10 However, the Truman administration did expend considerable energy selling the assumptions and prescriptions contained in NSC-68 to the US public. See, Steven Casey, 'Selling NSC-68: The Truman Administration, Public Opinion, and the Politics of Mobilization, 1950–51', *Diplomatic History*, Vol.29, No.4, 2005, pp.655–690.
11 NSC-64: The Position of the United States with Regard to Indochina, February 27 1950, *Foreign Relations of the United States 1950*, Vol.VI, *East Asia and the Pacific*, doc.480.
12 President Eisenhower Press Conference, April 7 1954, in William Appleman Williams, Thomas McCormick, Lloyd Gardner and Walter LaFeber (eds.), *America in Vietnam: A Documentary History* (New York: W. W. Norton, 1989), pp.156–157.
13 The major provisions of the 1954 Geneva Accords are summarised in *Pentagon Papers* (Gravel edition, Boston: Beacon Press, 1971), Vol.1, pp.270–282.
14 See George Herring, *America's Longest War: The United States and Vietnam, 1950–1975* (3rd ed., New York: McGraw-Hill, 1996), pp.61–72.
15 Article IV of the SEATO Treaty recognised that, "aggression by means of armed attack in the treaty area against any of the Parties or against any State or territory which the Parties by unanimous agreement may hereafter designate, would endanger its own peace and safety, and agrees that it will in that event act to meet the common danger in accordance with its

constitutional processes." A note explained that for the US, "recognition of the effect of aggression and armed attack" applied "only to communist aggression." For the text of the Treaty, see: http://avalon.law.yale.edu/20th_century/usmu003.asp.

16 Cited in Young, *The Vietnam Wars 1945–1990*, p.52.

17 See, Jessica M. Chapman, '"Staging Democracy": South Vietnam's 1955 Referendum to Depose Bao Dai', *Diplomatic History*, Vol.30, No.4, 2006, pp.671–703. Chapman points out that Eisenhower administration principals were, "more concerned with how the referendum would be perceived internationally than they were with how it would be experienced in South Vietnam." As a consequence, by "turning a blind eye to the contradictions between Diem's democratic rhetoric and his undemocratic practices", the US helped set the scene for the instability that would characterise Diem's government. See p.676.

18 Young, *The Vietnam Wars 1945–1990*, p.103.

19 See, Joseph G. Morgan, *The Vietnam Lobby: The American Friends of Vietnam, 1955–1975* (Chapel Hill, NC: University of North Carolina Press, 1997).

20 Cited in Herring, *America's Longest War*, p.47.

21 Cited in Young, *The Vietnam Wars 1945–1990*, p.77.

22 For example, in his memoirs, Lyndon Johnson recalled early conversations with Dean Rusk and Robert McNamara where they concluded that "outlays for military and economic assistance would probably have to increase as the Vietnamese stepped up their campaign against the Viet Cong." Johnson, *The Vantage Point*, p.46. Similarly, Marilyn Young has pointed out how the US understanding of the role of communism in the conflict in Vietnam, and the nature of communism, "cast Vietnamese who lived and worked north of the 17th parallel as more foreign to South Vietnam than the Americans, for the Americans were invited guests, while North Vietnam was an enemy country." Young, *The Vietnam Wars 1945–1990*, p.104.

23 Frederick Nolting, *From Trust to Tragedy: The Political Memoirs of Frederick Nolting, Kennedy's Ambassador to Diem's Vietnam* (New York: Praeger, 1988), p.123.

24 See, for example, the account in David Kaiser, *American Tragedy: Kennedy, Johnson, and the Origins of the Vietnam War* (Cambridge, MA: Belknap Press, 2000), which reproduces Kennedy's own account, dictated on 4 November, at pp.276–278.

25 Michael R. Beschloss (ed.), *Taking Charge: The Johnson White House Tapes, 1963–1964* (New York: Simon & Schuster, 1997), p.123.

26 Robert Dallek, *Lone Star Rising: Lyndon Johnson and his Times 1908–1960* (New York: Oxford University Press, 1991), p.292.

27 Brian VanDeMark, *Into the Quagmire: Lyndon Johnson and the Escalation of the Vietnam War* (New York: Oxford University Press, 1995), p.9.

28 Ibid.

29 Dallek, *Lone Star Rising*, p.292. See also Johnson, *The Vantage Point*, p.47.

30 Dallek, *Lone Star Rising*, p.383.

31 Ibid., p.444.

32 Rick Perlstein, *Before the Storm: Barry Goldwater and the Unmaking of the American Consensus* (New York: Nation Books, 2009) captures this domestic context.

33 Johnson, *The Vantage Point*, p.51.

34 A point made by Fredrik Logevall, 'The Indochina Wars and the Cold War, 1945–1975', in Melvyn P. Leffler and Odd Arne Westad (eds.), *The Cambridge History of the Cold War: Volume II, Crisis and Détente* (Cambridge: Cambridge University Press, 2010), p.289.

35 Paper Prepared by the Vice-President (undated, May 1961), *Foreign Relations of the United States 1961–1963*, Vol.I, *Vietnam 1961* (print edition, Washington, DC: Government Printing Office, 1988), doc.59.

36 Robert Dallek, *Flawed Giant: Lyndon Johnson and his Times 1961–1973* (New York: Oxford University Press, 1998), p.18.

37 Dallek, *Flawed Giant*, p.13. On his return, he recommended that: "Our mission people must, by example and by subtle persuasion encourage the Saigon government from the President down to get close to the people, to mingle with them, to listen for their grievances and to act on them. Handshakes on the streets of Vietnamese leaders and people is the concept that has got to be pursued. And shirt-sleeves must be the hallmark of Americans. Unless we get this approach which we do not now have, on the part of Vietnamese officials or Americans this effort is not going to succeed." Report by the Vice President (undated), *Foreign Relations of the United States 1961–1963*, Vol.I, *Vietnam 1961*, doc.60.

38 Dallek, *Flawed Giant*, p.16.
39 Memorandum for the Record of Meeting, November 24 1963, *Foreign Relations of the United States 1961–1963*, Vol.IV, *Vietnam, August–December 1963*, doc.330. Johnson provides an account of this meeting in *The Vantage Point*, pp.43–44.
40 Memorandum for the Record of Meeting, November 24 1963, *Foreign Relations of the United States 1961–1963*, Vol.IV, *Vietnam, August–December 1963* (print edition, Washington, DC: Government Printing Office, 1991), doc.330.
41 Memorandum from Senator Mike Mansfield to the President, January 6 1964, *Foreign Relations of the United States 1964–1968*, Vol.I, *Vietnam 1964* (print edition, Washington, DC: Government Printing Office, 1992), doc.2: https://history.state.gov/historicaldocuments/frus1964-68v01/d2.
42 Memorandum From the President's Special Assistant for National Security Affairs (Bundy) to the President, January 9 1964, ibid., doc.8: https://history.state.gov/historicaldocuments/frus1964-68v01/d8.
43 Memorandum From the Secretary of Defense (McNamara) to the President, January 7 1964, ibid., doc.8.
44 Johnson's memoirs provide clear evidence of this. For example, reflecting on the situation he faced in 1965, he recalled that: "From all the evidence available to me it seemed likely that all of Southeast Asia would pass under Communist control, slowly or quickly, but inevitably, at least down to Singapore but almost certainly to Djakarta. I realize that some Americans believe they have, through talking with one another, repealed the domino theory. In 1965 there was no indication in Asia, or from Asians, that this was so." Johnson, *The Vantage Point*, p.151.
45 Memorandum From the Chairman of the Policy Planning Council (Rostow) to the Secretary of State, January 10, 1964, *Foreign Relations of the United States 1964–1968*, Vol.I, *Vietnam 1964*, doc.9: https://history.state.gov/historicaldocuments/frus1964-68v01/d9.
46 This is Dean Rusk's summary, contained in Letter From the Secretary of State to the Secretary of Defense (McNamara), February 5 1964, ibid., doc.36. The Joint Chiefs' memorandum of January 22 1964 is summarised at doc.17: https://history.state.gov/historicaldocuments/frus1964-68v01/d17, but not printed in the *FRUS* volume.
47 Telegram From the Secretary of State and the Secretary of Defense (McNamara) to the Ambassador in Vietnam (Lodge) and the Commander, Military Assistance Command, Vietnam (Harkins), January 31 1964, ibid., doc.25: https://history.state.gov/historicaldocuments/frus1964-68v01/d25.
48 Memorandum From the President's Special Assistant for National Security Affairs (Bundy) to the President, February 10 1964, ibid., doc.39: https://history.state.gov/historicaldocuments/frus1964-68v01/d39.
49 Memorandum of a Conversation Between the Joint Chiefs of Staff and the President, March 4 1964, ibid., doc.70: https://history.state.gov/historicaldocuments/frus1964-68v01/d70.
50 Beschloss, *Taking Charge*, pp.266–267.
51 Memorandum From the President's Special Assistant for National Security Affairs (Bundy) to the President, March 18 1964. *FRUS 1964–1968*, Vol.1, *Vietnam 1964*, doc.90: https://history.state.gov/historicaldocuments/frus1964-68v01/d90.
52 Ibid.
53 Memorandum From the Chairman of the Policy Planning Council (Rostow) to the Secretary of State, January 10 1964, ibid., doc.9: https://history.state.gov/historicaldocuments/frus1964-68v01/d9.
54 Memorandum of a Meeting, May 11 1964, ibid., doc.150: https://history.state.gov/historicaldocuments/frus1964-68v01/d150.
55 Memorandum From the Secretary of Defense (McNamara) to the President, March 16 1964, ibid., doc.84.
56 Notes Prepared by the Secretary of Defense (McNamara), May 14 1964, ibid., doc.154: https://history.state.gov/historicaldocuments/frus1964-68v01/d154.
57 Memorandum Prepared by the Directorate of Intelligence, Central Intelligence Agency, May 15 1964, ibid., doc.159: https://history.state.gov/historicaldocuments/frus1964-68v01/d159.
58 Cited in Beschloss, *Taking Charge*, p.362.
59 Ibid.

60 Ibid., pp.362–363.
61 Ibid., p.364.
62 Ibid., pp.364–365.
63 Ibid., p.367.
64 Ibid., p.368.
65 Ibid., p.370.
66 Memorandum From the Board of National Estimates to the Director of Central Intelligence (McCone), June 9 1964. *Foreign Relations of the United States, 1964–1968*, Vol.1, *Vietnam 1964*, doc.209: https://history.state.gov/historicaldocuments/frus1964-68v01/d209
67 Ibid.
68 Ibid.
69 Telegram from the Embassy in Vietnam to the Department of State, September 6 1964, ibid., doc.339.
70 Ibid.
71 Ibid.
72 See, for example, the Special National Intelligence Estimate, 'Chances for a Stable Government in South Vietnam', September 8 1964, ibid., doc.341.
73 Memorandum From the President's Special Assistant for National Security Affairs (Bundy) to the President, September 8 1964, ibid., doc.342.
74 Memorandum of a Meeting, White House, Washington, September 9 1964, 11 a.m, ibid., doc.343.
75 George W. Ball, *The Past Has Another Pattern: Memoirs* (New York: W. W. Norton, 1982), pp.381–383.
76 Ibid., p.383.
77 Ibid., p.384.
78 McNamara, *In Retrospect*, p.158.
79 Memorandum from the President's Special Assistant for National Security Affairs (Bundy) to President Johnson, January 27 1965, *Foreign Relations of the United States, 1964–1968*, Vol. II, *Vietnam, January–June 1965* (print edition, Washington, DC: Government Printing Office, 1996), doc.42.
80 Summary Notes of the 547th Meeting of the National Security Council, February 8 1965, ibid., doc.87.
81 Memorandum From the Director of the Bureau of Intelligence and Research (Hughes) to Acting Secretary of State Ball, February 8 1965, ibid., doc.90.
82 Memorandum for the Record, February 8 1965, ibid., doc.88.
83 Memorandum From Senator Mike Mansfield to President Johnson, February 8 1965, ibid., doc.92.
84 Memorandum From the President's Special Assistant for National Security Affairs (Bundy) to President Johnson, February 7 1965, ibid., doc.84.
85 Memorandum From the Deputy Director for Intelligence, Central Intelligence Agency (Cline) to the President's Special Assistant for National Security Affairs (Bundy), March 8 1965, ibid., doc.190.
86 Memorandum From the Joint Chiefs of Staff to Secretary of Defense McNamara, March 20 1965, ibid., doc.208.
87 Reproduced in Hunt (ed.), *A Vietnam War Reader*, pp.69–71. For Johnson's account, see *The Vantage Point*, pp.132–134.
88 Memorandum From the President's Special Assistant for National Security Affairs (Bundy) to President Johnson, June 30 1965, *Foreign Relations of the United States, 1964–1968*, Volume III, *Vietnam, June–December 1965*, doc. 33. That there were clear parallels had been pointed out by George Ball as part of what he characterised as his "rearguard action" over Vietnam. See, Ball, *The Past Has Another Pattern*, pp.395–396.
89 Memorandum From Bundy to Johnson, June 30 1965, ibid.
90 Memorandum for the Record (McCone), April 21 1965, *Foreign Relations of the United States, 1964–1968*, Volume II, *Vietnam, January–June 1965*, doc.266.
91 Editorial Note, *Foreign Relations of the United States 1964–1968*, Vol.III, *Vietnam June–December 1965* (print edition, Washington, DC: Government Printing Office, 1996), doc.16, https://history.state.gov/historicaldocuments/frus1964-68v03/d16.
92 Paper by Secretary of State Rusk, July 1, 1965, ibid., doc.39.

93 Memorandum From Secretary of Defense McNamara to President Johnson, July 1 1965, ibid., doc.38.
94 McNamara, *In Retrospect*, p.195.
95 Cited in Yuen Foong Khong, *Analogies at War: Korea, Munich, Dien Bien Phu, and the Vietnam Decisions of 1965* (Princeton, NJ: Princeton University Press, 1992), p.197. This was obviously also true of Johnson himself. As he told Senate Minority Leader Everett Dirksen during a 17 February 1965 telephone conversation: "When you are dealing with these people, you must have a self-enforcing treaty. They do not keep their word . . . That we know from Munich on, that when you give, the dictators feed on raw meat." Michael Beschloss, *Reaching for Glory: Lyndon Johnson's Secret White House Tapes, 1964–1965* (New York: Simon & Schuster, 2001), p.181.
96 Paper by the Under Secretary of State (Ball), undated, *Foreign Relations of the United States 1964–1968*, Vol.III, *Vietnam June–December 1965*, doc.40.
97 Memorandum From the President's Special Assistant for National Security Affairs (Bundy) to President Johnson, July 1 1965, ibid., doc.43.
98 Memorandum of a Meeting With President Johnson, February 17 1965, *Foreign Relations of the United States, 1964–1968*, Volume II, *Vietnam, January–June 1965*, doc.133. See Johnson, *The Vantage Point*, pp.130–131 for his account of the meeting.
99 Paper Prepared by Secretary of State Rusk, February 23 1965, ibid., doc.157.
100 See, for example, Notes of Meeting, April 2 1966, *Foreign Relations of the United States 1964–1968*, Vol, IV, *Vietnam 1966* (print edition, Washington, DC: Government Printing Office, 1998), doc.109.
101 Memorandum for Record, Saigon, July 11 1967, *Foreign Relations of the United States 1964–1968*, Vol.V, *Vietnam 1967* (print edition, Washington, DC: Government Printing Office, 2002), doc.236, note 2.
102 See, James McAllister, '"A Fiasco of Noble Proportions": The Johnson Administration and the South Vietnamese Elections of 1967', *Pacific Historical Review*, Vol.73, No.4, 2004, pp.619–651.
103 Telephone Conversation Between President Johnson and Former President Eisenhower, November 4 1967, *Foreign Relations of the United States 1964–1968*, Vol.V, *Vietnam 1967*, doc.384.
104 *Foreign Relations of the United States 1964–1968*, Vol.IV, *Vietnam 1966*, doc.80, note 2.
105 Telephone Conversion Between President Johnson and Secretary of State Rusk, February 22 1966, ibid., doc.81.
106 Memorandum of Conversation Between Secretary of Defense McNamara and the Ambassador at Large (Harriman), May 14 1966, ibid., doc.137.
107 Telephone Conversion Between President Johnson and Secretary of State Rusk, February 22 1966, *Foreign Relations of the United States 1964–1968*, Vol.IV, *Vietnam 1966*, doc.81.
108 Memorandum of Conversation Between the Ambassador at Large (Harriman) and Secretary of Defense McNamara, *Foreign Relations of the United States 1964–1968*, Vol.V, *Vietnam 1967*, doc.330.
109 Arthur M. Schlesinger, Jr. recorded in his journal entry for July 28 1966: "I find McNamara especially puzzling, as does RFK. When he talks to us, he dismisses the military value of bombing the north, asserts the importance of limiting the war, denies the possibility of a military victory and looks wistfully to the neutralisation of South Vietnam and the withdrawal of American troops. Nothing seems to alarm him more than the prospect of provoking a war with China. Yet publicly he is the spokesman for the widening of the war; and it is hard to believe that he urges his private views on the President with the force that he does with his old friends of Kennedy years." Arthur M. Schlesinger, Jr., *Journals 1952–2000* (New York: Penguin, 2008), p.250.
110 Cited in Young, *The Vietnam Wars*, p.169.
111 Schlesinger, Jr., *Journals*, p.251.
112 Memorandum From the President's Assistant (Jones) to President Johnson', November 2 1967, *Foreign Relations of the United States 1964–1968*, Vol.V, *Vietnam 1967*, doc.377.
113 See, Melvin Small, *Antiwarriors: The Vietnam War and the Battle for America's Hearts and Minds* (Lanham, MD: SR Books, 2004).
114 Jeff Shesol, *Mutual Contempt: Lyndon Johnson, Robert Kennedy, and the Feud That Defined a Decade* (New York: Norton, 1997).

115 McNamara, *In Retrospect*, pp.321–323.
116 Ball, *The Past Has Another Pattern*, p.383.
117 Letter to Hubert Humphrey, 11 April 1966, in Andrew Schlesinger and Stephen Schlesinger (eds.), *The Letters of Arthur M. Schlesinger, Jr.* (New York: Random House, 2013), p.318.
118 See, John Lewis Gaddis, *George F. Kennan: An American Life* (New York: Penguin, 2011), pp.590–594.
119 See, for example, Preston, *Sword of the Spirit, Shield of Faith*, Ch.26.
120 Hans J. Morgenthau, 'To Intervene or Not to Intervene', *Foreign Affairs*, Vol.45, No.3, April 1967, pp.425–436, at p.433.
121 He had set out this evidence and argument previously in W. W. Rostow, *The United States and the Regional Organization of Asia and the Pacific, 1965–1985* (Austin, TX: University of Texas Press, 1986). Now he updated the analysis in two further interventions: 'The Case for the Vietnam War', *Parameters*, Winter 1996–1997, pp.39–50; and 'Vietnam and Asia', *Diplomatic History*, Vol.20, No.3, 1996, pp.467–471, the latter as part of a roundtable discussion of McNamara's *In Retrospect*.
122 Rostow, 'The Case for the Vietnam War'.
123 Michael H. Hunt, *Lyndon Johnson's War: America's Cold War Crusade in Vietnam, 1945–1968* (New York: Hill and Wang, 1996), p.107.

5 Doctrine, dominoes and democracy in the Nixon-Kissinger foreign policy

Richard Nixon ran for the Republican presidential nomination in 1968 as the centrist candidate between Ronald Reagan, to his right, and Nelson Rockefeller to his left. He was elected president with 43 per cent of the popular vote – a further 13.5 per cent going to the segregationist George Wallace, whose nominee for vice-president, former USAF General Curtis LeMay, doubted Nixon's determination to retain a first-strike nuclear capability over the Soviet Union and commitment to winning the war in Vietnam. Wallace attracted blue-collar workers in the North as well as Southern voters and in 1969 the best-selling political analysis of the year – Kevin Phillips' *The Emerging Republican Majority* – drew upon the lessons from the Wallace campaign and Phillips' own work for Nixon in 1968. The book argued that if the Republicans pursued a 'Southern strategy' in future – attracting conservative voters who associated the Democrats with the Civil Rights campaign, welfare dependency, decaying moral standards, anti-war protestors, rising crime rates and higher taxes – they could dominate presidential elections. Nixon had come to similar conclusions by 1970 when he identified "disaffected Democrats, and blue collar workers, and . . . working class white ethnics" as his target groups, emphasising "anti-crime, anti-demonstration, anti-drugs, anti-obscenity."[1]

For the student of US foreign policy, the ideological imprimatur of Richard Nixon and Henry Kissinger is easy to discern and relatively undiluted by departmental input or bureaucratic wrangling. This reflects the fact that as President Nixon sought to concentrate power in the White House and conduct his own foreign policy, relegating the State Department to a marginal role on key issues. In the age of the 'Imperial Presidency' this was an easy task to accomplish and we have already seen the Department of State cowed in the early 1950s under the impact of McCarthy, Dulles and Eisenhower.[2] One corollary of the relegation of the significance of State under Nixon was the rise in the influence of the National Security Council and Kissinger, his National Security Advisor.[3] This approach to the organisation of foreign policy-making itself makes the Nixon administration of interest in assessing the extent to which US foreign policy exhibited ideologically informed variation at the micro-level across Cold War-era administrations. In centralising decision-making to such an extent, Nixon limited the capacity for foreign policy to emerge as the consequence of compromises between the vested interests of different government departments. These departments still fought their corner, and objected to policy which they saw as detrimental to US interests (for example, the Department of Defense's objections to Nixon's agreement to sell the Shah of Iran whatever conventional weapons he asked for), but they rarely got their way.

NIXON AND KISSINGER: BACKGROUNDS AND IDEOLOGICAL BASES OF FOREIGN POLICY

Kissinger once observed that the "convictions that leaders have formed before reaching high office are the intellectual capital they will consume as long as they continue in office."[4] This was certainly true of both himself and Nixon. Both brought a Realist view of the world to their practice of foreign policy, one rooted in their very different personal experiences. As Nixon conceded: "This combination was unlikely – the grocer's son from Whittier and the refugee from Hitler's Germany, the politician and the academic."[5] Their common outlook allowed them to work closely together on foreign policy, but the relationship was far from the symbiotic one that is sometimes assumed. Indeed, their relationship was also an oddly competitive one.[6] Such was Nixon's distrust of Kissinger, who, Nixon felt, sought to take the credit for foreign policy initiatives and analyses that were his, that, according to John Ehrlichman, "one of the reasons for the White House taping system was that Nixon wanted to be able to prove whose ideas were being carried out, and who was the originator."[7] This attests to both a sense of rivalry and to the importance of ideas in the administration's foreign policy. Their rivalry would lead Nixon to consider jettisoning Kissinger, but ultimately their shared world-view and moral outlook bound them together, as did their successes and, perhaps more significantly, their failures.

Nixon's political and personal experiences had left him with something of an ambivalent relationship to the democratic process and a self-image as an outsider, removed from the East Coast establishment. His family had not been able to afford to allow him to take up the scholarship to Harvard University he was offered and instead he studied law at the local Quaker Whittier College. This seemed to leave Nixon with a deep-seated need to prove himself. As one biographer puts it, in a political context this meant that:

> A sense of public mission and the personal drive to succeed were indelibly fused in Nixon's view of politics as an arena where the only possible outcomes were victory or defeat . . . Since victory was necessary to fulfill his good intentions, Nixon could justify to himself his use of unsavory means to defeat opponents who stood in his way. It was as if doing bad could be excused as necessary to do good.[8]

His record of adopting the politics of McCarthyism in the 1950s' election victories that paved his way to the vice-presidency testify to the bad, as do elements of his 1968 campaign and the obsession with re-election in 1972 that led to Watergate. But Nixon felt himself a victim too – over the 1952 trust fund/Checkers affair, the claims of vote-rigging in favour of Kennedy in the 1960 presidential election and the post-election use by the Kennedys of federal agencies to trawl his financial records in the hope of uncovering financial misconduct. He later claimed that he had simply "played by the rules of politics as I found them."[9]

Alongside this ambivalent relationship to the democratic process as practised in the US, Nixon developed an extreme conception of the meaning of American exceptionalism, which held that other countries were not necessarily equipped to make the transition to democracy. Moreover, this also held that no developing country could ever attain the *quality* of democratic progress that the US had enjoyed as a result of its unique historical experience. At times, this seemed to rest on an understanding of the prerequisites for development akin to that found in the modernisation theories of the late 1950s and early 1960s – for example, the stages of growth theory of Walt Rostow, which posited a number of sequential stages of economic development that countries would have to go through to arrive at the US ideal (termed "the age of high mass consumption"), but also emphasised that individual countries' prospects of achieving this end goal varied according to local conditions.[10]

Like Nixon, Kissinger too was an outsider, a refugee from the collapse of the Weimar Republic and rise of the Nazi regime, an experience that left him with the firm conviction that:

> democracies were weak and ineffective at combating destructive enemies. They were too slow to act, too divided to mount a strong defense, and too idealistic to make tough decisions about the use of force. This was the central 'lesson' of appeasement – the appeasement of the Nazi party within the Weimar system, the appeasement of Nazi Germany within the international system. Democracies needed decisive leaders, and they needed protections against themselves.[11]

One consequence of these lessons was Kissinger's consistent belief in the importance of order over justice. Invoking Goethe, he once explained to a Harvard colleague that: "If I had to choose between justice and disorder, on the one hand, and injustice and order, on the other, I would always choose the latter."[12] On the eve of his appointment as Nixon's National Security Advisor in 1968, Kissinger retained this core belief, writing on the 'Central Issues of American Foreign Policy' that the, "greatest need of the contemporary international system is an agreed concept of order."[13] By this time, Kissinger believed, the potential for the US to lead a Wilsonian crusade to "bring about domestic transformations in 'emerging countries'" was negated by the fact that what he termed "political multipolarity" (a product of what he saw as the decline of superpower authority during the 1960s) made it "impossible to impose an American design."[14]

Hence, his own personal experiences combined with his reading of history to lead him to view international politics through a rigidly Realist lens,[15] one that Nixon shared as a consequence of his anti-communism and understanding of the roots of victory in the Second World War.[16] For both of them, disorder or revolt in any one part of the world could not be considered the isolated event it might appear, no matter how 'insignificant' the country involved. As Kissinger explained in a 1968 essay:

> The essence of a revolution is that it appears to contemporaries as a series of more or less unrelated upheavals. The temptation is great to treat each issue as an immediate and isolated problem which once surmounted will permit the fundamental stability of the international order to reassert itself. But the crises which form the headlines of the day are symptoms of deep-seated structural problems.[17]

As a result of their life experiences, both Nixon and Kissinger, in the words of Kissinger biographer Jeremi Suri:

> had a dark view of human nature and democratic society, born of their own experiences with social prejudice . . . They did not believe that an expansion of freedoms would naturally make for a better society. Free citizens were often hateful and destructive . . . For Nixon and Kissinger, social improvement required firm national leadership to limit human excesses and restrict human hatreds. The same applied

to the international system, where competitive states would pummel one another to death without the force of imposed order from a superior power.[18]

These were the bases, then, of a distinctive Nixon-Kissinger approach to foreign policy. As Kissinger reflected in his memoirs: "Nixon and I wanted to found American foreign policy on a sober perception of permanent national interest, rather than on fluctuating emotions that in the past had led us to excesses of both intervention and abdication."[19] One consequence of this was that the language of foreign policy under Nixon and Kissinger was shorn of much of the vocabulary of exceptionalism and sense of guiding moral purpose that had been a characterisitic of it since at least the proclamation of the Truman Doctrine in 1947, to be replaced by a vocabulary of interests and alliances based on geopolitical rather than ideational grounds. As we shall see, a form of exceptionalism still applied and the language of 'freedom' still had its place, but both Nixon and Kissinger recognised that the purpose of national security and foreign policy was to protect core domestic values from external threats and that this did not automatically require the promotion of those core domestic values abroad.[20]

At the same time, neither saw themselves as being 'ideological', in effect falling into the trap about which Michael Freeden warns in his work on ideology.[21] In private discussions, Nixon liked to present himself as a flexible pragmatist.[22] For his part, Kissinger regarded 'ideology' as being something that the administration's Cold War adversaries possessed.[23] But their shared Realism was itself an ideological construct. For Kissinger in particular it was based on the lessons of nineteenth century European history. On this understanding, ideology was not the primary driver of foreign policy behaviour, which could be better explained by reference to the nature of the international system and the balance of power within it.[24] However, neither Nixon nor Kissinger were quite so sanguine about the role of ideology when they saw it as a factor destabilising pro-Western states and putting the international balance of power at risk,[25] as we shall see with regard to the case of Chile. Realism and anti-communism offered different analyses of contemporary developments and different policy prescriptions (as the intervention of Realists in the 1960s' debate about the Vietnam War demonstrated) and the tension between the two was never fully reconciled by Nixon and Kissinger. Nevertheless, Realism was clearly the dominant ideological guide to the Nixon foreign policy.

DOCTRINE AND DEMOCRACY

In July 1967, over a year before he won the 1968 presidential election, Nixon gave a speech to the Bohemian Club, a private men's club in San Francisco, in which he set out his own views on the principles that should govern US foreign policy and the role of ideas such as democracy and freedom within this vision. They were views informed by his trips across Europe, the Soviet Union, Asia, Latin America, Africa and the Middle East in the months preceding the speech.[26] The framework, of course, was set by the Cold War competition with the Soviet Union. Notwithstanding the fact that the Soviet Union was coming closer to achieving nuclear parity with the US and the fact that America's global prestige had taken a battering over Vietnam, Nixon saw grounds for optimism in that:

> Communism is losing the ideological battle with freedom in Asia, Africa, Latin America as well as in Europe. In Africa, the Communist appeal was against colonialism.

Now that the colonialists are gone, they must base their case on being for Communism. But African tribalism and rebellious individualism are simply incompatible with the rigid discipline a Communist system imposes.[27]

As a consequence: "All over the world, whether from East Germany to West, from Communist China to free China, from Communist Cuba to the free American republics, the traffic is all one way – from Communism to freedom."[28] Still, there was no room for complacency given Nixon's understanding of the goals of Soviet communism. Nixon warned that while it was important for the US to conduct negotiations with the Soviet Union aimed at reducing tensions:

we must always remember in such negotiations that our goal is different from theirs: We seek peace as an end in itself. They seek victory with peace being at this time a means toward that end. In sum, we can live in peace with the Soviet Union but until they give up their goal for world conquest it will be for them a peace of necessity and not of choice. As we enter this last third of the twentieth century the hopes of the world rest with America. Whether peace and freedom survive in the world depends on American leadership.[29]

But there was an interesting tension here. What exactly did 'freedom' entail, and how exactly did Nixon propose that the US lead in ensuring its survival or spread? At one level, and as understood by Lyndon Johnson in relation to Vietnam, 'freedom' simply meant anti-communism, or freedom from communism. This was its meaning for Kissinger, for whom 'freedom' and 'security' were near synonyms and had to be understood in globalist terms if 'freedom' was to be defended. For Nixon 'freedom' as it applied to the developing world was essentially understood in terms of economic opportunity. To a significant extent it meant the freedom of individuals to engage in private enterprise. "In every area of the world", Nixon explained, "private, rather than government, enterprise should be encouraged, not because we are trying to impose our ideas but because one works and the other doesn't."[30] However, it did not follow that political freedom need also be encouraged, so long as the economic sphere was not unduly circumscribed. As Nixon explained with reference to four key US allies of the day:

Thailand has a limited monarchy. Iran has a strong monarchy. Taiwan has a strong President with an oligarchy. Mexico has one-party government. Not one of these countries has a representative democracy by Western standards. But it happens that in each case their system has worked for them. It is time for us to recognize that much as we like our own political system, American style democracy is not necessarily the best form of government for people in Asia, Africa and Latin America with entirely different backgrounds.[31]

Nixon had only met Kissinger once, at a late 1967 Manhattan cocktail party, prior to offering him the post of National Security Advisor, but both had arrived independently at broadly the same conclusion. Democracy, Kissinger warned, was not an inevitable outcome of nationalism:

In the last century, democracy was accepted by a ruling class whose estimate of itself was founded outside the political process. It was buttressed by a middle class, holding a political philosophy in which the state was considered to be a referee of the ultimately important social forces rather than the principal focus of national consciousness . . . The pluralism of the West had many causes which cannot be duplicated elsewhere. These included a church organization outside the control of the state and therefore symbolizing the limitation of government power; the Greco-Roman philosophical tradition of justice based on human dignity, reinforced later by the Christian ethic; an emerging bourgeoisie; a stalemate in religious wars imposing tolerance as a practical necessity and a multiplicity of states. Industrialization was by no means the most significant of these factors. Had any of the others been missing, the Western political evolution could have been quite different.[32]

The key, then, was not to attempt to "transfer American institutions to new nations",[33] but to encourage local regimes to establish and embed a legitimacy that would help ensure global stability. This view coincided with Nixon's belief that developing countries did not necessarily have the capacity to achieve high degrees of democratic governance. He felt this particularly strongly with regard to African nations, an area towards which Nixon harboured a special disdain right to the end of his political career. As he complained in his Bohemian Club speech:

> Just ten years ago Ethiopia and Liberia were the only independent countries in Black Africa. Today there are thirty independent countries in Black Africa. Fifteen of these countries have populations less than the State of Maryland, and each has a vote in the UN Assembly equal to that of the United States. There were twelve coups in Black Africa in the last year. No one of the thirty countries has a representative government by our standards and the prospects that any will have such a government in a generation or even a half-century are remote.[34]

Hence, Nixon's conception of what 'freedom' meant outside the US was a product of both his own personal beliefs and of the *realpolitik* requirements of the Cold War conflict. It was, in essence, a communitarian vision, shorn of the cosmopolitanism discernible in much of the Kennedy administration's foreign policy discourse.

This world-view also informed the Nixon administration's approach to foreign aid. Nixon had long understood the importance to the US economy of access to raw materials in the developing world. This was one of the foreign policy topics that, as Eisenhower's Vice-President, Nixon would dicuss with Secretary of State John Foster Dulles. A note of a February 1958 conversation shows them discussing, "at some length the project for a study of economic warfare" which arose out of their concern that the Soviet Union "might develop a capability and purpose to wage economic warfare against our free enterprise system by getting control of raw materials. There might be a real question", they felt, "as to whether our classical free trade methods based upon profits by private enterprise could survive that kind of struggle."[35] This left Nixon with an understanding of the importance of US foreign aid in countering the attraction of centralised control and state planning in newly independent countries in the developing world.

US foreign aid was an important instrument in promoting stability under authoritarian rule but one that Nixon was capable of justifying in terms of American exceptionalism. In a May 1969 message to Congress, for example, he spoke of the, "moral quality in this

Nation that will not permit us to close our eyes to want in this world" and the, "record of generosity and concern for our fellow men, expressed in concrete terms unparalleled in the world's history, [that] has helped make the American experience unique."[36] At the same time, though, he did not limit his rationale to one rooted in American exceptionalism. Reflecting both his own Realist world-view and the economic realities of the day, he also accepted that US foreign aid was an important means towards ensuring the US interest in global stability:

> If we turn inward, if we adopt an attitude of letting the underdeveloped nations shift for themselves, we would soon see them shift away from the values so necessary to international stability. Moreover, we would lose the traditional concern for humanity which is so vital a part of the American spirit. In another sense, foreign aid must be viewed as an integral part of our overall effort to achieve a world order of peace and justice. That order combines our sense of responsibility for helping those determined to defend their freedom; our sensible understanding of the mutual benefits that flow from cooperation between nations; and our sensitivity to the desires of our fellow men to improve their lot in the world.[37]

Nixon and Kissinger were keen to avoid US foreign aid being made conditional on regime type or progress towards democracy. Behind the closed doors of a September 1969 meeting of the President's Task Force on Foreign Aid any Nixonian "concern for humanity" was qualified by criticism of the State Department's desire, "to give aid to every country in the world", resulting in what Nixon termed, "lots of 'Mickey Mouse programs'."[38] He argued that US foreign aid should only go to those countries where there was a major US interest and, "should not attempt to dictate the type of political system maintained in foreign countries, although many of the Task Force members will probably espouse socialist approaches and repeat many of the old tired ideas."[39] Kissinger warned the chairman of the Task Force that he would, "hear that leftist totalitarian approaches are completely acceptable but that the U.S. should oppose rightist approaches." This, Kissinger told him, "is particularly strange because we do not know what democracy means in a less developed country. This is another conceptual problem which must be tackled." He was "afraid that his academic colleagues were not very fertile in answering it."[40] Moreover, Kissinger's belief in linkage meant that the subject of foreign aid could not be considered in isolation or simply based on "abstract notions" such as democracy.

Kissinger complained that aid policy had "fallen into the hands of economists."[41] Nixon agreed, or came to agree. In a June 1971 Oval Office conversation with Kissinger it was his turn to complain that the IMF and World Bank were, "playing the role of God in judging not just the economic viability of loans, but whether or not loans should be made to nations that aren't live up [sic] to the moral criteria that we think governments should live up to." Complaining about the way in which Secretary of State William Rogers sought to establish this connection, Nixon told Kissinger: "I don't believe that has anything to do with a loan. The same argument that he argues is that it does, on the ground, that affects stability and so forth." Conversely, Nixon argued, "maybe a dictatorship is the most stable damn country to make it to, and if it is, make it to a dictatorship."[42]

TOWARDS THE NIXON DOCTRINE

As early as 1967 Nixon was moving towards articulating what would subsequently come to be termed the Nixon Doctrine. As he wrote in a piece on 'Asia After Viet Nam' published in *Foreign Affairs* towards the end of 1967

> I am not arguing that the day is past when the United States would respond militarily to communist threats in the less stable parts of the world, or that a unilateral response to a unilateral request for help is out of the question. But other nations must recognize that the role of the United States as world policeman is likely to be limited in the future.[43]

An increased reliance on regional allies providing for their own defence had clear implications. Their importance to US security meant that the US could not afford to impose its own system of government on them, for fear of alienating local elites and for fear that the consequences could not be anticipated or managed. This could lead to a 'loss' in the zero-sum calculations of the Cold War balance of power. Rather, inequalities and suffering could be mitigated through economic development on the US model without the need to insist on the development of liberal democratic structures. In this sense, the emerging Nixon Doctrine differed from the Truman Doctrine not only in the nature of its military commitment, but also in the conception of 'freedom' that underpinned it. As Nixon explained:

> Not all the governments of non-communist Asia fit the Western ideal of parliamentary democracy – far from it. But Americans must recognize that a highly sophisticated, highly advanced political system, which required many centuries to develop in the West, may not be best for other nations which have far different traditions and are still in an earlier stage of development. What matters is that these governments are consciously, deliberately and programmatically developing in the direction of greater liberty, greater abundance, broader choice and increased popular involvement in the processes of government.[44]

On the question of the feasibility or desirability of democracy promotion amongst its allies in the developing world, Nixon and Kissinger arrived at similar analyses at broadly the same time, albeit via different paths. The logic of these analyses was that the US, facing a world of greater turbulence and uncertainty than at the beginning of the 1960s, should move beyond the idealism of the Kennedy era. This had perpetuated what was, for Nixon and Kissinger, the myth that while other states had interests, the US simply assumed responsibilities. Writing in 1968, Kissinger advocated a more mature conception of the US national interest, rooted in stability in the international system, one that was "not necessarily amoral" because "moral consequences can spring from interested acts."[45] For Kissinger:

> A sense of mission is clearly a legacy of American history; to most Americans, America has always stood for something other than its own grandeur. But a clearer understanding of America's interests and of the requirements of equilibrium can give perspective to our idealism and lead to humane and moderate objectives, especially

in relation to political and social change. Thus our conception of world order must have deeper purposes than stability but greater restraints on our behavior than would result if it were approached only in a fit of enthusiasm.[46]

Just what these deeper purposes were remained unstated, and during the course of the following six years the evidence for their existence was far from overwhelming. In short, Nixon and Kissinger's foreign policy was rooted in a rejection of what they both saw as the excessive idealism of the early 1960s, and its replacement by their brand of Realism. The principal aim of this Realist approach was the maintenance of global stability in increasingly turbulent times, driven less by a mission to export American values than by a Bismarckian *realpolitik* calculation of the national interest.

In his 1969 inaugural address, Nixon spoke of an aim of global peace:

> Let us take as our goal: Where peace is unknown, make it welcome; where peace is fragile, make it strong; where peace is temporary, make it permanent . . . Let all nations know that during this administration our lines of communication will be open. We seek an open world – open to ideas, open to the exchange of goods and people – a world in which no people, great or small, will live in angry isolation . . . With those who are willing to join, let us cooperate to reduce the burden of arms, to strengthen the structure of peace, to lift up the poor and the hungry.[47]

This was a speech clearly aimed at multiple audiences. For the US audience it was designed as confirmation of campaign promises to end the war in Vietnam, holding out the possibility of negotiation over Cold War obstacles to improved relations with the Soviet Union, and a willingness to negotiate to bring about an end to China's international isolation. At the same time, however, it was a message that addressed politics at the global level. The corollary of this focus at the global level from day one of the administration was Nixon and Kissinger's belief in linkage.[48] This globalist outlook, belief in linkage, belief in the importance of the maintenance of a balance of power through military alliances and the emerging notion of a 'Nixon Doctrine' combined to have a decisive impact on the administration's understanding of the importance of regime complexion on the global periphery.

It was following a speech in Guam on 26 July 1969 that Nixon, in answering questions from reporters on the likely US response should future Vietnam-type situations arise in Asia, said that in future the US should avoid:

> becoming involved heavily with our own personnel . . . I want to be sure that our policies in the future, all over the world, in Asia, Latin America, Africa, and the rest, reduce American involvement. One of assistance, yes, assistance in helping them solve their own problems, but not going in and just doing the job ourselves.[49]

This was the clearest articulation by Nixon to date of a consistent global strategy and, as such, was quickly dubbed by reporters the 'Guam Doctrine' with some journalists, such as Stanley Karnow, making the link to the argument contained in Nixon's earlier *Foreign Affairs* piece. Nixon had not discussed with Kissinger the statement that arose in the question and answer session beforehand, as he had intended no major policy pronouncement while in Guam.[50] In fact, Nixon's visit there was a consequence of his wanting to be on hand to greet the return of the Apollo XI space mission which had splashed down in the Pacific the previous day. As such, questions were raised as to how far this represented the deliberate enunciation of a carefully considered new doctrine. Notwithstanding this, the Guam principle clearly represented a further articulation of the shift in Cold War strategy that Nixon had been contemplating for some time, in part in conjunction with Kissinger.[51] It was a clear response to the fact that the Truman Doctrine's commitment was without nuance and, as such, offered no basis for differentiation in terms of American interests. Nixon's statement represented a rejection of the need for the autopilot application of Containment, something that had culminated in the debacle in Vietnam. The Nixon Doctrine, then, as the 'Guam Doctrine' would be referred to by the following year, was not a rejection of the need to contain the Soviet Union, but an evolution towards a more nuanced basis for its application. As such it was a significant development in US Cold War foreign policy thinking. As Nixon noted in his *Memoirs*:

> In the past our policy had been to furnish the arms, men, and matériel to help other nations defend themselves against aggression. That was what we had done in Korea, and that was how we started out in Vietnam. But from now on, I said, we would furnish only the matériel and the military and economic assistance to those nations willing to accept the responsibility of supplying the manpower to defend themselves.[52]

The only exception would be where US allies or regional friends faced attack from the Soviet Union or China, in which case they were still to be covered by the US nuclear umbrella. Critics have argued that in practice the Nixon Doctrine lacked coherence and was not applied consistently, as a result of which administration actions did not always match administration rhetoric.[53] This was particularly the case over Vietnam and the extension of the war into Cambodia.[54] In fact over Vietnam the administration was itself divided about the weight to attach to the Nixon Doctrine both as it emerged pre-Guam and thereafter. Shortly before Nixon made his Guam comments, Defense Secretary Melvin Laird had coined the term 'Vietnamization', as a more positive expression of 'de-Americanization'. This process was to constitute the tangible expression of the application of the Nixon Doctrine to Vietnam.

Meanwhile, although Kissinger gave friends and former Harvard colleagues the impression that he was working hard to disengage from Vietnam, in practice he was planning for an intensification of bombing as the means to bring about the optimum outcome, telling aides: "I cannot believe that a fourth-rate power like North Vietnam doesn't have a breaking point."[55] As noted above, in their 1967 and 1968 writings both Nixon and Kissinger had been discussing a shift in US foreign policy very much along the lines of the Nixon Doctrine, a form of Nixon Doctrine in embryo. In practice, Kissinger's immediate post-Guam enthusiasm to see it applied to Vietnam seemed limited. One key difference, for example, was around the meaning of 'internal subversion'. Four days after Nixon's Guam statement, Kissinger gave a background briefing to reporters that suggested that Nixon's statement would result in little change:

Q. Does that mean that the United States now has decided not to supply any combat troops where a country is faced with internal subversion?

Dr. Kissinger: The general policy is that internal subversion has to be the primary responsibility of the threatened country. In an overwhelming majority of the cases, to which it is hard to think of an exception, the numbers involved are not tremendous. We are talking now of internal subversion.

Q. The numbers of what?

Dr. *Kissinger:* The numbers of guerrillas involved are not tremendous. Therefore, local manpower should have the predominant responsibility for meeting this. The United States stands ready to supply material assistance, advice and technical assistance where that is requested and where our interests so dictate. But the general policy is as I have indicated. You understand, of course, that it is never possible to be absolutely categorical about every last case, but this is the general policy as it now stands.[56]

Privately, he warned Nixon that the South Vietnamese were incapable of providing for their own defence and that to the American public troop withdrawals would be like, "salted peanuts . . . the more US troops come home, the more will be demanded."[57]

Nevertheless, by the time of Nixon's January 1970 State of the Union address the Nixon Doctrine was being presented as the intellectual heart of the administration's foreign policy. In February 1970, Kissinger told reporters that it represented, "a comprehensive, philosophical statement of American foreign policy", which made it clear that, "for better or worse our policies are not simply tactical responses to immediate situations", but were based on "a coherent picture of the world" which meant that, "the United States should not be the fireman running from one conflagration to the other, but can address itself to the longer-term problems of a peaceful international structure."[58] Still, it was far from constituting a fully thought-out strategy. Several grey areas remained; for example, the question of the point at which an insurgency backed by external support became so extensive as to represent an invasion by foreign troops, which Nixon had committed the US to oppose. As a January 1970 NSC document, listing "some hard issues" in relation to the Nixon Doctrine, pointed out:

> Our new Asian approach is, however, obscure on those cases where massive external intervention shades the nature of the conflict from insurgency towards conventional aggression, such as happened at some point (whether before or after American intervention is debatable to say the least) in South Vietnam. Laos, with 50,000 North Vietnamese troops, and perhaps 5,000 Chinese, is the obvious present case. Our equivocation there reflects not only what we inherited in the past and the linkage with Vietnam but also our uncertainty about how to apply our Asian doctrine in the future.[59]

However, there was more to the Nixon Doctrine than was outlined by Nixon in Guam. Although prompted by Vietnam it offered a global solution to the potential problem of US overstretch and the opposition of the US public and Congress to the commitment of US military forces to combat any and every challenge to global stability. It offered a formula through which, in Stanley Karnow's words, "by shifting the human burden to local surrogates, the United States could project its global power at a cost tolerable to Americans."[60] This was made more necessary given the indications by the beginning of 1970 that Nixon's honeymoon over Vietnam was coming to an end and that public opinion might turn against him unless American troops began to be withdrawn.

Out of this logic developed a darker side to the Nixon Doctrine. The purpose of furnishing arms and other matériel was not simply to deter external aggression. In the context of the Cold War competition both Nixon and Kissinger, like their immediate predecessors, understood 'aggression' as being something that could arise internally. Hence, the Nixon

Doctrine was intended to supply the means by which local elites could both help ensure global stability by acting as regional gendarmes, armed and trained by the US, and also sustain themselves in power by suppressing any opposition, which was, almost by definition, held to be ideologically hostile to US interests in stability. The primary mechanism for achieving this was the International Security Assistance Program, unveiled in September 1970. As Nixon explained at the time:

> The national security objectives of the U.S. cannot be pursued solely through defense of our territory. They require a successful effort by other countries around the world, including a number of lower income countries, to mobilize manpower and resources to defend themselves. They require in some cases, military bases abroad, to give us the necessary mobility to defend ourselves and to deter aggression. They sometimes require our financial support of friendly countries in exceptional situations . . . our security assistance programs must be formulated to achieve the objectives of the Nixon Doctrine, which I set forth at Guam last year. That approach calls for any country whose security is threatened to assume the primary responsibility for providing the manpower needed for its own defense. Such reliance on local initiative encourages local assumption of responsibility and thereby serves both the needs of other countries and our own national interest. In addition, the Nixon Doctrine calls for our providing assistance to such countries to help them assume these responsibilities more quickly and more effectively.[61]

Hence, the Doctrine built on Nixon and Kissinger's deep-rooted beliefs in the infeasibility of democracy promotion amongst authoritarian US friends and allies in the developing world to mandate the suppression of dissent so as to maintain in power local elites delivering stability. The impact and consequences of the application of the Doctrine to Iran – perhaps the country towards which the Doctrine was most clearly and consistently applied – illustrate well this aspect of its darker side. Arguably, the logic of the Doctrine was also to encourage local pro-US elites to seize back power from governments with the potential to challenge the maintenance of stability. Such logic would explain US attempts to first prevent the election of Salvador Allende, leader of the Chilean Socialist Party, as president of Chile and, second, having failed in this, to destabilise his government with the aim of bringing about its fall. In this the Nixon Doctrine was fundamentally anti-democratic. It placed a high premium on non-democratic friends and allies in the developing world, as these were the most reliable over the medium-long term. However, in this it became as inflexible as the doctrine it was designed to supplant. In particular, the mechanistic assumption that the election of a left-wing coaliton government in Chile represented a threat to US global interests, or challenged the global configuration of power, represented the ultimate failure of Kissinger's approach to foreign policy – one rooted in his insistence that no development in the world, no matter how isolated it might appear on the surface, was without import elsewhere. This mentality showed clear continuity with that of American policy-makers since Truman.

IRAN

As vice-president, Nixon had visited Iran in 1953 in the aftermath of the US and British-orchestrated overthrow of Mossadegh. Hence, his relationship with the Shah had a personal dimension that spanned almost the entire period of the Shah's rule. At that first meeting Nixon had been struck by their common understanding of regional security questions.[62] Both understood the importance of Iran's regional role. By virtue of its size Iran represented a huge land buffer that separated the Soviet Union from the oil-rich, soft underbelly of the Gulf, represented by the sheikhdoms of Saudi Arabia, Kuwait, Oman, Qatar and the UAE. Because of this, Iran became central to the application of the Nixon Doctrine to the Middle East, forming one of two 'twin pillars' with Saudi Arabia.[63] However, because of its geographical location, size and strategic depth, Iran was always the more important of these pillars. As Kissinger wrote in his memoirs: "The geopolitical importance of that country must impel any administration into seeking good relations with whatever group governs Iran."[64]

For the most part, US relations with Iran under the Shah encountered few stresses. Indeed, Kissinger characterised him as "for us that rarest of leaders, an unconditional ally."[65] Moreover, unlike other allies, he did not seek or require US aid. The arms that the US felt Iran required to perform its regional gendarme role, it could afford to pay for in cash. However, the Shah's own view of the scale of armaments necessary went well beyond that of US planners. US planners were well aware that Iran was far from a functioning democracy, and equally well aware that the scale of military spending the Shah envisioned for Iran could create and/or exacerbate discontent by diverting resources from infrastructure development programmes. Hence, considerations of global stability clashed with considerations of internal stability. Previously, the Kennedy administration had sought to emphasise the need for a social reform programme to cement the Shah's position inside Iran. The Shah had responded with the Kennedy-esque 'White Revolution', which had the effect of expanding the scope of governmental responsibility, but also of expectations attached to it – for example, with regard to land reform. The Nixon administration, however, resolved the national security/internal democracy dilemma not by ignoring the issue of internal democracy, but by arriving at the conclusion that Iran was not, at this point in its historical development, ready for a constitutional democracy. Instead Nixon concluded that the optimum form of government for the Iranians at that time was precisely the form of benign dictatorship provided by the Shah.

This attachment to an extreme form of American exceptionalism is evident in an April 1971 White House discussion involving US Ambassador to Iran Douglas MacArthur II, the nephew of General Douglas MacArthur. In this, Nixon conceded that the Shah was heading, "basically, let's face it a virtual dictatorship in a benign way." And anyway, Nixon went on " . . . when you talk about having a democracy of our type in that part of the world, Good God, it wouldn't work. Would it? . . . They don't know what it's called." MacArthur agreed: "They don't even know – they don't know what it is. You know what happened in the Congo? Belgium gave them a constitution, wonderful buildings, all the nice trappings, but these people had never practiced it at all." Nixon replied:

> let's look at Africa generally. And this country [Iran], at least has got some degree of civilization in its history. But those Africans, you know, are only about 50–75 years from out of the trees, some of them. But did you know that of all of Africa, of all those new countries, there is not one country that has a so-called parliamentary democracy that meets even the standards that we would half-way insist on for Vietnam . . . And it's got to be that way. They aren't ready. You know this. You've got to remember it

took the British a hell of a long time of blood, strife, chopping off the heads of kings and nobles and the rest before they finally got to their system.[66]

Intelligence community analyses of the Iranian political situation in the late 1960s/early 1970s stressed the limited gains emanating from the 'White Revolution' while conceding the absence of formal democratic structures. For example, a January 1969 National Intelligence Estimate, after noting how the Shah's, "successes in discomfiting his political enemies and in cutting down possible challengers have left him unrivaled at the center of power", went on to analyse the political situation:

> The Shah has succeeded in presenting himself as a nationalist reformer, but he has concentrated all political power in his own hands and the regime remains narrowly based. In the last analysis it depends on the army and security forces, which as far as we can tell are faithful to the Shah. His efforts to enlist the support of well-educated technocrats in important posts in government have borne fruit and many members of the once politically restive middle class have had their attention diverted to moneymaking. They were attracted by the scope for action they have been allowed in the economic field. Yet their support is not based on any widespread devotion to Iran's political system; an economic recession could quickly reduce their sense of commitment to the regime. This could also take place if the Shah's sense of infallibility should lead him to restrict further their participation in the decisionmaking process. Over the long term, economic development probably will not provide a satisfactory substitute for greater political participation. Hence, in a few years unrest may again begin to reach significant levels among politically aware elements. In time this could pose serious problems for the regime, particularly if dissent were to find support within the military.[67]

Hence, there were clear indications that the Shah's approach could put him on a collision course with the nascent middle and professional classes. It was in this context that the Shah's proposed spending on US weaponry attracted concern. The question of whether to meet his demands caused a split in the Nixon administration. There were those who felt that to do so would undermine the Shah by encouraging deficit spending, reducing social spending, thereby heightening internal opposition. On the other side, there were those who believed that to decline to sell the Shah everything he wanted would be to encourage closer relations between Iran and the Soviet Union and risk the loss of a strategically vital ally.

The issue came to a head in mid-1972, when Nixon was due to visit Tehran in an oft-delayed reaffirmation of the special relationship between the two countries. White House conversations held in advance of the trip show a president focused exclusively on the strategic benefits to the US of the relationship. In these Nixon declared himself "stronger than a horseradish" in his support of the Shah, revealed his admiration for the Shah's rule ("He runs a damn tight shop, right?"), and sought reassurance that Iran could play the regional role required of it by the 'Twin Pillars' strategy ("And these guys, they can probably fight pretty good if they have to.")[68] The key determinant of the policy outcome in terms of the tension between global security and internal democracy was to be found in Nixon's belief that Iran under the Shah was a dependable ally – both in terms of the stability of his own position and the fact of his relative disinterest in the Arab-Israeli conflict, which marked him out from other allies and potential allies. When Ambassador MacArthur offered his observation that: "You know, the Soviets have been able, by – through their polarization of this Arab-Israel conflict, they have been able to gain increasing influence in these places, there's no question about it. But a strong Iran helps counterbalance that", Nixon replied:

> But they're just one friend there. And it – Iran is not of either world, really, in a sense, I guess. But the point is, that by God if we can go with them, and we can have them strong, and they're in the center of it, and a friend of the United States, I couldn't agree more – it's something. 'Cause you look around there, it just happens that, who else do we have except for Europe? The Southern Mediterranean – it's all gone. Hassan will be here, he's a nice fellow, but Morocco, Christ, they can't last. Morocco, Tunisia, Libya, Algeria, the, the Sudan, naturally the UAR, all the little miserable countries around – Jordan, and Lebanon, and the rest. They're like – they go down like ten pins, just like that. That some of them would like to be our friends, but central to every one of those countries, even as far off as Morocco, is the fact that the United States is aligned with Israel, and because we're aligned with Israel, we are their enemy . . . That's what it is. Now this doesn't mean that we let Israel go down the drain, because that would play into the Soviet hands, too. But it does mean that right now we're in a hell of a difficult spot, because, because our Israeli tie makes us unpalatable to everybody in the Arab world, doesn't it?[69]

This firm attachment to the Shah led administration principals to rationalise away growing evidence of domestic unrest. This expressed itself in multiple forms, including student protests, terrorist attacks, the November 1970 attempt to assassinate Ambassador MacArthur and his wife in Tehran, émigré complaints about Nixon's proposed visit to Tehran, and the campaign of bombing that accompanied it when Nixon finally made his trip. Intelligence reports clearly stated that the growing violent opposition to the Shah represented a serious threat, more serious than the Shah's secret police, SAVAK, suggested, and that the repression with which SAVAK met this opposition simply exacerbated the problem.[70] However, the administration's globalist outlook left it blind to, or disbelieving of, the significance of such local events and it failed to act on these warnings.

Nixon's desire to maintain the Shah's full support also led to a significant shift in US policy towards Iraq at the Shah's request. For several years Iran (and Israel) had covertly funded the Kurdish revolt inside Iraq led by Mustafa Barzani, in a bid to ensure that the increasingly Soviet-allied Iraq was fully occupied with internal affairs and not in a position to threaten Iran or the wider region. Although Barzani had approached the Nixon White House for support prior to 1972, his approaches had been rejected on the grounds that: i.) the US did not interfere in the internal affairs of other countries, and; ii.) the formation of an independent Kurdish state was not a US aim, although given contemporaneous events in Chile the latter might reasonably be interpreted as being the more important consideration. However, the Shah returned to the subject of US support for Barzani during Nixon's May 1972 Tehran visit, which itself came just one month after the signing of the Soviet-Iraqi Treaty of Friendship and Cooperation. In this changed context Nixon agreed that a delegation from Barzani's group should meet with administration officials in Washington in July 1972, where they presented their struggle as being against the spread of Soviet influence in the Middle East (via the

Ba'athist regime in Iraq) and hence the same as that in which the US was itself involved. The Nixon administration had no interest in Kurdish independence *per se*, and assessed the merits of covert support for Barzani solely in terms of global linkage. As outlined by DCI Richard Helms, the case for covert financial and military aid to the Kurds rested on the grounds that:

> It is clearly in the interest of the USG and its friends and allies in the area that the present Iraqi regime be kept off balance, or even overthrown if that can be done without escalating hostilities on the international level. The most effective and secure means to achieve this end will be to furnish appropriate support to Barzani and the Kurds to enable them to maintain their resistance to the regime. The regime, despotic internally, is aggressively hostile in its intentions toward Iran, Kuwait, Jordan, Saudi Arabia, and the newly-formed Federation of Arab Emirates. The danger Iraqi hostility poses has become an increasingly significant factor in the area because of the steadily deepening Soviet support for Iraq, now institutionalized in the Soviet-Iraqi treaty of friendship and cooperation signed 9 April 1972. Soviet awareness of the threat Kurdish opposition represents to the Iraqi regime has been reflected recently in increased Soviet and East German pressure on Barzani to join the National Charter Front sponsored by the Soviets and the regime. Both the regime and the Soviets appreciate that if the Iraqi Army must be mobilized and redeployed for a renewed campaign against the Kurds, it is likely to become less subject to regime control, and the regime's capabilities for action against its neighbors be reduced.[71]

Hence, the logic of the Nixon Doctrine would be extended further. The decision to support the Kurdish bid for 'freedom' arose out of national security considerations, rather than as a value in itself. Moreover, national security requirements led to a distinction being made between the two non-democratic regimes in Iran and Iraq – the former was labelled a 'benign dictatorship', the latter 'despotic internally', and this distinction established the ideological groundwork for very different relationships. As a result, Barzani's organisation was able to receive up to US$3 million a year in funding via the CIA and up to US$2 million in supplies, excluding transportation costs. In this respect, the Nixon Doctrine arguably anticipated the Reagan Doctrine by a decade in covertly intervening inside Iraq on behalf of the Kurds. This support emboldened Barzani who expanded his military confrontation with Iraqi military forces so that, by the summer of 1974, a full-scale war was underway with Barzani and the Kurdistan Democratic Party (KDP) relying heavily on Iranian military support and US finance and weapons, and Iraq having to call up reservists to deal with the insurgency. During 1974–1975, the high water-mark of this insurgency, there were some 60,000 casualties. Its intensity created the very real possibility that Iran and Iraq would themselves be pushed into war, a possibility for which neither felt prepared.[72] Hence, during a 1975 Organization of the Petroleum Exporting Countries (OPEC) meeting the two sides reached an agreement on a range of outstanding issues, including an end to Iranian support for the KDP, and hence also to US support. This put the Iran-Iraq animosity on ice and led to the immediate crushing of the Kurdish insurgency, underlining the fact that US support for the KDP was always conditional because it was premised solely on considerations of *realpolitik*. Asked by a 1975 congressional hearing why aid to the Kurds had been so abruptly cut off, Kissinger famously explained that, "covert action should not be confused with missionary work."[73]

CHILE

Nixon's attitude towards South America was indelibly marked by his 1958 vice-presidential tour. Local reactions to Nixon ranged from mild protest (Argentina), to mass protest, rock and bottle-throwing (Peru) and a near mob lynching following an airport reception at which Pat Nixon's red suit was turned brown by the volume of spit raining down on the visiting dignitaries (Venezuela).[74] Nixon blamed his reception on organised communist agitation. Under his administration South America was accorded a low priority, Chile apart.

Nixon recognised the growth of social unrest across South America and the risk of this resulting in governments if not hostile then at least cooler towards the US than was traditional. At the same time, awareness of the limitations of US power meant that Latin America was a prefect region for the application of the Nixon Doctrine. In that region local militaries were an ideal vehicle for containing local left-wing anti-Americanism. Hence, in a 31 October 1969 speech directed at Latin America, Nixon explained that while the US had a "preference" for democracy, nevertheless it, "must deal realistically with governments in the inter-American system as they are."[75] In private conversation with Kissinger he went further, confessing his preference for dictatorships in the region.[76]

The Nixon administration's belief that the election of Salvador Allende at the head of the Unidad Popular coalition represented a threat to US interests was the combined product of a residual belief in a variant of the domino theory and the issue of linkage and US credibility in a global context. The anti-communist Nixon of the 1950s had been a firm believer in the domino theory. By 1969, however, this had been largely discredited. Even Kissinger, in a lengthy October 1969 review of post-1945 world politics, implicitly accepted that the theory was mistaken, writing that:

> as events in Greece, Burma, Malaysia, the Philippines, Guatemala, the Congo, Laos, and Indonesia show – the capacity of local communist parties to subvert or gain control of unstable states by 'wars of national liberation' or any other means has proved to be quite limited. This is true even when such parties are supported by an adjacent communist power, especially if the target states receive external assistance. South Vietnam now seems to be an exception, due to a combination of unique circumstances: the sophisticated use of modern military power by North Vietnam, the organizational genius of Ho Chi Minh in developing an extensive Viet Cong infrastructure, and his ability to exploit nationalist sentiment in the war against the French.[77]

Moreover, the domino theory was consciously de-emphasised by the administration once Vietnamization became the *leitmotif* of Nixon's Vietnam policy, for obvious reasons. Nevertheless, Nixon himself clearly felt that the domino theory still had a role in explaining the US involvement in Vietnam to the US public and US allies, and so it was still utilised on occasion.[78] This was particularly the case after Congress, in June 1970, rescinded the Gulf of Tonkin Resolution, removing the legitimating authority for the presence of US combat troops in Vietnam. For example, asked during a July 1970 television interview to explain why US troops remained in Vietnam in light of the withdrawal of congressional support, Nixon fell back on the domino theory:

> Now I know there are those who say the domino theory is obsolete. They haven't talked to the dominoes. They should talk to the Thais, to the Malaysians, to the

Singaporeans, to the Indonesians, to the Filipinos, to the Japanese, and the rest. And if the United States leaves Vietnam in a way that we are humiliated or defeated, not simply speaking in what is called jingoistic terms, but in very practical terms, this will be immensely discouraging to the 300 million people from Japan clear around to Thailand in free Asia; and even more important it will be ominously encouraging to the leaders of Communist China and the Soviet Union who are supporting the North Vietnamese. It will encourage them in their expansionist policies in other areas.[79]

At the same time, however, Nixon was keen to explain that he was not suggesting a vision of the domino theory in the 1950s' sense of the concept. Nixon's seeming confusion by 1970 over the applicability of the domino theory might be seen as a consequence of the fact that linkage, as championed by Kissinger in particular, offered a more diffuse and wide-ranging expression of the belief that lay at the intellectual heart of the domino theory. Linkage was based on the notion that a perceived or actual reverse for the US in any part of the world would have a deleterious impact on global stability because of its impact on others' perceptions of US power, commitment and, hence, credibility. The domino theory might have been largely discredited by 1970, but the concerns underpinning it lived on via the concept of linkage.

In the course of his July 1970 television interview, Nixon had told his interviewers that:

If the people of South Vietnam after they see what the Vietcong, the Communist Vietcong, have done to the villages they have occupied, the 40,000 people that they have murdered, village chiefs and others, the atrocities of Hue – if the people of South Vietnam, of which 850,000 of them are Catholic refugees from North Vietnam, after a blood bath there when the North Vietnamese took over in North Vietnam – if the people of South Vietnam under those circumstances should choose to move in the direction of a Communist government, that, of course, is their right.[80]

He went on to note that,

in no country in the world today in which the Communists are in power have they come to power as a result of the people choosing them . . . In every case, communism has come to power by other than a free election, so I think we are in a pretty safe position on this particular point."[81]

This apparent confidence, however, masked a growing concern. Just days earlier Nixon had asked for "an urgent review of US policy and strategy in the event of an Allende victory" in the upcoming Chilean elections.[82]

In his *Memoirs*, Nixon devoted just one carefully crafted page out of over 1,000 to his administration's efforts to undermine the Allende government.[83] In this, he presented the threat posed by Allende's election in essentially domino theory terms, recalling the warning of an Italian businessman to the effect that: "If Allende should win, and with Castro in Cuba, you will have in Latin America a red sandwich. And eventually, it will all be red."[84] On this reading, Nixon was faced with the difficult decision of having to undermine democracy to save it. It was, he explained, "a peculiar double standard that would require us alone to stand abjectly aside as democracies are undermined by countries less constrained by conscience."[85] Kissinger invoked a similar spectre at the time. During a 16 September 1970 briefing with a group of Midwest newspaper editors on the implications for the US of Allende's election victory (and as the administration sought ways of preventing Allende from actually assuming office), Kissinger explained:

> Now, it is fairly easy for one to predict that if Allende wins, there is a good chance that he will establish over a period of years some sort of Communist government. In that case you would have one not on an island off the coast which has not a traditional relationship and impact on Latin America, but in a major Latin American country you would have a Communist government, [ad]joining, for example, Argentina, which is already deeply divided, along a long frontier [ad]joining Peru, which has already been heading in directions that have been difficult to deal with, and [ad] joining Bolivia, which has also gone in a more leftist, anti-US direction, even without any of these developments.
>
> So I don't think we should delude ourselves that an Allende take-over in Chile would not present massive problems for us, and for democratic forces and for pro-US forces in Latin America, and indeed to the whole Western Hemisphere.[86]

In his memoirs Kissinger defended the administration's efforts to destabilise Allende in three different ways. First, in terms of linkage, as a consequence of the impact Allende's election had on US credibility globally at a time of multiple global challenges (although this rather neglected the fact that the effort to prevent his election had been under way in advance of these).[87] Second, and without irony, on the grounds that: "Allende represented a break with Chile's long democratic history and would become president not through an authentic expression of majority will but through a fluke of the Chilean political system."[88] Third, on the grounds that, "Allende's election was a challenge to our national interest. We did not find it easy to reconcile ourselves to a second Communist state in the Western Hemisphere."[89]

It was Kissinger who made most of the running in shaping the administration's response to Allende's election. He had previously quipped that South America was no more than "a dagger pointing at the heart of Antarctica" and in 1969 had told the Chilean Foreign Minister, Gabriel Valdés, that: "Nothing of importance can come from the South" because the "axis of history starts in Moscow, goes to Bonn, crosses over to Washington, and then goes to Tokyo. What happens in the South is of no importance."[90] (Nixon agreed, telling Donald Rumsfeld in 1971: "Latin America doesn't matter. People don't give one damn about Latin America. The only thing in the world that matters is Japan, China, Russia, and Europe."[91]) But now Kissinger's belief in linkage, bordering on the domino theory that he had earlier explained was essentially redundant, led him to abandon this earlier insouciance and instead to offer and champion the most alarmist assessments of the implications of Allende's victory. For example, a 3 November 1970 memorandum from Vernon Walters, the US military attaché in Paris, warned of how:

> We are engaged in a mortal struggle to determine the shape of the future of the world. Latin America is a key area in the struggle. Its resources, the social and economic problems of its population, its proximity to the US and its future potential make it a priority target for the enemies of the US. We must ensure that it is neither turned against us nor taken over by those who threaten our vital national interests.[92]

Kissinger forwarded this to Nixon and days later was writing to Nixon himself, warning that Allende's election, "poses for us one of the most serious challenges ever faced in this hemisphere" and that Nixon's "decision as to what to do about it may be the most historic and difficult foreign affairs decision you will have to make this year."[93] Taken at face value, this elevated the issue of Chile above those of relations with the Soviet Union and China and the task of extricating the US from Vietnam. Unintentionally echoing the flawed logic that had led the US into Vietnam in the first place, and which he had himself attacked, Kissinger now told Nixon that: "the example of a successfully elected Marxist government in Chile would surely have an impact on – and precedent value for – other parts of the world, especially in Italy; the imitative spread of similar phenomena elsewhere would in turn significantly affect the world balance and our own position in it."[94]

CONCLUSIONS

As time passes, Nixon's foreign policy appears less of a success than it did at the time, when the world's media followed him as he blazed a trail to China, met with the ailing Mao, was photographed at the Great Wall of China, and visited Moscow, met with Soviet leader Leonid Brezhnev and signed the SALT agreement. In retrospect, the achievement of the opening to China and détente with the Soviet Union are seen as having an air of inevitability given structural changes in the international system. Meanwhile, as time passes greater attention is given to areas that Nixon and Kissinger themselves regarded as merely peripheral to the core concerns of US foreign policy. At a time of challenge to the global power of the United States, the Nixon-Kissinger foreign policy was premised on the need to accommodate the Soviet Union, accepting it as a fixture in international relations. The task was to manage the Soviet Union via the carrot of détente and the potential stick of a system of regional alliances and, via Kissinger's vision of linkage, to use détente to secure Soviet (and Chinese) support to help bring about an end to the war in Vietnam. All other considerations were secondary, but at the same time linked. The extent of Soviet (and Chinese) influence over North Vietnam was far more limited than Nixon or Kissinger or their predecessors realised, and hence the whole concept of linkage was flawed. Linkage was premised on an international communism directed from Moscow that Kissinger and Nixon, in their speeches and writings, professed to no longer believe in. The need to maintain alliances to counter the Soviet Union dictated that there was little scope for policies that challenged the credentials of individual governments whose roles helped secure global stability, even at the cost of local turbulence.

This logic gave rise to the Nixon Doctrine, but its unstated corollary was continued support for pro-Western authoritarian regimes. The more the US relied on allies to act as regional policemen in Cold War hotspots, the greater the importance of resisting pressures for liberalisation that could result in radical nationalist regimes that gravitated towards Moscow (the only alternative to being a pro-US ally in the zero-sum Cold War world-view of Nixon and Kissinger).[95] Indeed, allies that had no need to go through the process of contesting regular elections were the most reliable, as they were unlikely to be replaced by governments less sympathetic to US strategy and goals.

Hence, the language of 'freedom' was accorded a lower emphasis in Nixon administration foreign policy, although it did retain a rhetorical presence that reflected its centrality as an idea in American political culture. Conversely, as we will see in the next chapter, the Reagan administration, which did not accept the status quo with the Soviet

Union as inevitable,[96] would make much more extensive use of the language of freedom in challenging what it saw (at some times with more justification than others) as spreading Soviet influence in areas such as Afghanistan, Cambodia, Central America and Southern Africa.[97] Hence, in the rhetorical armoury of President Reagan, the Contras seeking to overthrow the left-wing Sandinista government in Nicaragua became "the moral equivalent of our Founding Fathers",[98] whilst in Angola, UNITA leader Jonas Savimbi was lauded as a "freedom fighter." Savimbi was visiting Washington, at the culmination of an expensive public relations exercise designed to improve his image in the US, at the time of Reagan's 1986 State of the Union address, and so was on-hand to hear the President offer his support to international 'freedom fighters', saying that: "America will support with moral and material assistance your right not just to fight and die for freedom, but to fight and win freedom – in Afghanistan,; Angola; Cambodia and Nicaragua."[99] While it may be possible to see the seeds of the Reagan Doctrine in the Nixon Doctrine, in essence the Reagan Doctrine – the practice of arming, funding and offering diplomatic support to local guerrilla groups attempting to overthrow left-wing and/or pro-Soviet regimes in these areas – supplanted the Nixon Doctrine. Rollback replaced Containment. Amongst conservatives as well as liberal critics, the Nixon Doctrine was now viewed as having been far too accommodating to the Soviet Union and, as a consequence, fundamentally flawed.

In retrospect, the application of the Nixon Doctrine to Iran and downplaying of the importance of promoting democracy there had devastating consequences for which the US continued to pay a heavy price into the twenty-first century. It was the 1979 collapse of this one of the 'twin pillars' of the Nixon Doctrine in the Middle East that led to the US opening to Iraq, the building up of Saddam Hussein as a counter-weight to Iran, and all that flowed from it. However, it is with regard to Chile that the reputations of Nixon and Kissinger continue to suffer most. Nixon himself was clearly aware of the problem that Chile represented when he came to write his *Memoirs*.[100] Indeed, it is possible that the only way in which to write a positive account of Nixon's political life is to avoid discussing Chile, as Jonathan Aitken does in his 600-page biography.[101] There is some irony in all of this, as Mark Lawrence points out, in that the part of the world that Nixon and Kissinger considered the least important has come to have such a damaging impact on their reputations.[102]

Does the case of Chile, then, represent an application of the Nixon Doctrine? The argument here is that at one level it does. Local forces were covertly encouraged and supported in bringing 'stability' to a country that, for Nixon and Kissinger, risked becoming 'unstable'. It fitted the description of the Doctrine that Nixon provided in his *Memoirs* (and cited earlier). On the other hand, it was clearly something that went beyond the strict letter of the Nixon Doctrine, as Chile did not represent a case of internal subversion, but of electoral success in a country that the US Ambassador to Chile, Edward Korry, had informed Nixon in January 1970, represented, "one of the calmer and more decent places on earth; its democracy, like our own, has an extraordinary resilience . . . I see little that will endanger real US interests in the country, in the area or in the hemisphere."[103] Perhaps, then, the case of Chile simply points above all to the *flexibility* of the Nixon Doctrine. As Henry Kissinger told internal critics of the invasion of Cambodia: "We wrote the goddamn doctrine, we can change it."[104] Some might regard this very flexibility as being suggestive less of doctrine and more of codified expediency.

For Kissinger, the historical reckoning must take in his relationship with the Pinochet regime after 1973.[105] Reflecting his essentially *realpolitik* approach to the issue, he told an October 1973 staff meeting: "I think we should understand our policy – that however unpleasant they act, this government is better for us than Allende was."[106] In addition, such reckoning must involve questions about the state of his knowledge about Operation Condor – a co-ordinated effort by the military governments of Chile, Argentina, Uruguay, Paraguay, Bolivia and later Brazil to track down and eliminate left-wing opposition.[107] This too can be viewed as a logical outgrowth of the Nixon Doctrine of self-policing societies with US involvement restricted to arms and training, although also extending to diplomatic support.

This helps explain why increasingly the Nixon foreign policy has come to be viewed as having been anathema to American values, ushering in a corrective in the form of the Carter administration's attempt to link foreign policy with the promotion of human rights – targeting precisely those clients that had benefited most from the Nixon-Kissinger approach. Kissinger biographer Walter Isaacson has argued that, because of his background, Henry Kissinger stands outside the American foreign policy tradition, regardless of how much he wanted to be regarded as part of it. On this reading, Kissinger's Realism represented a "European-style philosophy of international affairs."[108] Kissinger, Isaacson argues, "never had an instinctive feel for American values and mores." He quotes Kissinger aide Lawrence Eagleburger, who reflected on the fact that:

> Henry is a balance-of-power thinker. He deeply believes in stability. These kind of objectives are antithetical to the American experience. Americans tend to want to pursue a set of moral principles. Henry does not have an intrinsic feel for the American political system, and he does not start with the same basic values and assumptions.[109]

Hence, the Kissinger practice of foreign policy can be separated from the wider US historical tradition. In a key respect, Kissinger was simply un-American, more of a Metternich. However, this is too convenient a line of argument and in itself a form of reassertion of the idea of American exceptionalism. Any explanation for the trajectory of US foreign policy in the first half of the 1970s clearly needs also to account for Nixon.

NOTES

1 Kabaservice, *Rule and Ruin*, pp.296, 305.
2 Arthur M. Schlesinger, Jr., *The Imperial Presidency* (New York: Houghton Mifflin, 1973).
3 Richard Nixon, *The Memoirs of Richard Nixon* (London: Arrow ed., 1979), p.340. For as assessment of Kissinger's impact on the influence of the NSC, and the rivalry with the Departments of State and Defense during the Nixon administration, see: David Rothkopf, *Running the World: The Inside Story of the National Security Council and the Architects of American Power* (New York: Public Affairs, 2005), Ch.6; Walter Isaacson, *Kissinger: A Biography* (New York: Simon & Schuster, 1992), Ch.10.
4 Henry Kissinger, *The White House Years* (London: Weidenfeld & Nicolson/Michael Joseph, 1979), p.54.
5 Nixon, *Memoirs*, p.341.
6 Illustrated in the way in which they discuss each other's contributions to foreign policy in their respective memoirs.
7 Cited in Gerald S. Strober and Deborah Hart Strober, *Nixon: An Oral History of His Presidency* (New York: Harper Perennial, 1996), p.124.
8 Iwan Morgan, *Nixon* (London: Arnold, 2002), p.18.

9 Ibid.
10 W. W. Rostow, *The Stages of Economic Growth: A Non-Communist Manifesto* (Cambridge: Cambridge University Press, 1960). See also, David Milne, *America's Rasputin: Walt Rostow and the Vietnam War* (New York: Hill and Wang, 2008), esp. Ch.2.
11 Jeremi Suri, *Henry Kissinger and the American Century* (Cambridge, MA: Harvard/The Belknap Press, 2007), p.8. The most detailed biographical treatment of Kissinger's early life is Niall Ferguson, *Kissinger 1923–1968: The Idealist* (London: Allen Lane, 2015).
12 Isaacson, *Kissinger*, p.76.
13 Henry A. Kissinger, 'Central Issues of American Foreign Policy', originally 1968, reprinted in Henry A. Kissinger, *American Foreign Policy: Three Essays* (London: Weidenfeld & Nicolson, 1969), p.57.
14 Ibid., pp.57–8.
15 For a discussion of Kissinger's Realism, see Isaacson, *Kissinger*, Ch.29; Robert D. Kaplan, 'Kissinger, Metternich, and Realism', *The Atlantic Monthly*, June 1999: www.theatlantic.com/issues/99jun/9906kissinger.htm.
16 Robert Dallek, *Nixon and Kissinger: Partners in Power* (London: Penguin/Allen Lane, 2007), p.90.
17 Kissinger, 'Central Issues', p.52.
18 Jeremi Suri, 'Henry Kissinger and American Grand Strategy', in Fredrik Logevall and Andrew Preston (eds.), *Nixon in the World: American Foreign Relations, 1969–1977* (New York: Oxford University Press, 2008), p.70.
19 Kissinger, *The White House Years*, p.914.
20 This utilises the definition of 'national security' provided by Leffler: Melvyn P. Leffler, 'National Security', in Michael J. Hogan and Thomas G. Paterson (eds.), *Explaining the History of American Foreign Relations* (2nd ed. Cambridge: Cambridge University Press, 2004), pp.123–136, at p.123; and the discussion of the relationship between core values in US domestic and foreign policy in Andrew Preston, 'Monsters Everywhere: A Genealogy of National Security', *Diplomatic History*, Vol.38, No.3, 2014, pp.477–500, at p.480.
21 Freeden, *Ideology*, Ch.1.
22 It is not unusual for biographers to agree. For example, to Roger Morris Nixon's politics were, "not of wing or doctrine so much as ceaseless self-advancement." Roger Morris, *Richard Milhous Nixon: The Rise of an American Politician* (New York: Henry Holt, 1990), p.740.
23 For example, at the end of a February 1970 in a discussion of recent shifts in the nature of the Cold War with reporters, Kissinger concluded by explaining that the administration accepted that: "there are still serious causes of tension, that ideology is not dead, even though it has changed some of its character, and that large areas of discord and hostility remain." White House Background Press Briefing by the President's Assistant for National Security Affairs, Washington, February 16 1970, *Foreign Relations of the United States, The Nixon-Ford Administrations. Vol.1: Foundations of Foreign Policy, 1969–1972*, doc.58, www.state.gov/r/pa/ho/frus/nixon/i/20700.htm.
24 As Kissinger explained in 1969, "we will judge other countries, including Communist countries . . . on the basis of their actions and not on the basis of their domestic ideology." Kissinger, *The White House Years*, p.66.
25 See, for example, ibid., pp.66–69, 662–664.
26 On the impressions he gained on these trips, see, Nixon, *Memoirs*, pp.280–283.
27 Address by Richard M. Nixon to the Bohemian Club, San Francisco, July 29 1967, *Foreign Relations of the United States, Foundations*, doc.2.
28 Ibid.
29 Ibid.
30 Ibid.
31 Ibid.
32 Kissinger, 'Central Issues', pp.82–83.
33 Ibid., p.84.
34 Nixon, Bohemian Club Address.
35 Ambrose, *Nixon: The Education of a Politician 1913–1962*, p.461.
36 Special Message From President Nixon to the Congress, May 28 1969, in Public Papers of the Presidents of the United States: *Richard Nixon, 1969*, p.411.

37 Ibid., p.417.
38 Memorandum of Conversation, San Clemente, California, September 2 1969, 11.45 a.m., *Foreign Relations of the United States, Foundations*, doc.35.
39 Ibid.
40 Ibid.
41 Ibid.
42 Cited in Lubna Z. Qureshi, *Nixon, Kissinger, and Allende: US Involvement in the 1973 Coup in Chile* (Lanham, MD: Lexington Books, 2009), p.13.
43 Richard M. Nixon, 'Asia After Viet Nam', *Foreign Affairs*, Vol.46, No.1, 1967, pp.113–125. Quote at p.115. Kissinger was reaching similar conclusions. In his 1968 'Central Issues of American Foreign Policy' essay, he wrote that the US was; "a superpower physically, but our designs can be meaningful only if they generate willing cooperation. We can continue to contribute to defense and positive programs, but we must seek to encourage and not stifle a sense of local responsibility. Our contribution should not be the sole or principal effort, but it should make the difference between success and failure. Kissinger, 'Central Issues', pp.93–94.
44 Nixon, 'Asia After Viet Nam', p.117.
45 Kissinger, 'Central Issues', p.93.
46 Ibid., p.94.
47 Public Papers of the Presidents of the United States: *Richard Nixon, 1969*, pp.3–4.
48 For an early outline with regard to the Soviet Union, see Letter from President Nixon to Secretary of Defense Laird, *Foreign Relations of the United States, Foundations*, doc.10.
49 Cited in Jeffrey Kimball, 'The Nixon Doctrine: A Saga of Misunderstanding', *Presidential Studies Quarterly*, Vol.36, No.1, March 2006, pp.59–74. Quote at p.64.
50 Kissinger, *The White House Years*, p.224.
51 Nixon had clearly not planned in advance to articulate a doctrinal shift whilst in Guam (although readers of his *Memoirs* could be forgiven for thinking otherwise). H. R. Haldeman's diary entry for the period makes this clear. H. R. Haldeman, *The Haldeman Diaries: Inside the Nixon White House* (New York: Berkley Books ed., 1995), p.91.
52 Nixon, *Memoirs*, p.395.
53 For example, Kimball, 'The Nixon Doctrine'.
54 Kissinger, *The White House Years*, p.225.
55 Karnow, *Vietnam*, p.596.
56 *Foreign Relations of the United States, Foundations*, doc.30. Compare this with the firmer conception of the boundaries of the Doctrine provided by Nixon in a meeting on the same day at which Kissinger was present: "Where problem is internal subversion, countries must deal with problem themselves. We will help – but not American ground forces. Even when there is foreign exported revolution. Not talking about invasion by conventional troops." Memorandum of Conversation, Bangkok, July 29 1969, 4 p.m., *Foreign Relations of the United States, Foundations*, doc.31.
57 Memorandum, Kissinger to Nixon, September 10 1969, reproduced in Kissinger, *The White House Years*, pp.1480–1482. Quote at p.1481.
58 White House Background Press Briefing by the President's Assistant for National Security Affairs, Washington, February 16 1970, *Foreign Relations of the United States, Foundations*, doc.58.
59 Paper Prepared in the National Security Council Staff, 'The Nixon Doctrine for Asia: Some Hard Issues', n/d, *Foreign Relations of the United States, Foundations*, doc.54.
60 Karnow, *Vietnam*, p.594.
61 Message From President Nixon to the Congress, 'Foreign Assistance for the Seventies', Washington, September 15 1970, *Foreign Relations of the United States, Foundations*, doc.70.
62 Gary Sick, *All Fall Down: America's Tragic Encounter With Iran* (New York: Penguin, 1986), p.8.
63 On this strategy, see Howard Teicher and Gayle Radley Teicher, *Twin Pillars to Desert Storm: America's Flawed Vision in the Middle East from Nixon to Bush* (New York: William Morrow, 1993).
64 Kissinger, *The White House Years*, p.1265.
65 Ibid., p.1261.
66 Conversation Among President Nixon, Ambassador Douglas MacArthur II, and General Alexander Haig, Washington, DC, 8 April 1971, *Foreign Relations of the United States,*

1969–1976, Documents on Iran and Iraq, 1969–1972, doc.122, www.state.gov/r/pa/ho/frus/nixon/e4/71804.htm.

67 NIE 34–69, 'Iran', 10 January 1969, *Foreign Relations of the United States, Iran and Iraq, 1969–1972*.

68 Conversation Among President Nixon, Ambassador Douglas MacArthur II, and General Alexander Haig, Washington, DC, 8 April 1971, ibid.

69 Ibid.

70 For example, Memorandum, State Department Bureau of Intelligence and Research, 'Iran: Internal Dissidence – A Note of Warning', 12 June 1972, ibid.

71 Memorandum from the President's Deputy Assistant for National Security Affairs (Haig) to Kissinger, 28 July 1972 (forwarding memorandum from Helms, dated 18 July 1972), ibid.

72 On the mid-1970s Kurdish insurgency, see Charles Tripp, *A History of Iraq* (2nd ed. Cambridge: Cambridge University Press, 2002), pp.211–214. The figure of 60,000 casualties comes from Said K. Aburish, *Saddam Hussein: The Politics of Revenge* (London: Bloomsbury, 2000), p.120.

73 Isaacson, *Kissinger*, p.653.

74 Ambrose, *Nixon*, pp.458–482; Nixon, *Memoirs*, pp.185–193.

75 Cited in Mark Atwood Lawrence, 'History from Below: The United States and Latin America in the Nixon Years', in Logevall and Preston (eds.), *Nixon in the World*, p.274.

76 Ibid.

77 Memorandum From the President's Assistant for National Security Affairs (Kissinger) to President Nixon, Washington, October 20 1969, *Foreign Relations of the United States, Foundations*, doc.41.

78 See, for example, his comments of 1 April 1969, following a meeting with Australian Prime Minister John Gorton. *Foreign Relations of the United States, Foundations*, doc.17.

79 Interview with President Nixon, Los Angeles, California, July 1 1970, *Foreign Relations of the United States, Foundations*, doc.67.

80 Ibid.

81 Ibid.

82 Cited in Dallek, *Nixon and Kissinger*, p.232.

83 Nixon, *Memoirs*, pp.489–490.

84 Ibid., p.490.

85 Ibid., pp.489–490.

86 Kissinger, *The White House Years*, p.673.

87 Ibid., p.654.

88 Ibid.

89 Ibid.

90 Cited in Seymour Hersh, *The Price of Power: Henry Kissinger in the White House* (New York: Summit Books, 1983), p.263. Valdés replied "Mr Kissinger, you know nothing of the South", to which Kissinger replied, "No, and I don't care." Ibid. See Chs.21 and 22.

91 Cited in Lawrence, 'History from Below', p.269.

92 Cited in Dallek, *Nixon and Kissinger*, p.238.

93 Ibid., p.239.

94 Ibid. Perhaps Nixon's Italian businessman had also spoken with Kissinger.

95 As Kissinger wrote in 1968: "A bipolar world loses the perspective for nuance; a gain for one side appears as an absolute loss for the other. Every issue seems to involve a question of survival. The smaller countries are torn between a desire for protection and a wish to escape big-power dominance. Each of the superpowers is beset by the desire to maintain its preeminence among its allies, to increase its influence among the uncommitted, and to enhance its security vis-à-vis its opponent." Kissinger, 'Central Issues', p.56.

96 On this difference, see, James Mann, *The Rebellion of Ronald Reagan: A History of the End of the Cold War* (New York: Viking, 2009), esp. Ch.3.

97 On the Reagan administration's interventionism (the Reagan Doctrine), see James M. Scott, *Deciding to Intervene: The Reagan Doctrine and American Foreign Policy* (Durham, NC: Duke University Press, 1996); Peter Schweizer, *Victory: The Reagan Administration's Secret Strategy That Hastened the Collapse of the Soviet Union* (New York: The Atlantic Monthly Press, 1994).

98 www.pbs.org/wgbh/amex/reagan/peopleevents/pande08.html.

99 Patrick E. Tyler and David B. Ottaway, 'The Selling of Jonas Savimbi: Success and a $60,000 Tab', *Washington Post*, 9 February 1986.
100 See, also, the damage limitation approach evident in his 1977 interviews with David Frost. The transcript covering that portion of the interviews focusing on Chile has now been published in, David Frost with Bob Zelnick, *Frost/Nixon* (Basingstoke: Macmillan, 2008).
101 Jonathan Aitken, *Nixon: A Life* (Washington, DC: Regnery Publishing, 1993).
102 Lawrence, 'History from Below', p.271.
103 Dallek, *Nixon and Kissinger*, p.231.
104 William Shawcross, *Sideshow: Kissinger, Nixon and the Destruction of Cambodia* (London: The Hogarth Press, 1986), p.145.
105 On this, see Tanya Harmer, 'Fractious Allies: Chile, the United States, and the Cold War, 1973–76', *Diplomatic History*, Vol.37, No.1, 2013, pp.109–143.
106 Quoted in Rabe, *The Killing Zone*, p.145.
107 See, John Dinges, *The Condor Years: How Pinochet and His Allies Brought Terrorism to Three Continents* (New York: The New Press, 2004); Greg Grandin, *Kissinger's Shadow: The Long Reach of America's Most Controversial Statesman* (New York: Metropolitan Books, 2015), pp.151–154.
108 Isaacson, *Kissinger*, p.761. Earlier, however, Isaacson concedes that the clash between idealism and Realism in US foreign policy is one that can be traced back to Thomas Jefferson and Alexander Hamilton. Ibid., p.654.
109 Ibid., p.764.

6 The exceptionalism of Ronald Reagan: ideology and Cold War, from intensification to end

Richard Nixon resigned as president in August 1974 in response to the threat of impeachment, to be replaced by his Vice-President Gerald Ford. The Watergate scandal, growing social and economic problems and persistent divisions over Vietnam continued to reverberate after Nixon's departure. The Republican landslide victory coalition of 1972 began to disintegrate. Many activists disliked what they perceived as Nixon's appeasement of communism in its various forms (détente, diplomatic relations with China and withdrawal from Vietnam). The continued growth of big government at home and associated diseases – flagging economic performance, moral decay, the promotion of minorities and 'welfare dependency' – were also linked in the conservative imagination to a decline in America's standing in the world. This turned Republican activists towards Ronald Reagan's bid for the nomination in 1976. Reagan felt the same connections as the activists and even Ford, the incumbent and as a presidential frontrunner, felt obliged to stress the role of "Morality in Foreign Policy", thereby setting a pattern; "when moderate conservatives won, they secured their victories only by appeasing the militants."[1]

Ford won the nomination but lost the 1976 presidential election to Jimmy Carter, a former Governor of Georgia, a born-again Christian and the only Democrat between 1960 and 2016 to carry Mississippi and Alabama in his near-sweep of the South. As President, Carter saw himself as part of a Democratic tradition that had produced the New Deal, New Frontier and Great Society. But he was also separate from that tradition – separated by the "fire-break" of the Vietnam War,[2] as well as by the recent revelations of Watergate and the Church Committee hearings into aspects of the Cold War conduct of the CIA. One expression of this was evident in a speech Carter gave at Notre Dame University in May 1977, given as his administration sought to take the first steps towards normalisation of relations with Vietnam.[3] In the speech he spoke of how the US had "fought fire with fire, never thinking that fire is better quenched with water. This approach failed", he told his audience, "with Vietnam the best example of its intellectual and moral poverty."[4] A rejection of the logic that had ensnared the US in Vietnam was a central element of Carter's overarching vision of America's approach to the rest of the world, one that evoked Woodrow Wilson and drew on his own religious beliefs. As he wrote in his memoirs: "Our country has been strongest and most effective when morality and a commitment to freedom and democracy have been most clearly emphasized in our foreign policy." However, Carter felt that since the time of the Truman administration, "persistent support" for such an approach had often been missing:

Much of the time we failed to exhibit as an American characteristic the ideal-ism of Jefferson or Wilson. In the process we forfeited one of our most effective ways to meet threats from totalitarian ideologies and arouse the spirit of our own people. Because of the heavy emphasis that was placed on Soviet-American competition, a dominant factor in our dealings with foreign countries became whether they espoused an anti-communist line. There were times when right-wing monarchs and military dictators were automatically immune from any criticism of their oppressive actions. Our apparent commitment was to protect them from any internal political movement that might result in the establishment of a more liberal ruling group. Instead of promoting freedom and democratic principles, our government seemed to believe that in any struggle with evil, we could not compete effectively unless we played by the same rules or lack of rules as the evildoers.[5]

This emphasis on morality was nowhere more evident than in the Carter administration's commitment to the promotion of human rights, the expansion of which Carter "hoped and believed" could become "the wave of the future around the world."[6] Yet the practical application of the principle proved problematic and divisive. Added to the problems of definition with which the administration wrestled there was the question of consistency. Were America's allies really to be punished because they did not live up to American standards with regard to human rights (a proposition which, as we saw in the last chapter, was incompatible with Richard Nixon's Realism-informed approach to foreign policy)? Were some simply too valuable to risk alienating, especially in the zero-sum arena of the global Cold War? Should a focus on human rights drive policy towards the Soviet Union at the risk of jeopardising progress on arms control? What should be the balance between focusing on the behaviour of Third World dictators (of particular concern in lib-eral circles) and the Soviet record on human rights (the conservative preference)? Carter later explained that he was familiar with but rejected the "widely accepted arguments that we had to choose between idealism and Realism, or between morality and the exer-tion of power."[7] Yet in practice the human rights policy came to be applied selectively, with the most significant blind-spot concerning the Shah of Iran (seemingly a textbook example of the "right-wing monarchs" Carter criticised his predecessors for support-ing regardless of their human rights record). Moreover, his most senior foreign policy principals – Secretary of State Cyrus Vance and National Security Advisor Zbigniew Brzezinski – each seemed to represent one of these tendencies of idealism and Realism – with Vance the post-Vietnam liberal and Brzezinski emphasising the primacy of security over development and the importance of thinking in globalist terms that could not help but recall Henry Kissinger.[8]

Brzezinski did not completely reject the emphasis that the Carter administration attached to human rights but felt that the US should aim for a "proper balance between human-rights imperatives and the uglier realities of world politics." In particular, he rec-ognised that the policy was only likely to impact on state behaviour in those states over which the US held some leverage and as a result became particularly concerned about the impact of the policy on emerging regional powers in Latin America. As he recalled in his memoirs:

Concerned that our human-rights policy was in danger of becoming one-sidedly anti-rightist, in a talk with the President on August 7, 1978, I said that we are 'running the risk of having bad relations simultaneously with Brazil, Chile, and Argentina' because of the way State was implementing our human rights policy.[9]

Rather than provide balance, however, the appointment of Vance and Brzezinski produced a bitter personal rivalry, one that intensified as international events – in particular, a spate of revolutionary upheaval in the developing world and Soviet intervention in Afghanistan – led to the collapse of détente and the emergence of a 'Second Cold War'.[10] In this context, Carter's approach to foreign policy was seen to have failed, a failure symbolised by his administration's inability to free the US hostages held in Tehran following the storming of the US Embassy there on 4 November 1979. Ronald Reagan's time had come.

Commentators and scholars have regularly labelled the Nixon-Kissinger period as non-ideological and the Reagan administration as the opposite, with Reagan often described as a Cold War ideologue[11] who placed the ideological contest between the United States and the Soviet Union at the heart of his administration.[12] However, as we have set out to demonstrate in this book, all presidencies have an ideological character to them. What is most important is to understand the ideological continuities across administrations and the particularities of specific presidencies. Categorising Reagan as 'ideological' is almost too easy because he spoke in blunt anti-communist and proudly nationalist language from his prime-time entry into American politics endorsing Barry Goldwater at the Republican Party Convention in 1964 to the very end of his presidency. In his 1964 'A Time for Choosing' speech Reagan argued that people all over the world needed to choose an ideological side and not to be silent "about the millions of people enslaved in the Soviet colonies in the satellite nations." Further he endorsed the hard right anti-communist position that Soviet influence needed to be rolled back across the world. By the end of Reagan's presidency, as conditions changed significantly in the Soviet Union under Mikhail Gorbachev, Reagan came to see a greater value in arms negotiations with the Soviets. Nonetheless in his Farewell Address from the Oval Office on January 11 1989 he still simplistically contrasted communism and Americanism in a manner that he had done throughout his career. "Nothing is less free than pure communism", he explained, whereas America was "the shining city" that John Winthrop had hoped it would be.[13] Freedom was a concept Reagan never tired of claiming was at the heart of the American way of life. The hyperbolic nature of this belief in freedom was frequently on display – for example, in a speech Reagan gave to the Conservative Political Action Conference in 1983, where he proclaimed that: "The task that has fallen to us as Americans is to move the conscience of the world, to keep alive the hope and dream of freedom. For if we fail or falter, there'll be no place for the world's oppressed to flee to."[14]

This constant emphasis on the virtues of 'freedom' as a guiding force of American public and foreign policy was at the centre of Reagan's nationalist and anti-communist ideology. The meta concept of freedom was employed by Reagan to justify all manner of policies, from tax cuts to the funding of what he called the "freedom fighters of Afghanistan"[15] and the Contra "freedom fighters" in Nicaragua.[16] The Reagan Doctrine of aiding and arming anti-communist and anti-leftist insurgent groups in order to undermine and roll back left-wing regimes in the Third World, was regularly presented as part of Reagan's push for greater freedom. At the same time, it was an explicit rejection of Containment, of the more accommodationist Nixon-Kissinger approach to the Soviet Union as a factor in the international system, and of the Carter administration's attempts to link foreign policy to human rights.[17] Its logic depended on an understanding of international communism as a monolithic force advancing under the direction and at the behest of Moscow, and as such risked reintroducing pasts errors rooted in ideology to the conduct of US foreign policy.

The Reagan Doctrine built on Reagan's dictum that the USSR and communists the world over "fear the infectiousness of even a little freedom, and because of this in many ways their system has failed."[18] This simple freedom-loving world-view contrasted not just two systems of government but two ways of living. The bluntest ideological expression of this was in Reagan's notorious Westminster speech in 1982 when he claimed that, "the march of freedom and democracy will leave Marxism-Leninism on the ash-heap of history as it has left other tyrannies which stifle the freedom and muzzle the self-expression of the people."[19] Seeing Reagan's speeches as ideological is not difficult because that is the way Reagan saw the distinctions he was trying to draw between America and the Soviet Union – as an ideological battle. James Graham Wilson, a historian at the US State Department, characterised Reagan's Westminster speech as an "ideological crusade."[20] This tone of ideological combat was to the fore in Reagan's 1985 Address to the General Assembly of the United Nations, in which he set out how:

> When we enjoy these vast freedoms as we do, it's difficult for us to understand the restrictions of dictatorships which seek to control each institution and every facet of people's lives – the expression of their beliefs, their movements, and their contacts with the outside world. It's difficult for us to understand the ideological premise that force is an acceptable way to expand a political system.[21]

However, claiming to be on the side of freedom became a justification for a range of deadly foreign policies in the Third World. This agenda also contributed to nuclear arms negotiations being halted, thus increasing Cold War tensions as the Reagan administration rejected the premises of the SALT negotiations and pushed for victory over the USSR rather than coexistence. The limitations of this freedom-espousing ideology, which lacked the subtlety to deal with both complex conflicts in the Third World and nuclear arms negotiations, will be highlighted throughout the chapter.

REAGANISM: THE MAN AND HIS ADMINISTRATION

Sean Wilentz in his study of the Reagan era is typically drawn to the man himself and thus writes of Reaganism: "Although it had tens of millions of followers, its theory resided not in a party, a faction, or a movement, but in the mind and the persona of one man: Ronald Wilson Reagan."[22] Richard Reeves, seemingly forgetting about Wilsonianism, goes as far as to say that: "No other President became a noun in that way."[23] The term 'Reaganism' was coined, Reeves argues, because Reagan viewed "the world in terms of ideas." Within the administration, and outside of it, people were calling the administration the 'Reagan Revolution', suggestive of a particularly 'ideological' moment in time.[24] The ideological nature of the Reagan presidency is most apparent in the period directly after his inauguration in 1981 and during the 1984 re-election campaign when Reagan made his pitch for four more years in the Oval Office: "We came together in a national crusade to make America great again, and to make a new beginning. Well, now it's all coming together."[25] Both domestically and internationally Reagan clearly thought that words, including declarations of greatness and strength, mattered. He used declarative language to present the

Cold War as an ideological struggle where there would be a winner and a loser. At least as far back as 1977 Reagan had shown his confidence that America would reign supreme when he explained to Richard Allen: "we win and they lose."[26] Given this mindset, once elected president in 1980 Reagan and his staff set about reanimating what they saw as the ideological Cold War. The contrast to the previous administrations in terms of language was stark. James Mann writes: "The Nixon veterans reacted to Reagan's first term Soviet policies with a peculiar blend of horror and admiration. They were taken aback by Reagan's rhetoric and by his emphasis on moral concerns and ideals, rather than geo-politics, as the basis for American foreign policy."[27]

Like all presidencies Reagan's was of course bigger than the man himself. Nonetheless, it is useful to have a strong sense of Reagan's own ideas and persona because these shaped the direction of many of his important policies, or at least they often gave the hard-liners in his administration extensive licence to act. The development of the Reagan Doctrine flowed directly from Reagan's own conviction, reflecting that of the New Right he represented, that the Soviets had made gains in the 1970s across the world via a new period of Third World revolutions and these needed to be rolled back.[28] These ideas were strongly supported by hard-liners in the administration such as Richard Clark, Jeane Kirkpatrick, William Casey and Caspar Weinberger. At the National Security Council a literal interpretation of Reagan's anti-communist outlook was taken to extremes as Oliver North and John Poindexter broke the law to ensure that the anti-Sandinista Contras received arms (discussed further later in this chapter).[29] However, despite the frequent and declarative statements Reagan often made about his beliefs, Reagan's own personal management style was often very hands-off and lacking in detailed guidance. There was an aloof and elusive private side to the Reagan presidency that has often contradicted the image of Reagan as the "great communicator" or the jovial public president.[30] The private Reagan has in fact often confounded biographers trying to understand the sources of his ideas. There are a few key explanations for why Reagan is a perplexing figure. Before the 2016 election of Donald Trump, Reagan was the oldest person to be elected president. Reagan, it is worth remembering, was shot and nearly killed on March 30 1981. There is also the suggestion that Reagan's Alzheimer's disease which he informed the American people about in 1994 was already apparent by 1984.[31] Reagan had a regular habit of getting facts and people's names wrong and his tendency to confuse fact with fiction is well documented.[32] Reagan's grasp of detail was notoriously thin on many policy fronts, from the state of apartheid in South Africa to the names of countries in Latin America. To deal with this lack of knowledge or engagement the CIA made movies for Reagan so he could learn about countries of importance to the US.[33] Close associates like his speech-writer Peggy Noonan note how forgetful and vague Reagan often was.[34] Reagan's vagueness and hands-off management style created a space that led to considerable rivalry and conflict in his administration, complicating the view that Reaganism was a clear or coherent ideology. Both Noonan and Donald Regan (Reagan's first Secretary of the Treasury) note that the President was far more open to influence and was a more chaotic leader than is generally acknowledged. In his biography *For the Record*, Regan referred to the early days of the administration as the "guesswork presidency."[35] Another intriguing story is the important role Suzanne Massie, the author of *Land of the Firebird: The Beauty of Old Russia*, seemingly played in tempering and broadening Reagan's view of the Soviet people, often to the chagrin of Reagan's staff who tried to cut off her access to the President.[36] James Mann records that after the October 1986 Reykjavik summit with Soviet leader Mikhail Gorbachev, "hawkish officials in the Pentagon, the CIA, and other agencies" feared Gorbachev's influence on Reagan in their one-on one-meetings.[37] These peculiarities of the Reagan presidency are all worth keeping in mind to guard against reifying what Reaganism supposedly is. Nonetheless, Reagan's speeches, his record of supporting anti-leftist movements and his general attitude towards the Soviet Union provide a strong basis from which we can ana-lyse his ideological predilections.

REAGAN'S ANTI-COMMUNISM

Given Reagan's famous denunciations of the Soviet Union and statements from adminis-tration insiders like Jeane Kirkpatrick on its self-consciously assertive ideological nature,[38] it is not surprising that a conventional wisdom emerged claiming Reagan's administration had reanimated the Cold War as an ideological battle, not just a territorial and military contest.[39] It also contested the meaning of past events, as Reagan had done during the 1980 presidential election campaign when he referred to the Vietnam War as "a noble cause" in which the United States was intervening to defend "a small country newly free from colonial rule . . . against a totalitarian neighbor bent on conquest."[40] For Colin Dueck, in his foreign policy Reagan "pursued a fundamentally daring, ideologically charged strat-egy of aggressive anti-Communist containment and indirect rollback."[41] Robert Patman similarly outlines this orthodox reading when he writes: "Unlike some of his less ideologi-cal predecessors, President Reagan had a firm belief in the power of ideas and enthusi-astically engaged with Moscow in the 'competition of ideas and systems'", adding that "Reagan's willingness to take on the Soviets in the area of ideology was psychologically important."[42] Furthermore there was a belief that Reagan's ideological approach made the Soviet Union's leadership stand up and take notice.[43] Richard Crockatt argues that: "Reagan was, in short, the most unashamedly ideological of the post-war presidents",[44] and pursued "a small number of large ideas relentlessly and with supreme confidence."[45] An example of this confidence in American 'know-how' was Reagan's belief that a highly improbable nuclear missile defence shield – formally the Strategic Defense Initiative (SDI), but more often referred to as 'Star Wars' – could be developed.[46]

One consequence of Reagan's ardent anti-communist ideology was a tendency to exaggerate the threat that left-wing governments and movements in Latin America and elsewhere posed to the USA. Florid claims regarding extensive Soviet influence and the deprivations of freedom committed by leftist governments were presented by Reagan as justifications for the US to fund right-wing governments and militias around the globe.[47] The gap that existed between the depiction of the threat to freedom and actually existing states of democratic governance enjoyed in pro-US states in Central America was only off-set by the invocation of the stark spectre of international communism, as in a March 1983 speech on Central America in which Reagan advised that:

> The problem is that an aggressive minority has thrown in its lot with the Commu-nists, looking to the Soviets and their own Cuban henchmen to help them pursue political change through violence. Nicaragua, right here, has become their base. And these extremists make no secret of their goal. They preach the doctrine of a 'revolu-tion without frontiers.' Their first target is El Salvador . . .
>
> Make no mistake. We want the same thing the people of Central America want – an end to the killing. We want to see freedom preserved where it now exists and its rebirth where it does not. The Communist agenda, on the other hand, is to exploit

human suffering in Central America to strike at the heart of the Western Hemisphere. By preventing reform and instilling their own brand of totalitarianism, they can threaten freedom and peace and weaken our national security.[48]

William LeoGrande has highlighted the pattern that this insistence on a Soviet-orchestrated threat in Central America gave rise to:

As soon as the administration declared that vital interests were at stake in Central America and upped the ante of military aid or advisers, Congress and the public began seeing visions of Vietnam. To calm these fears, Reagan was forced to deny that he had any intention of sending US troops to fight. This put him in the odd position of arguing that vital interests were at risk, but that he would limit his response to sending more aid and perhaps a few more advisers. The inconsistency was obvious. Liberal members of Congress scoffed at the administration's dire warnings of impending disaster, arguing that both the threat and the US interests at stake were being grossly inflated.[49]

This is not to say that the deployment of ideas of freedom and democracy in relation to the administration's Central America policy was without effect. As Thomas Carothers has pointed out, the emphasis on freedom and democracy, "almost by dint of repetition . . . gained some real currency in the government and led to the growing conviction on the part of some US officials and members of the policy community that the United States can and should use military force to promote democracy abroad."[50] Similarly, the repeated invocation of freedom and democracy played a part over time in neutralising opposition in the US to funding the Contras on human rights grounds. The human costs of these policies were significant and disturbing. The globalised understanding of regional conflict encouraged an environment in which death squads organised by local elites flourished.[51] However, the American people were often wilfully ignorant of the growing US role in the region, reminding us of Orwell's famous suggestion that: "The nationalist not only does not disapprove of atrocities committed by his own side, but he has a remarkable capacity for not even hearing about them."[52] Congress at times supported the Reagan administration's military support to these anti-communist and pro-American forces and at times opposed them. LeoGrande argues that Reagan's "quest for bipartisan acquiescence to his Nicaragua policy was, in large measure, an attempt to return to the pre-Vietnam era of congressional-executive relations when presidents made foreign policy and Congress rubber-stamped it."[53] When Congress withheld its rubber-stamp members of the Reagan administration approached foreign and private individuals to fill the funding gap, most infamously with regard to the Contras.

Reagan had little time for, or interest in, claims of moral equivalence regarding US and Soviet behaviour during the Cold War. He believed that the moral superiority of the American system would be demonstrated via the outcome of the Cold War contest. This rejection of moral equivalence is perhaps most explicit in the infamous March 1983 'evil empire' speech, delivered to the National Association of Evangelicals in Orlando, Florida. In this he shared his belief:

that communism is another sad, bizarre chapter in human history whose last pages even now are being written. I believe this because the source of our strength in the quest for human freedom is not material, but spiritual. And because it knows no limitation, it must terrify and ultimately triumph over those who would enslave their fellow man.[54]

He urged his audience, when discussing nuclear freeze proposals to, "beware the temptation of pride – the temptation of blithely declaring yourselves above it all and label both sides equally at fault." To see any similarities in American and Soviet behaviour was, according to Reagan, "to ignore the facts of history and the aggressive impulses of an evil empire, to simply call the arms race a giant misunderstanding and thereby remove yourself from the struggle between right and wrong and good and evil."[55] This was not just a fervently ideological outlook, it also presented the Cold War as a morality play with clear biblical overtones. John Lewis Gaddis has argued that the speech was, at least in part, an attack on the international standing that the Soviet Union had acquired through détente and an attempt to strip away any post-détente notions of equivalence of international standing.[56] Nevertheless, given Reagan's "fascination with the biblical story of Armageddon"[57] it is not surprising that many people around the world saw Reagan's talk of "evil"[58] and of America winning the Cold War, as reckless.

America's Cold War allies were far from sanguine about Reagan's characterisation of the Soviet Union and the Cold War contest. In New Zealand public concern about Reagan's language and intentions led to the Labour Party campaigning and coming to power on a pledge to not allow American nuclear ships into New Zealand harbours, despite the nation being a member of the ANZUS alliance. In Western Europe, fears regarding what Reagan might do, led to widespread concern and protest over the placement of a new generation of US intermediate-range nuclear missiles in the UK, Netherlands, Belgium, Italy and West Germany. This was the context in which the Campaign for Nuclear Disarmament was revitalised and European Nuclear Disarmament was launched, in April 1980, to campaign for a nuclear-free Europe.[59] Alarm was fuelled not merely by the revival of familiar Cold War rhetoric but by talk of 'limited nuclear war' – the 'Schlesinger Doctrine' – emanating from NATO and Washington, DC. It helps to explain why West German peace activism took on the dimensions of a mass movement focusing its oppositional energies on the NATO decisions. West Germany was one of the anticipated 'theatres' in which limited nuclear war would take place and from which Pershing and Cruise missiles would seek to prevail against Soviet SS-20s.[60] While some of its members talked openly about prevailing in nuclear war, the Reagan administration was clear about its intent to increase defence spending.[61] Protests on the streets against the perceived bellicosity of the Reagan administration increased in the early 1980s in Britain, West Germany, Belgium, the Netherlands, Denmark, Sweden and Norway – the so-called 'Arch of Angst'.[62]

REAGAN'S NATIONALISM

As Michael Freeden argues, nationalism is a thin-centred ideology. It is strong on emotions and sentiment but not particularly prescriptive; in other words, it generally does not provide clear policies beyond motherhood notions such as 'strengthening America'. This does not mean that nationalists do not try to put their ideas into action: often the results are crude and at times brutal. Nationalism is often Janus-faced: it has a hard-power seeking side that remembers defeats more than victories and a more symbolic and forward looking side that sees the future as golden. The more poetic side of American nationalism is represented by the belief in American exceptionalism. During the late 1970s and 1980s Reagan's supporters in the New Right and neoconservative movements believed in a dangerous version of American exceptionalism, which tended to assert that America during the 1970s had been too timid in its support of anti-communist movements and in projecting the essential goodness of American power around the world. These supporters also had a strong predilection to dismiss Cold War arms negotiations, compromises and summits (in short détente) as signs of weakness and appeasement. Furthermore, the New Right and the neoconservatives promoted a simplistic anti-communism that lacked nuance and tended to see all socialist and communist governments as birds of a feather. The hubris of toughness combined with a belief that America was innately virtuous in its motives and actions abroad characterised both the New Right and the neoconservatives in the 1970s.[63] These nationalist beliefs harmonised with Reagan's whose record of conviction on this score identified him as a true believer in this type of conservative nationalism as far back as the 1950s.

Reagan's 1980 election campaign (and arguably the 1984 re-election campaign too) was based on a belief in American greatness, and the rejection of even the mildest suggestion that America was in relative decline or in a 'malaise'. In 1979 President Carter gave a speech on resources and the environment that was quickly dubbed by the media as his 'malaise' speech, even though Carter never used that word in his pronouncements. A Reagan presidency promised no such concern about limits. Instead supply-side economics and taking the fight to the Soviets was sold with a smile and wisecracks. This was Reagan's way of proclaiming that America's best days lay ahead and that success was the American way. Once elected, his administration drew heavily on the Heritage Foundation's *Mandate for Leadership* released in January 1981 which explicitly aimed to move American politics to the right as quickly as possible.[64] The document added weight to the popular idea within the administration of raising the defence budget significantly.[65]

Dallek effectively shows the connections between Reagan's nationalism and that of his supporters in the New Right and beyond, when he writes:

> Those upwardly mobile, middle-class Americans who make anti-communism an extension of their fight for greater personal freedom at home also derive a sense of status from their militancy against the Soviets abroad. Indeed, both groups use the crusade against communism as a demonstration of their Americanism and their importance in preserving the nation. Superpatriotism, pride in country, pride in flag, pride in America's men and women in uniform are central elements of this 'cold war fundamentalism'.[66]

This nationalism had a clear enemy.

It has become fashionable to argue that Reagan's 1980 campaign speeches and his strident anti-communism expressed in office was simply rhetoric and that the actions of the Reagan administration subsequently were more moderate.[67] However, as Odd Arne Westad reminds us most people in Europe, and the US, thought the incoming Reagan administration would be moderated on coming to power and so:

> the first months of the Reagan administration became a bit of a shock: from day one it was the radicals – for instance, those who believed in a strict monetarist agenda in the economy or the need to roll back Soviet influence in the Third World – who created the administration's agenda, even though they were mostly dependent on

establishment figures such as Reagan's two secretaries of state, Alexander Haig (1981–82) and George P. Shultz (1982–89) to implement it.[68]

In foreign affairs this radical nationalism was projected via vastly increased defence spending and the more aggressive policies adopted towards Central America.[69] Combined with Reagan's confident talk about the boundless possibilities and goodness of the United States and his aggressive pronouncements about the Soviet Union, this discourse projected a strong sense of national superiority.

The bellicose orientation was put into policy in the first term as hawkish aides like Richard Pipes drafted policy papers that marked a departure from the approaches of Carter, Ford and Nixon.[70] An important policy directive early on was NSDD-75, approved in January 1983, which outlined a policy towards the Soviet Union comprising three elements: "external resistance to Soviet imperialism; internal pressure on the USSR to weaken the sources of Soviet imperialism; and negotiations to eliminate, on the basis of strict reciprocity, outstanding disagreements."[71] The primary focus of US policy was to be on the first of these: "To contain and over time reverse Soviet expansionism by competing effectively on a sustained basis with the Soviet Union in all international arenas – particularly in the overall military balance and in geographical regions of priority concern to the United States." All three elements, NSDD-75 advised, would require US policy to have "an ideological thrust which clearly affirms the superiority of U.S. and Western values of individual dignity and freedom, a free press, free trade unions, free enterprise, and political democracy over the repressive features of Soviet Communism." Although direct intervention was largely discouraged, NSDD-75 and companion policy directives were aggressive in their posture. As Dueck has argued: "In a sense these directives were a return to early cold war American strategy. They aimed at not only the containment but the rollback, where possible, of Soviet power."[72] Summing up this approach to the Cold War, Westad states:

> From the outset the Reagan administration was much more intent than any previous US government had been in using economic warfare against its enemies through hitting at their trade, currency, and credit. 'Make them scream,' was a much heard slogan in the corridors of power, especially during Reagan's first period, when the administration's ideological militancy was at its peak.[73]

In terms of arms negotiations, the approach of the administration in its first year was to push for the so-called 'Zero Option' proposal, the brainchild of Assistant Secretary of Defense Richard Perle, under the terms of which the Soviets would get rid of their East European-based nuclear weapons and in return the US would commit to not placing the new generation of Pershing II and Cruise missiles in Western Europe.[74] Even the ultra-Realist Al Haig thought the proposal was one-sided and unrealistic. In his memoir he writes:

> The fatal flaw in the Zero Option as a basis for negotiations was that it was not negotiable. It was absurd to expect the Soviets to dismantle an existing force of 1,100 warheads, which they had already put into the field at the cost of billions of rubles, in exchange for a promise from the United States not to deploy a missile force that we had not yet begun to build and that had aroused such violent controversy in Western Europe. Caspar Weinberger, in his enthusiasm for the Zero Option, could not concede this point.[75]

Perle had not expected the Soviets to agree, but saw that their inevitable refusal would legitimate the new US deployments by presenting the USSR as obstructing the peace initiative. Along with pushing the Zero Option the Reagan administration rejected Soviet calls for a 'no first use' agreement. This stance on nuclear negotiation, Reagan's aggressive rhetoric and the significant increase in US military spending led to the Soviets viewing the US under Reagan as being on the offensive and even that a nuclear attack could be "imminent."[76]

In terms of military spending in March 1981 the White House proposed the largest peacetime military budget in US history. The Reagan administration proposed that by 1983 defence spending would be US$222.8 billion, representing a US$33.8 billion increase. This pattern of spending planned to outlay $1.6 trillion over five years. It meant that defence spending was consuming more than 30 per cent of the federal budget.[77] As LaFeber rightly points out, this upward trajectory in defence spending was initiated in the last year or so of the Carter administration as détente collapsed and gave way to the 'Second Cold War' and policy changed dramatically towards the Soviet Union. Still, the overall impact of the increase in spending during the Reagan administration was significant. In 1985 the defence budget was US$294.7 billion, a doubling from the level of 1980, with an expensive new initiative – SDI ('Star Wars') – announced in 1983 requiring a new line of military expenditure. The Soviets were alert to the implication of this vast increase in spending which meant that they were now caught up in an arms race that could consume up to 27 per cent of their GDP while consuming only seven per cent of that of the US.[78]

For many it seemed this arms build-up was not just for show and that American policy was unconcerned about global public opinion. Once the Zero Option was rejected by Moscow, the Reagan administration went ahead with the deployment of Pershing II and Cruise nuclear missiles in Western Europe with little sign that it was willing to reconsider this policy. In the same year that the first of these missiles were deployed, the US invaded Grenada and engaged in a major military exercise in Europe, Able Archer 83, simulating a nuclear attack on the Soviet Union. Michael Mandelbaum writes: "Collectively, [these incidents] helped create the impression of a president prepared to use force in support of American interests."[79] Militarism is often the hard edge of nationalism and the Soviet leadership undoubtedly viewed early 1980s' American militarism as part of a strategy of confrontation. During the first term of the Reagan administration this stance strengthened the hand of hard-liners in the Kremlin. Over time some argue it broke the back of Soviet militarism; however, this claim remains highly speculative.

REAGAN AND AMERICAN EXCEPTIONALISM

Reagan's nationalism drew on more than patriotism and national pride, it was also fuelled by his strong belief in American exceptionalism. For Lou Cannon this amounted to "an innocent and unshakable belief in the myth of American exceptionalism."[80] Similarly, Peter Rodman claims that Reagan "was an unashamed believer in American exceptionalism" who thought that America had a moral calling to be "the last best hope of man on earth."[81]

Three core beliefs tend to undergird exceptionalist thinking: a belief in the exceptionalism of *birth* (a conviction that America's founding is unique and is a blueprint for greatness), the exceptionalism of *opportunity* (that America is blessed by a physical and economic frontier of ever expanding opportunities)[82] and the exceptionalism of *role* (a belief in America's ability and calling as a nation to achieve great things for America and the world). We can see the interaction of these clearly in Reagan's January 1989 Farewell Address, for example, when he spoke of how:

> I know I've said this before, but I believe that God put this land between the two great oceans to be found by special people from every corner of the world who had that extra love for freedom that prompted them to leave their homeland and come to this land to make it a brilliant light beam of freedom to the world. It's our gift to have visions.[83]

At times like this, 'freedom' could have the appearance of being a distinctly American value.

Exceptionalism is ultimately a dangerous concept because the notion that America is a uniquely blessed nation involves an implicit rejection of any possibility of moral equivalence with other states and, at the same time, has a deep resonance with many Americans. As a result, assertions of superiority are commonplace in political speeches in the US and are made by politicians from all sides. Hundreds of American politicians over the years have claimed that America is the "greatest nation ever." [84] In his 1984 State of the Union address Reagan declared: "we can be proud to say: We are first; we are the best; and we are so because we're free. America has always been greatest when we dared to be great."[85] The notion that America had a unique and providential founding[86] has been a perennial touchstone of American political culture. The core elements of this narrative are that America was founded by pilgrims seeking religious freedom who created a 'city on a hill' and whose offspring fought the British for their freedom and liberty. These ideals were codified by the Founding Fathers in the sacred documents of the Declaration of Independence and the Constitution, thus establishing the world's first constitutional democracy. Freedom, egalitarianism, democracy and other values can be given particular emphasis depending on who is telling this story; similarly, the story can be given a more secular or religious bent according to the narrator's beliefs. However, the common thread is that these grand beginnings set America on a path to greatness. From the notion of America having an exceptional birth, Reagan drew the conclusion that America's founding created a blueprint for America's role in the world. For example, in his 1983 State of the Union address he explained that:

> America's leadership in the world came to us because of our own strength and because of the values which guide us as a society: free elections, a free press, freedom of religious choice, free trade unions, and above all, freedom for the individual and rejection of the arbitrary power of the state. These values are the bedrock of our strength. They unite us in a stewardship of peace and freedom with our allies and friends in NATO, in Asia, in Latin America, and elsewhere.

A corollary of this was that:

> As the leader of the West and as a country that has become great and rich because of economic freedom, America must be an unrelenting advocate of free trade. As some nations are tempted to turn to protectionism, our strategy cannot be to follow them, but to lead the way toward freer trade.[87]

America's founding and the mythology surrounding it inspired the particularly liturgical exceptionalist language that Reagan was drawn to regularly repeat. Predictably, Reagan was fond of the Puritan preacher John Winthrop's famous 1630 'city on a hill' sermon. Reagan's configuration of this was to call America a "shining city."[88] In an election debate with John Anderson in 1980 Reagan claimed of America that: "We can meet our destiny, and that destiny is to build a land here that will be for all mankind a shining city on a hill."[89] As president in 1986 Reagan pronounced at a Republican Party rally that his "fondest hope, my grandest dream" for future generations was that "they would always find here in America a land of hope, a light unto the nations, a shining city on a hill."[90] As we saw earlier, he returned to this theme in his Farewell Address.

These statements often saw Reagan combine the exceptionalism of *birth* with that of *role*.[91] As Reagan told it, America had been born with a special and unique responsibility in the world: in an October 28 1980 presidential election debate with Jimmy Carter he spoke of "this mission, this responsibility for preserving peace, which I believe is a responsibility peculiar to our country, that we cannot shirk our responsibility." Reagan's favourite quote was from Thomas Paine: that "America had the chance to make the world over again"; an argument that philosophically seems rather more liberal than conservative. The conservative element to his use of Paine was Reagan's calling for spiritual and moral renewal, for a restoration of the past, rather than something entirely new. Reagan was consistently clear in his belief that the American people had been singled out by God to perform a special role in human history. In a 1982 speech on strategic arms reduction, he explained: "I've always believed that this land was set aside in an uncommon way, that a divine plan placed this great continent between the oceans to be found by a people from every corner of the Earth who had a special love of faith, freedom, and peace."[92] Reagan would repeat these words in a later speech, in June 1990, explaining how:

> You may think this a little mystical, and I've said it many times before, but I believe there was a divine plan to place this great continent here between the two oceans to be found by peoples from every corner of the Earth. I believe we were preordained to carry the torch of freedom for the world.[93]

The flip side of Reagan's belief that God had a divine plan for America was his flirtation with the notion that the Cold War could lead to Armageddon. Westad picks up on this theme when he writes that for the Reaganites,

> the Cold War was an apocalyptic struggle that had to be won. According to the president, 'we live today in a time of climactic struggle for the human spirit, a time that will tell whether the great civilized ideas of individual liberty, representative government, and the rule of law under God will perish or endure.'[94]

Aides and speechwriters largely steered Reagan away from such talk of Armageddon, instead encouraging him to focus on a more hopeful version of American exceptionalism.

Reagan's religiously imbued exceptionalism was undoubtedly important as it underpinned his conviction that America had a special role to play in the world and that this was a benign role, never a selfish one. His last State of the Union Address – full of religious imagery on the rise, fall and restoration of America – provides a further illustration of how exceptionalism was central to his nationalist ideology. In it he asked:

How can we not believe in the greatness of America? How can we not do what is right and needed to preserve this last best hope of man on Earth? After all our struggles to restore America, to revive confidence in our country, hope for our future – after all our hard-won victories earned through the patience and courage of every citizen – we cannot, must not, and will not turn back. We will finish our job. How could we do less? We're Americans.[95]

Also evident here is Reagan's great optimism in America, another recurring element in his nationalism.

THE REAGAN DOCTRINE

Reagan's anti-communism had a significant impact on American foreign policy towards the Third World where left-wing governments and movements were portrayed as part of a global push against vital US interests and US values. According to Reagan's Manichean world-view the opponents of leftist or anti-American forces were generally seen as right-eous "freedom fighters", even when their records of human rights abuses strongly suggested otherwise. These views shaped the Reagan Doctrine, which was often implemented in a clandestine manner by the CIA and the NSC who took on board Reagan's simple bromides and turned them into policies which provided military training and aid to various pro-US militias across the world.

In designating the Third World a crucial battle ground in the Cold War, the Reagan Doctrine placed Afghanistan near the top of the list of priorities for intervention. An early Reagan administration policy directive on Afghanistan stated the aim of military aid was to "make Moscow pay a price" and "make Moscow get out."[96] The application of the Reagan Doctrine in Afghanistan built on the assistance offered to anti-Soviet forces by the Carter administration. The first major increase in aid in the Reagan era, directed to traditionalist and Islamist movements in Afghanistan, occurred in late 1982. This included the supply of a range of weapons.[97] Policy was again recalibrated in 1986 when Stinger missiles were supplied to the Afghans: a decision pushed by the CIA Director William Casey and George Shultz.[98] At other points Congressmen such as Charlie Wilson, Gordon Humphrey and Paul Tsongas had pushed for greater funding of the Afghan mujahideen.[99] The actual delivery and use of US military funding in Afghanistan was extremely complicated because of how factionalised the Afghan opposition was and because of the significant role the Soviets and the Pakistanis played in Afghanistan. These factors point immediately to how fraught outside intervention was likely to be. James Scott argues that in the early 1980s there were seven major anti-government factions receiving support from the refugee community and foreign governments. According to Steve Coll, the supply of military aid worked in the following manner:

The United States, through the CIA, provided funds and some weapons, and generally supervised support for the mujahideen, but day-to-day operations were handled by the Pakistani Inter-Services Intelligence agency (ISI). Saudi Arabia agreed to match U.S. financial contributions to the rebels and distributed funds to the ISI. China sold weapons to the CIA and also donated a small number directly to Pakistan. Egypt was also involved.[100]

Islamist groups often received the lion's share of this funding, something that has haunted the Americans well beyond the end of the Cold War.

In 1988 the situation in Afghanistan began to change as the Soviet Union announced a significant troop withdrawal. However, foreign policy experts give little praise to the US in this period as the decade-long Soviet occupation came to an end. Scott argues that liberals, and then moderates, in America recognised that a change of circumstances in Afghanistan called for a new policy that looked for a political solution to what was, in essence, a civil war into which the Soviet Union had intervened. However, driven by anti-communist fervour the "hard-liners" – those who had designed the Reagan Doctrine – "failed to grasp" the new situation and instead they assumed that "the most radical factions of the mujahidin" continued to be "the primary recipients of the assistance." Scott concluded in 1996 that: "Ironically, the failure of the exile groups and local factions to make peace prompted the formation in late 1994 of a new force calling itself Taliban."[101] He suggests the Americans significantly contributed to the continuation of misery by giving most of their military aid to factions "most responsible for the persistence of the conflict" and for not taking enough of an interest in diplomatic solutions even as the Soviet presence and influence diminished. Similar conclusions are reached by Steve Coll.[102]

In 1979 the Sandinistas had overthrown the long-time pro-American Somoza dynasty in Nicaragua, bringing to power a revolutionary government that Reagan was instinctively opposed to. In order to undermine and overthrow the Sandinistas, the Reagan administration organised, trained and armed the Contras, largely recruited from the remnants of Somoza's National Guard but with little local support and a record of brutality that included targeting civilians and infrastructure (in other words using terrorist tactics).[103] Reagan's oft-repeated references to these forces as "freedom fighters" was ideological cant,[104] but consistent with his claim that "the Nicaraguan people are trapped in a totalitarian dungeon, trapped by a military dictatorship that impoverishes them while its rulers live in privileged and protected luxury and openly boast their revolution will spread to Nicaragua's neighbours as well."[105] The human rights abuses committed by the Contras led to Congress placing restrictions from 1982–1984 on US military aid via the Boland Amendment. Some within the administration, particularly at the NSC, were determined to either ignore or get around these restrictions and continue to find ways to support the Contras. The first step was to strongly encourage private individuals and other governments to provide aid to the Contras. In an extension of this search for Contras funding, members of the NSC arranged to sell military equipment to Iran – a supposed sworn enemy of the US since the Islamic Revolution of 1979 and subsequent hostage crisis – at an inflated price and syphon off the profits for the Contras, thus sustaining their insurgency without Congress ever knowing. Once exposed, the Iran-Contra scandal led to members of the Reagan administration being convicted of criminal offences. The episode constituted a major violation of the Constitution, arguably graver than Watergate, and could have led to the impeachment and dismissal of Reagan if tighter accountability standards had been applied.[106]

Why would the White House undermine America's commitment to international law and to the US constitution and the rule of law at home? Anti-communist ideological fervour is the obvious explanation.[107] These policies also took a terrible toll on the Nicaraguan people.[108] Westad writes that:

> In Nicaragua it left 30,000 dead (as historian William LeoGrande points out, relative to the population this was more than the United States lost in the Civil War, the two

world wars, and the Korean and Vietnam Wars combined). The country had over 100,000 refugees and an economy with inflation out of control and massive unemployment. In tiny El Salvador the effects were even worse; 70,000 dead, death squads roaming the countryside, villages destroyed, lives shattered.[109]

Here too, the US provided considerable military aid to right-wing forces during the Reagan period. Lastly, Scott argues that the conflict in Nicaragua failed to open up peace-seeking negotiations until "Reagan Doctrine assistance ended"; once US intervention had stopped "the Central American states managed to settle the conflict themselves and the Sandinistas and contras reached a cease-fire agreement." Scott goes as far to suggest that "In fact, the commitment of the White House to the Reagan Doctrine appears to have delayed resolution of the conflict."[110] A similar conclusion has been drawn in relation to US interventions in Angola.[111] As in Afghanistan the US decided to provide Stinger missiles to the rebels in Angola in 1986. As in Nicaragua the Americans were worried about Soviet and Cuban influence in southern Africa. The Reagan Doctrine had it that pushing back against this influence was necessary even if that meant siding with South Africa, despite Congress having placed sanctions on the apartheid regime. Although clearly contradicting Congress' anti-apartheid stance, hard-line anti-communists in the Reagan administration did not seem that concerned as they sought an open alignment with South Africa in Angola. Reagan, because of his ideological precepts, was receptive to advisers who suggested alliances with the anti-communist UNITA and the anti-communist South African government. George Shultz summarised this situation in the following manner: "Ronald Reagan . . . was . . . disposed to give the benefit of the doubt to an anti-Communist leader, even if authoritarian and dictatorial."[112] Reagan boasted in his Farewell Address at the Republican National Convention in August 1988 that in the 2,765 days of his administration "not one inch of ground" had "fallen to the Communists." However, as we have demonstrated, this came at a high human cost as ideological fervour often determined foreign policy decisions.

ARMS NEGOTIATION: DID REAGAN BECOME A REALIST?

There are broadly two approaches to explaining the end of the Cold War. In the first of these, it is held that "most of what Reagan and the first Bush accomplished would have been achieved by almost anyone who was president during the 1980s and early 1990s; the end of the Cold War resulted primarily from developments within the Soviet Union."[113] In this view, Reagan added a particular, and at times surprising, flavour to arms negotiations with Gorbachev, but the collapse of the USSR was by the late 1980s well underway and Gorbachev was wrestling with the challenge of trying to save the communist project, while accepting the need for radical reform in the USSR, including a vast reduction in military spending. The second involves the line of argument advanced by John Lewis Gaddis and other conservative historians that Reagan was a key actor (perhaps *the* key actor) in the ending of the Cold War. However, this emphasis on agency underplays the importance of structural factors outside the United States' control in ending the Cold War. Moreover, while it is premised on the importance of agency it underplays the agency of Gorbachev relative to that of Reagan.[114] American ideas mattered regarding stalling arms negotiations in the early 1980s and the type of peace that was achieved at the end of the Cold War, but material factors in the USSR clearly got ahead of American foreign policies and ideas in the mid-to-late 1980s. When it came to nuclear arms negotiations, Reagan rejected détente, the establishment approach to the Cold War that had been dominant throughout the 1970s, and instead set America on a new path in his first term. Détente, "[I]sn't that what a farmer has with his turkey – until Thanksgiving day?" Reagan asked when running for the presidency.[115] Not only did Reagan reject the assumptions underpinning détente he also rejected the deterrence theory of Mutually Assured Destruction (MAD) which "surprised the Kremlin, most American arms control experts, and many of his own advisers" as it had been the theory at the heart of the managed Great Power peace since the 1950s.[116] In Reagan's typically folksy and publicly appealing manner he said MAD was like two cowboys "standing in a saloon aiming their guns to each other's head – permanently."[117] If you couple these unorthodox strategic views with Reagan's fervent anti-communism and exceptionalist nationalism it is not surprising that the first term of the Reagan administration caused alarm about the possibility of nuclear war, in America and around the world. Reagan did not just believe the Cold War could be won, he wanted a missile defence shield (SDI) to be built to protect America from a nuclear weapons attack, thus potentially undermining the deterrence element of the US-USSR nuclear stalemate when viewed from Moscow. Reagan's strongly anti-communist rhetoric, development of SDI and placement of new tactical nuclear weapons in Western Europe had the Soviets concerned that a nuclear attack in the early years of the Reagan administration was quite possible. This general fear helps explain the Soviet response to the Able Archer 83 military exercises in Western Europe in 1983 which were interpreted as possibly being a cover for a pre-emptive nuclear attack.[118]

Within the scholarship on Reagan and arms negotiations with the Soviets there are two lines of argument, which overlap, that claim Reagan moderated his strident anti-communism, nationalism and militarism towards the Soviets from around late 1983 onwards. The first argument is that Reagan's abhorrence of nuclear weapons and genuine fear of a misunderstanding precipitating nuclear war led him to tone down his rhetoric and be more willing to meet with Soviet leaders to reduce nuclear tensions from the end of 1983 onwards. This view is most credibly advanced by Beth Fischer in *The Reagan Reversal* and by James Mann in *The Rebellion of Ronald Reagan*. The second line of argument is more ideological and has most notably been outlined by Melvyn Leffler in *For the Soul of Mankind* where he contends that Reagan became more of a Realist in his second term as his Realist advisers, particularly his Secretary of State George Shultz, had greater influence on his outlook towards the USSR and the need to engage in arms negotiations. Both theses have their merits and are based on credible research; however, they both underplay the more significant changes that were taking place in the USSR and across Eastern Europe. According to Fischer there were three significant events that led to Reagan taking a more cautious and conciliatory approach to nuclear war. In October 1983 Reagan attended his first Pentagon briefing on nuclear war; during his first two years as president he had not attended these briefings feeling it was not sensible to rehearse a nuclear apocalypse. According to Fischer the briefing had a profound impact on Reagan and heightened his fears that nuclear war was possible during his presidency.[119] The second event was the Able Archer 83 military exercise. Fischer writes that: "Though there was no nuclear exchange, Reagan viewed the incident as a nuclear 'near-miss'. Exercise Able Archer had brought the world to the brink of an inadvertent nuclear war, he believed."[120] The third factor was the impact of a film on the former Hollywood actor. On November 20 1983 more than 100 million Americans watched a television movie, *The Day After*, which focused on daily life in Lawrence, Kansas and

Kansas City, Missouri in the aftermath of a limited but devastating nuclear exchange between the US and the USSR. Reagan watched a pre-screening of the movie and was significantly affected. Other scholars and commentators have in recent work picked up on these concerns of Reagan's and his more conciliatory tone with Gorbachev at the four nuclear summits they held, to argue Reagan was at heart a nuclear abolitionist and that this came to the fore in his second term. Reagan in these accounts is often presented as more of an idealist and peacemaker than conventional wisdom has it. The problem with these accounts of a more peaceable Reagan is they suffer from a selective bias, just as the argument that Reagan became a Realist in his second term does. It ignores how the Reagan Doctrine was often expanded and demonstrated some of its worst excesses in the second term. It highlights instead Reagan's willingness with Gorbachev to eliminate vast amounts of their nuclear weaponry, and possibly, for a brief moment at the Rey-kjavík summit, all nuclear weapons. It does not highlight the continued high levels of military spending in Reagan's second term, the continued development of the provocative SDI programme, the drive to maximise US advantages as the Soviet Union collapsed and the fact that Reagan still continued to deliver a number of highly nationalist and anti-communist speeches in his second term. Reagan did tone his rhetoric down from 1984 onwards and did become more Realist as he seemed to better grasp the need to peacefully coexist with the Soviets, but this moderation was relative and certainly not a complete change in direction, as some such as Fischer suggest.

More important than Reagan moderating his position was the change of direction Gor-bachev was taking in the USSR with *glasnost* and *perestroika*. Once Gorbachev admitted that the USSR had serious problems that needed addressing, the burdensome faults of the Soviet system became open to change and reform – with the aim in Gorbachev's vision of saving socialism – and generated a momentum of their own. Socialism was not saved, rather the USSR began to unravel, allowing America to negotiate from a position of con-siderable strength drawing on Realist and nationalist understandings of power politics and national interest to emerge as the sole superpower, following the 50-year struggle with the Soviet Union. One of the consequences of the demise of the USSR, was that the highly questionable and often simplistic ideological ideas that had been promoted by the Reagan administration became overly determined as superior and even naturally trium-phant ideas, as theses like the "end of history" emerged. However, the ideologies of the Reagan administration when put in to practice were often deleterious, particularly when applied to the Third World.

NOTES

1 E. J. Dionne Jr., *Why the Right Went Wrong: Conservatism – From Goldwater to Trump and Beyond* (New York: Simon & Schuster, 2016), p.80.
2 John Dumbrell, *American Foreign Policy: Carter to Clinton* (Houndmills: Macmillan, 1997), p.13.
3 On this, see Cécile Menétrey-Monchau, *American-Vietnamese Relations in the Wake of the War: Diplomacy After the Capture of Saigon, 1975–1979* (Jefferson, NC: McFarland, 2006); Robert D. Schulzinger, *A Time for Peace: The Legacy of the Vietnam War* (New York: Oxford University Press, 2006), Ch.1.
4 Quoted in Michael S. Sherry, *In the Shadow of War: The United States Since the 1930s* (New Haven, CT: Yale University Press, 1995), p.344.

5 Jimmy Carter, *Keeping Faith: Memoirs of a President* (London: Collins, 1982), pp.142–143.
6 Ibid., p.144.
7 Ibid., p.143.
8 For a comparative analysis of their thinking, see Gerry Argyris Andrianopoulos, *Kissinger and Brzezinski: NSC and the Struggle for Control of US National Security Policy* (Houndmills: Palgrave Macmillan, 1991).
9 Zbigniew Brzezinski, *Power and Principle: Memoirs of the National Security Adviser 1977–1981* (New York: Farrar, Strauss, Giroux, 1983), p.128.
10 Fred Halliday, *The Making of the Second Cold War* (London: Verso, 1983).
11 In a variety of works Reagan is described as an ideologue. M. Stephen Weatherford and Lorraine M. McDonnell, 'Ideology and Economic Policy', in Larry Berman (ed.), *Looking Back on the Reagan Presidency* (Baltimore, MD: Johns Hopkins University Press, 1990) pp.122–155. Dueck writes that in 1980 Reagan "had campaigned on a remarkably ideological platform." He argues that Reagan was a rare ideologue in the Oval Office: "he was generally businesslike and flexible in a tactical sense, in pursuit of a fundamentally daring, ideologically charged foreign policy strategy combining elements of indirect rollback with aggressive anti-Communist containment." Dueck, *Hard Line*, pp.205, 208.
12 Jeane Kirkpatrick, *The Reagan Phenomenon, and Other Speeches on Foreign Policy* (Washington, DC: American Enterprise Institute, 1983), pp.7–8.
13 Ronald Reagan, Farewell Address, 11 January 1989, www.presidency.ucsb.edu/ws/?pid=29650. In this speech, Reagan expanded on his vision of the shining city, explaining that: "I've spoken of the shining city all my political life, but I don't know if I ever quite communicated what I saw when I said it. But in my mind it was a tall, proud city built on rocks stronger than oceans, windswept, God-blessed, and teeming with people of all kinds living in harmony and peace; a city with free ports that hummed with commerce and creativity. And if there had to be city walls, the walls had doors and the doors were open to anyone with the will and the heart to get here. That's how I saw it, and see it still."
14 Ronald Reagan, Conservative Political Action Conference Speech, 18 February 1983, www.reaganfoundation.org/media/128735/political-action.pdf.
15 Reagan called for supporting the Afghan "freedom fighters" as a candidate. In his presidential nomination acceptance speech, he asked: "Can we doubt that only a Divine Providence placed this land, this island of freedom, here as a refuge for all those people in the world who yearn to breathe free? Jews and Christians enduring persecution behind the Iron Curtain; the boat people of Southeast Asia, Cuba, and of Haiti; the victims of drought and famine in Africa, the freedom fighters of Afghanistan, and our own countrymen held in savage captivity." See: Ronald Reagan, Presidential Nomination Acceptance Speech, 17 July 1980, http://presidentialrhetoric.com/historicspeeches/reagan/nominationacceptance1980.html.
16 Ronald Reagan, Address to the Nation on Central America, 9 May 1984, https://catalog.archives.gov/id/7450175.
17 On this, see also Henry Nau, *Conservative Internationalism: Armed Diplomacy under Jefferson, Polk, Truman, and Reagan* (Princeton, NJ: Princeton University Press, 2005).
18 Ronald Reagan, Address to Eureka College Graduating Class of 1982, 9 May 1982, www.presidency.ucsb.edu/ws/?pid=42501.
19 Ronald Reagan, Address to the British Parliament, 8 June 1982, https://millercenter.org/the-presidency/presidential-speeches/june-8-1982-address-british-parliament.
20 James Graham Wilson, *The Triumph of Improvisation: Gorbachev's Adaptability, Reagan's Engagement, and the End of the Cold War* (Ithaca, New York: Cornell University Press, 2014).
21 Ronald Reagan, Address to the General Assembly of the United Nations (40th Anniversary on "Fresh Start" with Soviet Union), 24 October 1985, ww.presidency.ucsb.edu/ws/?pid=37963.
22 Sean Wilentz, *The Age of Reagan: A History 1974–2008* (New York: Harper, 2008), p.129.
23 Richard Reeves, *President Reagan: The Triumph of Imagination* (New York: Simon & Schuster, 2005), p.xvi, xii.
24 Martin Anderson, *Revolution: The Reagan Legacy* (San Diego, CA: Harcourt Brace Jovanovich, 1988).
25 Ronald Reagan, Presidential Nomination Acceptance Address, 23 August 1984, www.presidency.ucsb.edu/ws/index.php?pid=40290.
26 Nau, *Conservative Internationalism*, p.174.

27 Mann, *The Rebellion of Ronald Reagan*, p.32.
28 Halliday, *The Making of the Second Cold War*, Chs.4 and 5.
29 North produced a best-selling memoir focused on the Iran-Contra affair before going on to become a conservative talk-show host and celebrity; Oliver L. North with William Novak, *Under Fire: An American Story* (London: HarperCollins, 1991).
30 See, Frances Fitzgerald, *Way Out There in the Blue: Reagan, Star Wars, and the End of the Cold War* (New York: Touchstone, 2000).
31 As far back as 1989 doctors had "expressed their belief he was suffering from the degenerative disease." Stephen Lowman, 'President Reagan suffered from Alzheimer's while in office, according to son', *Washington Post*, 14 January 2011, http://voices.washingtonpost.com/political-bookworm/2011/01/president_reagan_suffered_from.html.
32 For example, Garry Wills, *Reagan's America: Innocents at Home* (London: Heinemann, 1985) pp.168–169.
33 Mann, *The Rebellion of Ronald Reagan*; Steve Coll, *Ghost Wars: The Secret History of the CIA, Afghanistan, and bin Laden, from the Soviet Invasion to September 10, 2001* (New York: Penguin Books, 2005), pp.149–150.
34 Edmund Morris, *Dutch: A Memoir of Ronald Reagan* (London: HarperCollins, 2000).
35 Cited in Beth A. Fischer, *The Reagan Reversal: Foreign Policy and the End of the Cold War*, (Columbia, MO: University of Missouri Press, 1997), p.72. This point is driven home by Donald Regan's answer to Reagan's speechwriter Peggy Noonan when she asked: "What will history find out about the president that it doesn't know now?" Regan replied: "That he was used. The people around the president used him like you wouldn't believe. History will tell the story. He was used mercilessly – and the historians will tell it." In her memoirs Noonan also recounts other staff making similar claims and there is no doubt there was a constant jockeying amongst principals and advisers as they tried to shield Reagan from each other's influence. See also Lou Cannon, *President Reagan: The Role of a Lifetime* (New York: Public Affairs, 2000).
36 Mann, *The Rebellion of Ronald Reagan*, p.109.
37 Ibid., p.107.
38 Kirkpatrick, *The Reagan Phenomenon*.
39 Andrew E. Pusch, 'Ronald Reagan and the Defeat of the Soviet Empire', *Presidential Studies Quarterly*, Vol.27, No.3, 1997, pp.451–466, at p.454; Westad, *The Global Cold War*, pp.360–361.
40 Ronald Reagan, Speech at the Veterans of Foreign Wars Convention, 18 August 1980, www.presidency.ucsb.edu/ws/?pid=85202.
41 Dueck, *Hard Line*, p.189.
42 Patman, 'Reagan, Gorbachev and the Emergence of "New Political Thinking"', p.599. Patman also notes that: "A second major feature of Reagan's strategy was a sustained ideological offensive against the Kremlin. From the outset, the Reagan administration attacked the USSR with the same rhetorical fervour that Moscow had always reserved for its own attacks on the West. . . . Such strong language signalled that the administration rejected in principle the perpetuation of the possible co-existence of a free world and a communist world. Reagan made it clear that, unlike most previous presidents, his opposition was not confined to aspects of Moscow's external behaviour but centred on the Soviet system itself. While Reagan tempered his 'evil empire' rhetoric in the election year of 1984, he made no apologies for this anti-Soviet message. It was linked to the imperative of negotiating from strength." Ibid., p.582.
43 Ibid., p.594; Stephen Sestanovich, *Maximalist: America in the World from Truman to Obama*, (New York: Random House Publishing, 2014), p.213.
44 Richard Crockatt, *The Fifty Years War: The United States and the Soviet Union in World Politics, 1941–1991* (London: Routledge, 1995), p.305.
45 Ibid., p.335.
46 On Reagan's personal belief in this see, for example, Richard Aldous, *Reagan & Thatcher: The Difficult Relationship* (London: Hutchinson, 2012), Chs.7–8.
47 See, for example, the case of the claims made in the 1981 White Paper, 'Communist Support for the Salvadoran Insurgency' discussed in Michael McClintock, *The American Connection, Volume One: State Terror and Popular Resistance in El Salvador* (London: Zed Books, 1985), pp.288–291.

48 Ronald Reagan, Remarks on Central America and El Salvador at the Annual Meeting of the National Association of Manufacturers, 10 March 1983, www.presidency.ucsb.edu/ws/?pid=41034.
49 William M. LeoGrande, *Our Own Backyard: The United States in Central America, 1977–1992* (Chapel Hill, NC: University of North Carolina Press, 1998), p.202.
50 Thomas Carothers, *In the Name of Democracy: US Policy Toward Latin America in the Reagan Years* (Berkeley, CA: University of California Press, 1991), p.78.
51 McClintock, *The American Connection, Volume One*; *The American Connection, Volume Two: State Terror and Popular Resistance in Guatemala* (London: Zed Books, 1985).
52 George Orwell, 'Notes on Nationalism' (1945), included in George Orwell, *Decline of the English Murder and Other Essays* (Harmondsworth: Penguin, 1980), pp.155–179, at p.166.
53 LeoGrande, *Our Own Backyard*, p.475.
54 Ronald Reagan, Address to the National Association of Evangelicals, 8 March 1983, https://nationalcenter.org/ReaganEvilEmpire1983.html.
55 In the same speech he asked his audience to: "pray for the salvation of all of those who live in that totalitarian darkness – pray they will discover the joy of knowing God. But until they do, let us be aware that while they preach the supremacy of the state, declare its omnipotence over individual man, and predict its eventual domination of all peoples on the Earth, they are the focus of evil in the modern world." Ibid.
56 John Lewis Gaddis, *The Cold War* (London: Allen Lane, 2005), p.225.
57 Fischer, *The Reagan Reversal*, pp.106–108.
58 Reagan also used the term "evil" in the 1984 presidential debate: "I believe that many of the things they have done are evil in any concept of morality that we have." Ronald Reagan, 'Presidential Debate with Walter Mondale (Defense and Foreign Policy)', 21 October 1984, https://millercenter.org/the-presidency/presidential-speeches/october-21-1984-debate-walter-mondale-defense-and-foreign.
59 Mark Phythian, 'CND's Cold War', *Contemporary British History*, Vol. 15, No. 3, 2001, pp.133–156.
60 On the thinking underpinning the Reagan administration's approach to nuclear weapons, see Robert Scheer, *With Enough Shovels: Reagan, Bush and Nuclear War* (New York: Random House, 1982); and J. Peter Scoblic, *U.S. vs. Them: Conservatism in the Age of Nuclear Terror* (New York: Penguin, 2009), esp. pp.125–131.
61 Geir Lundestad, *The United States and Western Europe Since 1945: From "Empire" By Invitation to Transatlantic Drift* (Oxford: Oxford University Press, 2003), pp.211–212.
62 Ibid., p.212.
63 The New Right helped bring Reagan and Reaganism to power through grassroots campaigning, fundraising and the deliberate strategy of targeting liberal congresspersons which was remarkably successful in moving the Senate to the right in the late 1970s and early 1980s. See Dueck, *Hard Line*, pp.196, 201–202.
64 *The New York Times* in 2002 called it "the manifesto of the Reagan revolution." Mark Dowie, 'Learning from the Right Wing', *New York Times*, 6 July, 2002.
65 Ronald Reagan, 'Address to the Nation on Defense and National Security', March 23 1983, www.presidency.ucsb.edu/ws/?pid=41093.
66 Robert Dallek, *Ronald Reagan: The Politics of Symbolism* (Cambridge, MA: Harvard University Press, 1999), p.133.
67 Lou Cannon and Time contributors, *The Reagan Paradox: The Conservative Icon and Today's GOP* (New York: Time Books, 2014); Peter Beinart, *The Icarus Syndrome: A History of American Hubris* (New York: HarperCollins, 2010).
68 Westad adds: "The radicals' strength was in their sense of mission and in their firm belief that they were fulfilling the mandate the president had been given in the election. Reagan's own occasional involvement with policy making also seemed to confirm that he supported the radical options over the more moderate ones that came from the bureaucracy at the Pentagon and the State Department." Westad, *The Global Cold War*, pp.337–338.
69 Ibid., pp.344–345.
70 Mann, *The Rebellion of Ronald Reagan*, p.31.
71 NSDD-75, available at: https://fas.org/irp/offdocs/nsdd/nsdd-75.pdf.
72 Dueck, *Hard Line*, p.214.
73 Westad, *The Global Cold War*, p.359.

74 See, Ronald E. Powaski, *Return to Armageddon: The United States and the Nuclear Arms Race, 1981–1999* (New York: Oxford University Press, 2000), Ch.1.

75 Alexander M. Haig, Jr., *Caveat: Realism, Reagan, and Foreign Policy* (New York: Macmillan, 1983), p.229.

76 Fischer, *The Reagan Reversal*, pp.124–125.

77 Ibid., p.126.

78 Alvin S. Felzenberg, *The Leaders We Deserved (and a Few We Didn't): Rethinking the Presidential Rating Game* (New York: Basic Books, 2008), p.106.

79 Michael Mandelbaum, 'The Luck of the President', *Foreign Affairs* Vol.64, No.3, 1985, pp.393–412, at p.399.

80 Cannon, *President Reagan*, p.793.

81 Peter W. Rodman, *More Precious Than Peace* (New York: Scribner, 1994), p.234. See also, Trevor McCrisken, *American Exceptionalism and the Legacy of Vietnam: US Foreign Policy since 1974* (New York: Palgrave Macmillan, 2003), pp.90–91; Ronald Reagan, 'Remarks at the Annual Washington Conference of the American Legion, February 22 1983', *Public Papers*, 1983, pp.264–271.

82 Ronald Reagan, First Inaugural Address, 20 January 1981, www.presidency.ucsb.edu/ws/?pid=43130.

83 Ronald Reagan, Farewell Address, 11 January 1989, www.presidency.ucsb.edu/ws/?pid=29650.

84 Barack Obama, Remarks at 2012 Democratic National Convention, 6 September 2012; Mitt Romney, Remarks at 2012 Republican National Convention, 30 August 2012; Marco Rubio, Keynote Speech at 2010 CPAC Conference, 18 February 2010; Sarah Palin, Speech at "Showdown in Searchlight" Tea Party Express Rally, 27 March 2010; Newt Gingrich, Speech at American Solutions Event, 21 October 2010; Samantha Power, United Nations Confirmation Hearing, 17 July 2013.

85 Ronald Reagan, State of the Union Address, 25 January 1984, www.presidency.ucsb.edu/ws/?pid=40205.

86 Ronald Reagan, Speech at the VFW Convention, 18 August 1980, www.presidency.ucsb.edu/ws/?pid=85202.

87 Ronald Reagan, Address Before a Joint Session of the Congress on the State of the Union, January 25 1983, www.presidency.ucsb.edu/ws/index.php?pid=41698.

88 Fitzgerald, *Way Out There in the Blue*, p.24.

89 Ronald Reagan, Ronald Reagan and John Anderson Debate, 21 September 1980, www.debates.org/index.php?page=september-21-1980-debate-transcript.

90 Ronald Reagan, Remarks at a Republican Rally, Costa Mesa, California, November 3 1986, *Public Papers of the Presidents of the United States: Ronald Reagan*, 1986. Similarly, on this theme of America being a beacon, in an August 1984 speech he told his audience that: "Greatness lies ahead of us. In this springtime of hope, some lights seem eternal; America's is." Ronald Reagan, Presidential Nomination Acceptance Address, 23 August 1984.

91 For example, see Ronald Reagan, Presidential Debate with Jimmy Carter, 28 October 1980, https://millercenter.org/the-presidency/presidential-speeches/october-28-1980-debate-ronald-reagan.

92 Ronald Reagan, Address to the Nation on Strategic Arms Reduction and Nuclear Deterrence, November 22 1982, *Public Papers*, 1982, p.1510. As Robert Dallek has observed: "For Reagan and some lower-middle-class Christian fundamentalists, anticommunism is also a crusade to restore traditional assumptions about God, family, and country to a central place in American life." Dallek, *Ronald Reagan*, p.133.

93 Ronald Reagan, Heritage Foundation Annual Board Meeting, Carmel, California, 22 June 1990.

94 Ronald Reagan, The Agenda is Victory, 26 February 1982, http://reagan2020.us/speeches/The_Agenda_is_Victory.asp; Westad, *The Global Cold War*, p.358.

95 Ronald Reagan, State of the Union Address, 25 January 1988, www.presidency.ucsb.edu/ws/?pid=36035.

96 Scott, *Deciding to Intervene*, p.59.

97 Ibid., pp.43, 51.

98 On the impact of the introduction of Stinger missiles, see Alan J. Kuperman, 'The Stinger Missile and US Intervention in Afghanistan', *Political Science Quarterly*, Vol.114, No.2, 1999, pp.219–263.

99   Scott, *Deciding to* Intervene, pp.47, 51.
100 Steve Coll, 'Anatomy of a Victory: CIA's Covert Afghan War', *Washington Post*, 19 July 1992; Scott, *Deciding to Intervene*, pp.48–49.
101 Ibid., pp.80–81.
102 Coll, *Ghost Wars*, pp.62–63.
103 Scott, *Deciding to Intervene*, p.188.
104 For example; "Our policy has consistently supported the efforts of those who seek democracy throughout Central America and who recognize that the freedom fighters are essential to that process." Ronald Reagan, 'Address to the Nation on Aid to the Nicaraguan Democratic Resistance', 2 February 1988, www.presidency.ucsb.edu/ws/index.php?pid=34932. See also, Ronald Reagan, Address to the Nation on Central America, 9 May 1984, https://catalog.archives.gov/id/7450175.
105 Westad, *The Global Cold War*, p.344.
106 See, Lawrence E. Walsh, *Firewall: The Iran-Contra Conspiracy and Cover-Up* (New York: Norton, 1997), the account by the Independent Counsel in the Iran-Contra investigation. From 1987 onwards Reagan was able to get away with claiming he could not remember details relating to the Iran-Contra initiative. See, *New York Times,* 'The President Can't Remember', 25 February 1987, www.nytimes.com/1987/02/25/opinion/the-president-cant-remember.html. At John Poindexter's trial in 1990 Reagan took this to extremes, claiming "I don't remember" or a variation of it at least 124 times. Ethan Bronner, 'Iran-Contra Deposition – Reagan Testimony Bares Memory Loss, But Not Much Else', *Boston Globe*, February 23 1990, http://community.seattletimes.nwsource.com/archive/?date=19900223&slug=1057639http://community.seattletimes.nwsource.com/archive/?date=19900223&slug=1057639; Also see, Malcolm Byrne, 'How the Reagan White House Bungled its Response to the Iran-Contra Revelations', *Daily Beast*, November 3 2014, www.thedailybeast.com/how-the-reagan-white-house-bungled-its-response-to-iran-contra-revelations.
107 Colin Dueck endorses this conclusion when he writes: "The Iran-Contra arms scandal provided evidence, among other things, of the fierce determination of many inside the Reagan administration to support anti-Communist insurgents overseas, even to the point of provoking a domestic political and legal scandal." Dueck, *Hard Line*, p.224.
108 Scott, *Deciding to Intervene*, p.192.
109 Westad, *The Global Cold War*, p.347.
110 Scott, *Deciding to Intervene*, pp.190–191.
111 Ibid., pp.148–149.
112 Ibid., p.126.
113 H. W. Brands, Review of Joseph S. Nye, Jr. *Presidential Leadership and the Creation of the American Era*, *Political Science Quarterly*, Vol.129, No.1, 2014, pp.134–136.
114 For something of a corrective, see William Taubman, *Gorbachev: His Life and Times* (New York: Norton, 2017).
115 Gaddis, *The Cold War*, p.217; Dueck, *Hard Line*, pp.198–199.
116 Reagan was opposed to the notion that a tactical nuclear war could be won. Leffler writes: "He was appalled that there were still men in the Pentagon who claimed a nuclear war was '"winnable." I thought they were crazy'." Leffler, *For the Soul of Mankind*, p.359.
117 Fischer, *The Reagan Reversal*, p.104.
118 See Nate Jones (ed.), *Able Archer 83: The Secret History of the NATO Exercise that Almost Triggered Nuclear War* (New York: The Free Press, 2016): Scoblic, *U.S vs. Them*, pp.131–135.
119 Fischer, *The Reagan Reversal*, p.110.
120 Ibid, pp.110, 129.

7 George W. Bush administration: terrorism, Iraq and freedom

How would US foreign policy respond to the end of the Cold War and how would ideology contribute to framing understandings of the role America should play in a changed world? The first president to confront these questions was Ronald Reagan's former Vice-President, George H. W. Bush. His administration responded to the end of the Cold War by strengthening and expanding America's alliance network and by further promoting global economic liberalisation. The major military intervention of his presidency, the 1991 Gulf War, on the surface has parallels with the invasion of Iraq led by his son's administration in 2003. However, the two wars were guided by different beliefs and goals. The 1991 Gulf War was justified as necessary to protect the sovereignty of Kuwait, which Saddam Hussein's Iraqi army had invaded and occupied in 1990. Iraq's disregard for its neighbour's sovereignty was not only strongly admonished by the US; on the day of the invasion, the UN Security Council passed Resolution 660 condemning Iraq. Soon after, Security Council Resolution 661 imposed economic sanctions on Iraq and Resolution 662 authorised a naval blockade to uphold those sanctions. These resolutions gave a strong liberal internationalist backing to the Bush Snr. administration's demand that Saddam's forces leave Kuwait. America was also undoubtedly concerned that global oil supplies could be heavily compromised by Saddam's control of oil-rich Kuwait; a fear that was shared by a wide range of nations. When Saddam Hussein did not withdraw from Kuwait, America led a broad coalition of nations into war. Although there is an argument to be put that diplomacy should have been tried for longer in 1991 and that the American-led military were too brutal in routing the Iraq army, particularly as they retreated, the American approach adopted in the first Iraq war stands in marked contrast to that adopted in the second Iraq war. In 1991, once Iraqi forces were dispatched from Kuwait, the idea of 'going into Baghdad' was quickly quashed by leading figures within the first Bush administration. Bush Snr's Secretary of Defense Dick Cheney claimed:

> I was not an enthusiast about getting U.S. forces and going into Iraq . . . We were there in the southern part of Iraq to the extent we needed to be here to defeat his forces and to get him out of Kuwait, but the idea of going into Baghdad, for example, or trying to topple the regime wasn't anything I was enthusiastic about. I felt there was a real danger here that you would get bogged down in a long drawn-out conflict, that this was a dangerous, difficult part of the world . . . I don't think it would have been worth it.[1]

It is startling to compare Cheney's attitude in 1991 with that in 2003 when he claimed that conquering Iraq would now be relatively easy and welcomed by the Iraqi people.[2] In *Plan of Attack*, a book that draws on detailed discussions with leading members of the Bush Jnr. administration, Bob Woodward writes that:

> After Sept. 11, 2001, Cheney said, the president understood what had to be done. He had to do Afghanistan first, sequence the attacks, but after Afghanistan – 'soon thereafter' – the president knew he had to do Iraq. Cheney said he was confident after Sept. 11 that it would come out okay.[3]

This chapter will explore the change of circumstances, thinking and beliefs that led America to enter into a highly destructive war in Iraq in 2003 that has had devastating consequences for the region and increased the threat of terrorism. Specifically, it will explore the ideas that underpinned the US approach to the 'War on Terror' and the decision to invade Iraq.

Before discussing the second Bush administration, it is worth noting the ABC (anything but Clinton) critique that Bush mounted against President Clinton's foreign policies during his 2000 campaign and before the September 11 2001 (9/11) attacks. This opposition was largely rhetorical, and with the benefit of hindsight, we can see that the foreign policy of the Clinton administration had much in common with that of Bush Snr. Meanwhile, George W. Bush's foreign policy was often a significant departure from the liberal-realist consensus that largely guided America's international relations after 1945.[4] In this chapter we will argue that Bush took up a neoconservative approach to the 'War on Terror' that was ideologically hubristic and often untethered from the facts on the ground. Not only did the Bush administration deem it necessary to invade Afghanistan and Iraq; it claimed that to reduce the threat of terrorism towards the US, the administration needed to bring liberal democracy and market capitalism to these countries.[5] This stridently ideological and imperial project was profoundly unsuccessful and extremely costly. In contrast, the foreign policy aims of the Clinton administration seem in retrospect rather modest. The Clinton administration inherited from the first Bush administration a policy of containing Saddam Hussein. It carried out this policy by pushing for the UN Special Commission (UNSCOM) and International Atomic Energy Agency (IAEA) arms inspectors to have unrestricted access to Iraq and by conducting various heavy aerial bombing campaigns, such as Operation Desert Fox in December 1998, now thought to have destroyed any remaining chemical weapons stockpile.

Bill Clinton's foreign policy followed a similar path to that of Bush Snr. with an emphasis on economic globalisation and maintaining America's vast military superiority with the overall goal of cementing Americans as the undisputed and sole superpower in the post-Cold War era. One obvious area of difference lay in Clinton's greater willingness to consider what has been called "liberal humanitarian intervention" in Somalia and the former Yugoslavia. Intervention, however, proved to be politically and militarily hazardous in both cases. The shooting down of two US Black Hawk helicopters in Mogadishu in 1993 and a violent street battle involving US forces quickly reduced congressional and popular support for committing troops on the ground in the civil wars of the 1990s.[6] This led to America staying on the sidelines during the genocide in Rwanda in 1994 where the Hutu militia killed around one million Tutsis and moderate Hutus.[7] Bill Clinton has described American inaction during this genocide as one of the biggest regrets of his presidency.[8] When the administration did intervene, it was generally criticised by leading

Republicans and this critique of Clinton's efforts extended to George W. Bush arguing against the US trying to nation-build during his run for the presidency in 2000. Bush Jnr.'s position was heavily influenced by his chief foreign policy adviser Condoleezza Rice who, during the presidential campaign, caricatured Clinton administration efforts in Bosnia as social work. As she told the *New York Times*, "we don't need to have the 82nd Airborne [Division] escorting kids to kindergarten."[9] Given the Bush Jnr. administration's subsequent attempts at nation-building in Afghanistan and Iraq, these criticisms seem ironic to say the least.

Overall, the Bush Snr. and Clinton legacy was to hand George W. Bush an America that was the undisputed global superpower. The flip side of America's unrivalled primacy in the last decade of the twentieth century was arguably significant foreign policy complacency; reflecting this, George W. Bush entered office with very limited foreign policy experience or knowledge and without any grand plans for US foreign policy. He had staked a claim on the very absence of nation-building ambitions abroad in the presidential debates against Al Gore in 2000, in which he announced that America should play a more modest role in the world. Bush declared in the second presidential debate with Gore that:

> I think one way for us to end up being viewed as the ugly American is for us to go around the world saying, 'we do it this way, so should you'. I think the United States must be humble and must be proud and confident of our values, but humble in how we treat nations that are figuring out how to chart their own course.[10]

These words seem chimerical in light of later events and claims such as Bush's 2003 statement that the invasion of Iraq was a good thing for the people of Iraq: "As people throughout Iraq celebrate the arrival of freedom, America celebrates with them. We know that freedom is the gift of God to all mankind, and we rejoice when others can share it."

THE BUSH DOCTRINE

"We meet at a time of great consequence for the security of our nation, a time when the defense of freedom requires the advance of freedom." George W. Bush[11]

The simplest explanation for why the foreign policy actions of the Bush administration turned out to be the opposite of what was promised during the 2000 campaign is the impact of events. It is often claimed that the 9/11 terrorist attacks changed everything. This is not a baseless claim, as the foreign policy neophyte George W. Bush was in many ways certainly transformed as a president by the 9/11 attacks.[12] After 9/11 he began to use messianic language frequently and talked not just of revenge but of re-ordering nations that harboured or sympathised with terrorists. As this powerful language soon revealed, ideas were crucial to the emerging Bush Doctrine. Bush's earliest response to the 9/11 attacks framed them as an assault on "freedom." Soon after he was calling for a "War on Terror", a particularly ideological framing of what some argued would have been better dealt with as a matter of policing and criminal justice. George W. Bush's belief in the power of ideas – particularly the idea of freedom – to reshape the world is most apparent in his attitude and speeches soon after the attacks. Karen Hughes, a close adviser to the President who had worked with him during his time as Texas Governor, was told by Bush as they were drafting a speech to give to a joint session of Congress immediately after the

9/11 attacks that: "This is a defining moment. We have an opportunity to restructure the world toward freedom, and we have to get it right."[13] There was often a sense of religious righteousness and spiritual revivalism in the way Bush presented his post-9/11 freedom agenda.

However, the '9/11 changed everything' argument misses some important points. First, Bush had talked about the transformative power of the idea of freedom during his 2000 campaign and in his first inaugural address, where he stated that

> Through much of the last century, America's faith in freedom and democracy was a rock in a raging sea. Now it is a seed upon the wind, taking root in many nations. Our democratic faith is more than the creed of our country. It is the inborn hope of our humanity, an ideal we carry but do not own, a trust we bear and pass along.[14]

This idea that democracy and freedom were universal human values that America had a responsibility to "pass along" became more aggressively and imperially stated after the 9/11 attacks. Bush quickly connected the idea of protecting freedom in America with a plan to bring 'freedom' to other nations. This became a key part of his War on Terror, based on the principle that free peoples and nations would cooperate with America and not support terrorists. Speaking on 9/11 Bush claimed that: "America was targeted for attack because we're the brightest beacon for freedom and opportunity in the world." By 20 September, in his address to a joint session of Congress, the ideas justifying a War on Terror were crystallising, with freedom doing much of the ideological work. The attack was committed by "enemies of freedom" with the consequence that: "Freedom and fear are at war. The advance of human freedom – the great achievement of our time, and the great hope of every time – now depends on us. Our nation – this generation – will lift a dark threat of violence from our people and our future."[15] As melodramatic and messianic as this might sound, scholars such as Robert Jervis and Adam Quinn are right to point out that this rhetoric had much in common with the rhetoric of earlier presidents.[16] What differentiated Bush was that he put these ideas more directly and dramatically into action than any other post-Second World War president.

Our second example of continuity is the Bush administration's unilateralist tendencies, which were quite apparent before the 9/11 attacks. As Jervis reminds us, prior to 9/11,

> the Bush administration walked away from the Kyoto Treaty, the International Criminal Court, and the protocol implementing the ban on biological weapons rather than trying to work within these frameworks and modify them . . . On a smaller scale, it forced out the heads of the Organization for the Prohibition of Chemical Weapons and the Intergovernmental Panel on Climate Change.[17]

A pattern of unilateralism was already established. Others have rightly pointed out that unilateral tendencies have always been apparent in the modern Republican Party.[18] Furthermore, neoconservatives from the late 1970s onwards had been advocating a more activist military posture for the United States that was more unilateralist.[19] It will be argued further into this chapter that these neoconservatives had important positions in the Bush administration from its outset and were well-placed to put their case for removing Saddam Hussein, with or without the support of America's traditional allies.

This brings us to our third objection to the '9/11 changed everything' argument. The idea of a military attack on Iraq to bring about regime change had been pushed by a number of members of the Bush administration, specifically Donald Rumsfeld, Paul Wolfowitz, Douglas Feith and John Bolton, during the 1990s. Once in office, Wolfowitz (Bush's Deputy Defense Secretary from 2001–2005) was particularly vocal on the need to remove Saddam. The President also entertained the idea of removing Saddam from the beginning of his time in office. Paul O'Neill, Bush Jnr.'s first Secretary of the Treasury, claims that regime change in Iraq was raised by Condoleezza Rice and Bush at the first NSC meeting, held just ten days after Bush's inauguration. O'Neill summarised the situation at the end of this first meeting:

> Bush had assignments for everyone. [Colin] Powell and his team would look to draw up a new sanctions regime. [Donald] Rumsfeld and [General Hugh] Shelton, he said 'should examine our military options.' That included rebuilding the military coalition from the 1991 Gulf War, examining 'how it might look' to use US ground forces in the north and south of Iraq and how the armed forces could support groups inside the country who could help challenge Saddam Hussein. [DCI George] Tenet would report on improving our current intelligence. O'Neill would investigate how to financially squeeze the regime. Meeting adjourned. Ten days in, and it was about Iraq.[20]

9/11 gave the idea of removing Saddam more traction, but the idea was on the table from the earliest days of the George W. Bush administration.

Before the war in Iraq was launched in 2003 the Bush administration outlined its foreign policy values, worldview and goals in a series of speeches and documents – most notably in Bush's West Point Academy commencement address of 1 June 2002 and the highly prescriptive National Security Strategy of 2002 (NSS 2002). Bush reiterated these principles in numerous speeches. The starkness and lack of subtlety in these statements and documents is most useful for scholarly purposes. It allows us to outline the ideological contours of Bush's foreign policy outlook, regularly referred to as the Bush Doctrine. Edward Rhodes, a critic of Bush's foreign policy, writes of the NSS 2002: "The prose is magnificent in its stark clarity and its avoidance of moral or political ambiguity."[21] One of many examples of this in the NSS 2002 is the statement that: "In pursuit of our goals, our first imperative is to clarify what we stand for: the United States must defend liberty and justice because these principles are right and true for all people everywhere. No nation owns these aspirations, and no nation is exempt from them."[22]

Realists tend to be sceptical of the role of ideas in guiding foreign policies. However, with Bush even Realists had to pay attention to the impact of ideology on foreign policy. One of the doyens of the Realist school, Robert Jervis, describes the impact of ideas in the following manner: "the Bush Doctrine may well have started out being a rationalization for certain actions, but over time started to guide behavior."[23] In summarising the Bush Doctrine, Jervis argued in a 2003 article that it had four core elements:

> a strong belief in the importance of a state's domestic regime in determining its foreign policy and the related judgement that this is an opportune time to transform international politics; the perception of great threats that can be defeated only by new and vigorous policies, most notably preventative war; a willingness to act unilaterally when necessary; and, as both a cause and a summary of these beliefs, an overriding

sense that peace and stability require the United States to assert its primacy in world politics.[24]

In a subsequent book Jervis organised these beliefs under four categories: the promotion of democracy and liberalism; a sense of great threat that justifies preventive war; a willingness to act unilaterally; and a commitment to maintaining American hegemony.[25]

Before discussing the core ideological elements of the Bush Doctrine in detail three issues will be briefly considered: how liberal was the Bush Doctrine? What should we make of Bush's claims that the doctrine was promoting God-given, universal human desires? And how important was the promotion of continued US primacy to the Bush Doctrine? The short answer to the third question is that primacy was very important. Moreover, primacy enabled the Bush administration to pursue an extremely ambitious global agenda. This sense of having the power to change the world is outlined in the opening lines of the NSS 2002, which proclaims:

> The United States possesses unprecedented – and unequalled – strength and influence in the world. Sustained by faith in the principles of liberty, and the value of a free society, this position comes with unparalleled responsibilities, obligations, and opportunity. The great strength of this nation must be used to promote a balance of power that favors freedom.[26]

The meaning of this strange phraseology "a balance of power that favors freedom" will be discussed further into this chapter. Before doing that, it is worth exploring the continuities of the Bush doctrine with earlier liberal doctrines.

Oz Hassan states the case for seeing the Bush Doctrine as hijacking liberalism in the following manner:

> by defining the events of 9/11 as an attack on 'freedom' the Bush Administration was able to make this transition by almost seamlessly appropriating a liberal internationalist discourse. As a result the initial assertion that primacy was the preferred grand strategy by the Administration turned into a large liberal grand strategy that drew upon hegemonic stability theory, democratic peace theory, neoliberal economics and modernization thesis to justify and operationalize promoting democracy in the Middle East.[27]

The problem with this argument is that these are not solely liberal ideas, in fact this militaristic take on these ideas had been adopted by a group of self-styled neoconservatives in the 1990s who were more willing than most liberals to argue for 'humanitarian' military intervention in the Balkans and elsewhere and, after the 9/11 attacks, pre-emptive intervention on anti-terrorist grounds. The ideas Hassan calls liberal, are in this case better described as neoconservative. This is not to deny that there was overlap between liberal interventionists and neoconservatives on Iraq, as there had been during the 1990s on intervention in the former Yugoslavia. However, before the 9/11 attacks, arguing for troops on the ground to bring about regime change in Iraq was confined largely to neoconservative advocacy groups such as the Project for the New American Century (PNAC).[28] In all of these cases liberals tended to be less convinced of the efficacy of unilateral military intervention compared to the neoconservatives.

For Realists like Jervis or Quinn the ideas in the Bush Doctrine have much in common with the liberal ideologies of Woodrow Wilson and his subsequent admirers. Quinn argues that after 9/11 "what emerged was something that bore significant resemblance to the Roosevelt-Wilson-Truman internationalist ideology, but adapted for the threats of a new era."[29] This activist view of liberalism has also been praised by the neoconservative Robert Kagan who has heavily criticised the Realist tradition for being "minimalist." In Kagan's framing of liberalism it

> has upheld an activist foreign policy that reflects American ideals as well as interests, and it runs from Hamilton through John Quincy Adams, Lincoln (the Civil War was a pivotal case, as the Union embraced a liberal 'foreign policy' toward the South), Theodore Roosevelt, Wilson, FDR, Truman, Kennedy, and ultimately to Reagan.[30]

In stark contrast to Kagan, liberal scholars like John Ikenberry or Daalder and Lindsey see Bush's foreign policies as a sharp break with the liberal approach. For Ikenberry, Bush's general disregard for international law, international institutions and multilateralism makes him an imperialist and illiberal president in the foreign policy arena. This illiberal posture is identified according to Ikenberry in the Bush administration's

> neo-imperial vision in which the United States arrogates to itself the global role of setting standards, determining threats, using force, and meting out justice. It is a vision in which sovereignty becomes more absolute for America even as it becomes more conditional for countries that challenge Washington's standards of internal and external behavior.[31]

Although liberalism encompasses a broader range of ideas and has more meanings than often suggested, in the end Ikenberry is right – the Bush Doctrine was more illiberal than liberal. The principal ideology that drove the Doctrine was neoconservatism.

Bush's certainty about the transformative power of ideas drew on his personal religiosity.[32] In his second inaugural address Bush claimed that "the ultimate goal" of US policy was "ending tyranny in our world",[33] elsewhere he asserted the goal of his administration was to "rid the world of evil."[34] Such pronouncements drew on biblical language to make dramatic statements about America's mission in the world being ultimately to bring about paradigmatic change. Bush seems to have believed wholeheartedly that this change would be life-altering for people everywhere. This replicated his own experience of being born again as a Christian, a transformation that Bush underwent in 1985 when he sought guidance from the evangelical preacher Billy Graham, whom he credits for helping him in giving up drinking alcohol altogether in 1986 and becoming a deeply religious person.[35] This personal journey gave Bush a certain inner confidence; before running for the presidency he confided to the Texan evangelical preacher James Robinson: "I feel like God wants me to run for President. I can't explain it, but I sense my country is going to need me. Something is going to happen . . . I know it won't be easy on me or my family, but God wants me to do it."[36] Bush's evangelical outlook was not just personal, it also extended to his view of the US role in the world, something we see in a number of his speeches where he pronounces that there are certain God-given political rights that all humans want. For example, Bush stated in 2003 that: "Americans are a free people, who know that freedom is the right of every person and the future of every nation. The liberty we prize is not America's gift to the world, it is God's gift to humanity."[37] Similarly, at a rally in 2004 he claimed that:

> I believe millions in the Middle East plead in silence for their liberty. I believe that, given a chance, they will embrace the most honorable form of government ever devised by man. I believe all these things, not because freedom is America's gift to the world, but because freedom is the Almighty God's gift to every man and woman in this world.

Sounding like an evangelical preacher in his second inaugural address Bush proclaimed that: "We have confidence because freedom is the permanent hope of mankind, the hunger in dark places, the longing of the soul."[38]

What are we to make of Bush's religious ideology and how it infused the Bush Doctrine and the occupation of Afghanistan and Iraq? The political rights that Bush calls God's gifts to the world are the same rights that influential neoconservatives were promoting. The overlap is powerful in its re-enforcing qualities, which seem to have insulated the Bush administration from facing up to the evidence of just how unsuccessful its policies in Afghanistan and Iraq had been. Bush's own religious certitude, coupled with a belief system that was promoted by a particularly brash and self-righteous group of intellectuals and policy experts, was a deadly combination that propelled America into war in Iraq in 2003 with unrealistic expectations that Americans would be treated as liberators. When they were not, Bush kept repeating claims that America was bringing 'freedom' and 'democracy' to the Iraqis as if proclaiming those words over and over would make them happen. This heady mix of religious faith and overconfident ideology created America's greatest foreign policy disaster since the Vietnam War.

It was a fundamental belief of the Bush administration that US primacy needed to be maintained and in fact strengthened so that the US would be unchallengeable into the foreseeable future. In his 2002 West Point speech, Bush bluntly asserted this: "America has, and intends to keep, military strengths beyond challenge – thereby making the destabilizing arms races of other eras pointless, and limiting rivalries to trade and other pursuits of peace."[39] A similar view was outlined by Condoleezza Rice in an October 2002 speech: "the United States will build and maintain 21st century military forces that are beyond challenge. We will seek to dissuade any potential adversary from pursuing a military build-up in the hope of surpassing, or equaling, the power of the United States and our allies."[40] This assertion of primacy is a reminder of the imperialist ideology at the heart of the administration's foreign policy. Imperial primacy was the priority, with ideas such as freedom and democracy promoted on America's terms. Democracy was promoted as long as political parties that the US supported were elected; the obvious example of this was the administration's negative response to the electoral success of Hamas in 2006 in Palestine.[41] Bush's commitment to primacy was not only foundational, it was continuous from the beginning to the end of his administration. It is another example of something that 9/11 did not change. In his first inaugural address he asserted that: "We will build our defenses beyond challenge, lest weakness invite challenge."[42] Given the costs of the War on Terror there is a strong case to be made that Bush did open the US up to challenge and squandered a good deal of the unrivaled position of power he inherited.

Notwithstanding the continuities there were three significant changes that 9/11 brought about. First, 'freedom' was no longer simply promoted as a magical idea for nations to think more about; freedom after 9/11 was presented as a justification for military intervention in Afghanistan and Iraq. Bush's 'freedom agenda' was now a war agenda. Second, this war was to be labelled the 'War on Terror'. This was more than just a war to fight terrorists; this was a war of ideas. The argument was constantly made that peoples that embrace liberty and democracy will not embrace terrorism. Third, this push to spread democracy was amplified as weapons of mass destruction (WMD) were not found in Iraq and the war therefore required a new core justification. Overall, this was a particularly ideological agenda, which will be discussed in detail below.

BUSH'S FREEDOM AGENDA

Defending and spreading freedom was at the ideological core of the Bush Doctrine. It was central to justifying the War on Terror in general and the invasion and occupation of Afghanistan and Iraq more specifically. Indicative of this, the invasion of Afghanistan, announced by Bush on October 7 2001, was officially named Operation Enduring Freedom. The President justified the war with the assertion that: "We defend not only our precious freedoms, but also the freedom of people everywhere to live and raise their children free from fear."[43] Similarly, the invasion of Iraq, launched on March 20 2003, was officially dubbed Operation Iraqi Freedom. Once again, the war was proclaimed by the US President as being good for the people of the nation being invaded: "Their lives and their freedom matter little to Saddam Hussein – but Iraqi lives and freedom matter greatly to us."[44] As the Iraq War proceeded and no WMD were found, the project of promoting freedom and democracy in Iraq became the principal public justification for the ongoing occupation. Moreover, the Bush administration and its supporters claimed that the spread of freedom to Iraq would make America safer. This view was expressed, for example, by the former Republican Speaker of the House of Representatives Newt Gingrich in a 2003 *Foreign Affairs* article:

> The United States supports the core values of constitutional liberty, the right to free speech (including a free press), independent judiciaries, free markets, free elections, transparency in government, the equality of women, racial equality and the free exercise of religious beliefs. Without these values, it is very hard to imagine a world in which U.S. safety can be secured. We should not confuse respect for others with acceptance of their values if they violate these principles.[45]

In a similar vein, in his second inaugural address Bush stated that: "The survival of liberty in our land increasingly depends on the success of liberty in other lands. The best hope for peace in our world is the expansion of freedom in all the world."[46]

What did spreading freedom mean for the Bush administration? In Afghanistan and Iraq, it meant free elections and the establishment of a market-based economy. As the NSS 2002 had explained: "Free markets and free trade are key priorities of our national security strategy." In Iraq this neo-liberal economic ideology was put in place under Paul Bremer's leadership of the Coalition Provisional Authority (CPA) in Iraq from 2003–2004. The priorities of the CPA were to privatise state-owned enterprises and open the Iraqi economy up to foreign investment. Tariffs on imports were largely suspended by the CPA and company taxation was cut. An Iraq stock market – the Baghdad Stock Exchange – was created and opened for business in June 2004. These policies were from the neo-liberal playbook dubbed the 'Washington Consensus' that had been promoted from the 1970s onwards by the World Bank, IMF and US Treasury Department in response to the debt crises in Latin America, often with negative consequences for the well-being of the people of Latin America.[47] In Iraq and Afghanistan, a relatively new and highly expensive element was added to the privatisation project, namely the contracting out of security and nation-building to private companies (some with links to the Bush administration). Although premised on a more free market approach to war, in the end the American taxpayer was hit with a substantial bill, revealing the hypocrisies of Bush's freedom agenda.[48] This outcome reflects the ideological mix of neo-liberal economics and neo-conservative nation-building that the Bush administration adopted in relation to the Iraq War.

The economic costs of the Iraq War were substantial. The *Financial Times* reported in 2013 that the US had, "overwhelmingly borne the brunt of both the military and reconstruction costs", making a lie of Paul Wolfowitz's claim on March 19 2003 that "We are dealing with a country that can really finance its own reconstruction, and relatively soon." Instead by 2013 the US had spent at least US$138bn on private security, logistics and reconstruction contractors, who "supplied everything from diplomatic security to power plants and toilet paper." The US firm Kellogg, Brown and Root, a former subsidiary of Halliburton, of which Dick Cheney was CEO and Chairman from 1995–2000, "was awarded at least $39.5bn in federal contracts related to the Iraq war" from 2003 to 2013.[49] It was reported in the *New York Times* in 2004 when, Kellogg, Brown and Root was still a subsidiary of Halliburton, that it was awarded a contract to "restore and operate Iraqi oil wells", without a bidding process. The value of the contract is classified but the *Times* claimed it could have been "worth as much as $7 billion."[50] The Commission on Wartime Contracting in Iraq and Afghanistan put out a report in 2011 that "estimated that defence contractors had wasted or lost to fraud as much as $60bn – or $12m a day – since 2001."[51] This experience of American companies profiting from the wars in Afghanistan and Iraq is an important element of Bush's freedom agenda that tends to be underplayed in the international relations literature. A noteworthy exception is Toby Dodge's scholarship which argues that the neo-liberal agenda was key to shaping policy within Iraq after the 2003 invasion. Dodge concludes that:

> The damage to state capacity directly resulting from Bremer's neo-liberal policies drove Iraq into civil war. It took three years and tens of thousands of Iraqi deaths for the Bush administration to realize that rebuilding the infrastructural and despotic capacity of the Iraqi state was the only way it could stabilize the situation and extricate US forces from what had become a deepening quagmire."[52]

Ideological analysis helps us explain this failure. How could Bush blithely and continuously claim that freedom needed to be spread in Iraq, as public order and safety was increasingly the obvious problem on the ground? Bush's ideological instincts and American mythology go some way to explaining this. Freedom was the touchstone idea that Bush turned to in the wake of the 9/11 attacks and continued to rely heavily on throughout his presidency. This was expressed in no uncertain terms in Bush's address to Congress on September 20 2001 when he stated: "Americans are asking, why do they hate us? They hate what we see right here in this chamber – a democratically elected government. Their leaders are self-appointed. They hate our freedoms – our freedom of religion, our freedom of speech, our freedom to vote and assemble and disagree with each other."[53] From the beginning of the War on Terror Bush made finding al-Qaeda terrorists not just a policing or military operation, but an ideological battle by claiming to Congress that: "All of this was brought upon us in a single day, and night fell on a different world, a world where freedom itself is under attack."[54] By portraying America as the ultimate defenders of global freedom, this gave his administration great license to act, not only on behalf of the American people, but on behalf of all of humanity. As Bush explained in the same speech, the "advance of human freedom – the great achievement of our time, and the great hope of every time – now depends on us."[55]

The obvious question is why and how did the idea of 'freedom' carry so much weight and power for Bush and his administration, allowing for so much to be proclaimed and done in its name? We have traced the uses to which the idea of freedom has been put and its centrality to the ideology of US foreign policy throughout this book. Franklin D. Roosevelt made the moral and ideological case for American support for the allies' cause in the Second World War with his declaration of American support of the "four freedoms." In the Cold War, freedom was central to American political rhetoric.[56] In his inaugural address in 1961 John F. Kennedy famously declared that America would "pay any price, bear any burden, meet any hardship, support any friend, oppose any foe to assure the survival and the success of liberty."[57] Lyndon Johnson was clear and undeviating in his insistence that he was defending freedom in Vietnam. As the American historian Eric Foner has written: "No idea is more fundamental to Americans' sense of themselves and as a nation than freedom. The central term in our political vocabulary, 'freedom' . . . is deeply embedded in the record of our history and the language of everyday life."[58] As the authors of *Habits of the Heart*, a study of American civic religion and political culture, contend, freedom is the "most resonant, deeply held American value."[59] Michael Foley in his comprehensive survey of the place of ideas in American politics agrees:

> The most abiding and durable self-characterization of the United States is that of freedom. The concept of freedom lies at the heart of American identity. It is at one and the same time a foundational ethic, a cultural reference point, a defining ideal, a controlling precept, a depiction of social reality, a medium of political exchange, a mobilizing source of aspiration, and a device of historical and political explanation.[60]

This history has been absorbed by the American people, according to public opinion scholars Herbert McClosky and John Zaller who assert that: "[n]o value in the American ethos is more revered."[61] As a result it is not surprising that freedom is the concept that presidents have most often used to justify their foreign policies. As Henry Nau has written, illustrating the point, Bush "waved the banner of freedom all over the planet, like Woodrow Wilson's League."[62]

Ronald Reagan's speechwriter Peggy Noonan has written about how she studied the speeches of earlier presidents in order to write with an authentic presidential "sound" and with what she calls the "grammar of the presidency."[63] Daniel T. Rodgers summarises this commonplace approach as "the work of the speechwriters' continuous, creative recycling of the words and gestures of their predecessors."[64] This creates a liturgical language of presidential speeches where ultimately ambiguous words like 'freedom' and 'liberty' take on purposeful and reassuring meaning. Like Reagan, George W. Bush never tired of proclaiming the special powers of the idea of freedom, without much knowledge of local conditions. In his memoir, *Decision Points*, Bush claims that Reagan's "moral clarity and call for their [the Soviet people's] freedom" was inspiring to Soviet dissidents and key to

American success in the Cold War. This simplistic view of freedom's winning ways was expressed in liturgical terms by Bush. Freedom is presented by Bush as an idea that has been promoted and protected by his political forefathers and whose time has come during his presidency to be granted to all people everywhere. If this sounds hyperbolic, it is worth recalling Bush's words from the NSS 2002: "the United States must defend liberty and justice because these principles are right and true for all people everywhere. No nation owns these aspirations, and no nation is exempt from them."

This is where ideology is particularly dangerous, because under Bush (as with earlier administrations) this ideological goal was often heedless of opposing argument and the weight of evidence on the ground in Afghanistan and Iraq.[65] At the 20th Anniversary of the National Endowment for Democracy in 2003 Bush claimed that:

> The advance of freedom is the calling of our time; it is the calling of our country. From the Fourteen Points to the Four Freedoms, to the Speech at Westminster, America has put our power at the service of principle. We believe that liberty is the design of nature; we believe that liberty is the direction of history. We believe that human fulfillment and excellence come in the responsible exercise of liberty. And we believe that freedom – the freedom we prize – is not for us alone, it is the right and the capacity of all mankind.[66]

This echoed the theme of Bush's 'Mission Accomplished' speech of May 1 2003 aboard the aircraft carrier USS Abraham Lincoln:

> Our commitment to liberty is America's tradition, declared at our founding, affirmed in Franklin Roosevelt's Four Freedoms, asserted in the Truman Doctrine and in Ronald Reagan's challenge to an evil empire. We are committed to freedom in Afghanistan, Iraq and in a peaceful Palestine. The advance of freedom is the surest strategy to undermine the appeal of terror in the world. Where freedom takes hold, hatred gives way to hope. When freedom takes hold, men and women turn to the peaceful pursuit of a better life. American values and American interests lead in the same direction. We stand for human liberty.[67]

Both speeches point to an American tradition of promoting freedom that has noted highpoints. Both speeches have an exceptionalist quality to them, which sees America playing a special role in the world.[68] The language is liturgical in the way it repeats certain mantras and pieties about America and its role in advancing the idea of freedom. This presidential belief in the powers and benefits of 'freedom' is one thing to espouse; however, putting these beliefs into action is behaviour of a different order. After 9/11 Bush used the US military to put these abstract ideological ideas into action as part of his War on Terror.[69]

THE WAR ON TERROR

In his 1964 State of the Union address President Lyndon Johnson declared a "war on poverty" which aimed "not only to relieve the symptom of poverty, but to cure it and, above all, to prevent it." Ronald Reagan famously quipped a generation later that "we waged a war on poverty, and poverty won." Reagan had his own domestic policy war, this time it was the 'war on drugs' and it is not flippant to suggest that in the 'war' on drugs, drugs often won. The same could be said of Bush's 'War on Terror' – that the threat from terrorism increased greatly in the wake of the Bush administration's expansive response to the 9/11 attacks. As many commentators have written, a war on a violent tactic is a peculiar formulation, the "equivalent" argues Anatol Lieven of "declaring 'aerial bombing' or 'tanks' the enemy."[70] The War on Terror was presented as a war of ideas in which freedom, elections and market-based economies were promoted by the Bush administration as the path to joining the civilised world. This doctrine was outlined with very few caveats by Bush's National Security Advisor Condoleezza Rice in 2003 when she claimed that:

> To win the War on Terror, we must win also win a war of ideas . . . Terror lives when freedom dies. True peace will come only when the world is safer, better and freer. That is why we are helping Afghans and Iraqis build representative governments that will serve the decent aspirations of their people. That is why we are committed to building a global trading system that is more and more free, to expand the circle of prosperity into the Americas, Africa, and the Middle East.[71]

Along with freedom, representative democracy and free market economics, the other key idea promoted as part of the War on Terror was pre-emption (the notion that the US had the right to engage in pre-emptive attacks on terrorists and 'rogue states' to prevent possible future attacks on itself).[72] Before we address pre-emptive war, we will discuss the Bush administration's ideational formation that 'free' democratic nations would form a coalition to put pressure on, and at times attack, the unfree and undemocratic. At the top of the list of suspect nations were the three states – Iran, Iraq and North Korea – that Bush identified in his 2003 State of the Union address as an "Axis of Evil." The Bush administration's NSS 2002 had envisioned a coalition of freedom-favouring states emerging that would confront rogue states and terrorists. The awkward phraseology Bush used for this coalition was "a balance of power that favors freedom." The term "balance of power" in the NSS 2002 is a complete departure from the traditional idea of 'balance of power' politics as practised via the Nixon-Kissinger foreign policy. Indeed, Bush's "balance of power that favors freedom" is quite the opposite of the more traditional understanding: it conceives of the US leading a global order with the notion of freedom at its core.[73] After the 9/11 attacks, the Bush Doctrine contended that it was no longer enough to support the expansion of human freedom only in principle. Now the administration was claiming intervention was required by freedom-enjoying states to rid the world of terrorism. The case was put starkly in Bush's introduction to the NSS 2002, with the assertion that:

> In building a balance of power that favors freedom, the United States is guided by the conviction that all nations have important responsibilities. Nations that enjoy freedom must actively fight terror. Nations that depend on international stability must help prevent the spread of weapons of mass destruction. Nations that seek international aid must govern themselves wisely, so that aid is well spent. For freedom to thrive, accountability must be expected and required.[74]

The NSS 2002 made it clear that this was not merely an abstract commitment, stating: "Through our willingness to use *force* in our own defense and in defense of others, the United States demonstrates its resolve to maintain a balance of power that favors freedom."[75] The emergence of a coalition of states willing to act as one was largely an act of wishful thinking by the Bush administration and a notion that disintegrated almost

entirely when it came to invading Iraq in 2003. Indeed, many of America's traditional
allies as well as three out of the five permanent members of the Security Council opposed
the invasion. Most other nations could not see the supposed connections between Saddam
Hussein's Iraq and al-Qaeda and most wanted to let the international weapons inspection
regime continue.[76] The Bush administration saw things differently; a new Bush Doctrine
now trumped Containment. Bush argued in early 2003 that after 9/11, "the doctrine of
containment just doesn't hold any water, as far as I'm concerned."[77]

In NSS 2002 a policy of pre-emption was outlined, with seven explicit and five implicit
references to the concept in the document. The idea of pre-emptive war was a dramatic
departure from the international norms on war that America had played a key role in
establishing after the Second World War. These norms emphasised that military power
should be maintained for self-defense rather than for offensive attack. Bush argued that
the attacks of 9/11 had changed American thinking and a new doctrine of attack before
being attacked was now "common sense."[78] This new approach to warfare was outlined
in NSS 2002 which contended that:

> Given the goals of rogue states and terrorists, the United States can no longer solely
> rely on a reactive posture as we have in the past. The inability to deter a potential
> attacker, the immediacy of today's threats, and the magnitude of potential harm that
> could be caused by our adversaries' choice of weapons, do not permit that option. We
> cannot let our enemies strike first . . . To forestall or prevent such hostile acts by our
> adversaries, the United States will, if necessary, act preemptively.[79]

The clear weakness of this thinking was not only that the doctrine of pre-emption placed
America outside international law, but also that it relied on accurate intelligence about
the threats posed to America by rogue states or non-state actors. The evidence the Bush
administration used to claim that Iraq posed a significant threat to the US turned out
to be not just faulty but manipulated and exaggerated. As Kaufmann has outlined the
administration

> made four main arguments to persuade the public of their case against Saddam
> Hussein: (1) he was an almost uniquely undeterrable aggressor who would seek any
> opportunity to kill Americans virtually regardless of risk to himself or his country;
> (2) he was cooperating with al-Qa'ida and had even assisted in the September 11,
> 2001, terrorist attacks against the United States; (3) he was close to acquiring nuclear
> weapons; and (4) he possessed chemical and biological weapons that could be used
> to devastating effect against American civilians at home or U.S. troops in the Middle
> East."

However, as Kaufmann points out: "Virtually none of the administration's claims held up,
and the information needed to debunk nearly all of them was available both inside and
outside the U.S. government before the war."[80]

In Bush's opening letter to NSS 2002 he appealed to "common sense" to address attacks
"before they are fully formed" using the "best intelligence."[81] Common sense would suggest the best intelligence would need to show that an attack was imminent. However,
Bush in an early 2004 interview dismissed this requisite for pre-emption. Discussing the
decision to invade Iraq, he told NBC's Tim Russert: "I believe it is essential – that when we
see a threat, we deal with those threats before they become imminent. It's too late if they

become imminent. It's too late in this new kind of war, and so that's why I made the deci-sion I made."[82] Given that the concept of imminence is central to notions of pre-emption, what Bush was really implementing was a strategy of prevention that guarded against the emergence of future risk rather than against actually-existing risk. In a review essay on the memoirs of the American protagonists of the Iraq War Melvyn Leffler argues that fear drove their thinking and policies.[83] We are more inclined to see this reckless thinking as being driven by hubris.[84] It is based on a sense that, first, success in Afghanistan had been easily achieved and, second, that invading Iraq offered an opportunity to take an expansive and long-term approach to eradicating terrorism by transforming the Middle East.[85] This thinking has turned out to be not only wrong, but highly destructive. Neo-conservative ideology played a significant role in encouraging this reckless thinking. As we will argue in the conclusion to this chapter, the neoconservatives (within and outside of the Bush administration) strongly advocated invading Iraq from the 1990s onwards. Once events in Iraq started to go very badly and no WMD were found, Bush doubled down on the neoconservative justification of the war, with the democratisation of Iraq now presented as one of the central reasons for invading and continuing to occupy the country.[86] Despite Bush's utopian rhetoric of bringing freedom, democracy and market capitalism to Iraq, on the ground the very negative trajectory of the Iraq War was forcing the US to change tactics, with David Petraeus' application of COIN Doctrine from 2007 onwards marking, "the complete jettisoning of the neo-liberal policy prescriptions that had driven US policy up to that point."[87] Under this approach Iraqi civilians were placed at the centre of what all occupations tend to become: a hearts and minds campaign. The spokesperson for the multi-national force in Iraq, William Caldwell, wrote of the COIN approach that "our success in Iraq depends on our ability to treat the civilian population with humanity and dignity."[88] For all the administration's florid rhetoric and use of state of the art military technology in Iraq, a way forward for a post-Saddam Iraq needed to be placed in the hands of the Iraqis as they searched for a political solution to the chaos America had created. The original sin of invading and occupying Iraq caused continuing problems for the Obama administration. To claim this sin was righted by the 'surge' of 2007 was yet another example of a tactic used by Republican politicians; of recasting reality in terms that suited them politically.[89] That they enjoyed some success in doing this meant that key lessons went unlearned. The fact that the supposed success of the 'surge' could paper over so much destruction and chaos is testimony to the power of rhetoric and wishful thinking when America goes abroad. It is also testimony to the collective amnesia regarding American foreign interventions that go wrong. The power of ideology helps explain these tendencies.

A NEO-CONSERVATIVE WAR?

The case of Iraq provides the clearest possible evidence of how American nationalism, with its exceptionalist and militaristic tendencies, is a powerful and potentially destructive ideology. In the wake of the 9/11 attacks a strident American nationalism was animated by President George W. Bush as he called for revenge.[90] Neoconservative ideologues seized on this moment to push the case for targeting not just al-Qaeda, but Saddam Hussein's regime in Iraq which they claimed would be a likely supplier of weapons of mass destruc-tion to terrorists in the future. Bush was particularly drawn to neoconservative arguments that the correct response to the threat of terrorism was to export American-style freedom and democracy to Afghanistan and Iraq via military intervention. Subsequently, Bush's speeches and the NSS 2002 were heavily influenced by neoconservative ideas.[91]

So who were the neoconservatives and what did they believe? It is useful to see them as a group of like-minded intellectuals spanning three generations with overlapping but not entirely similar beliefs. The first generation of neoconservatives forged the movement out of personal and intellectual friendships in the 1960s and 1970s. The core members – Irving Kristol (the so-called 'Godfather of Neoconservatism'), Daniel Bell, Nathan Glazer, Daniel Patrick Moynihan and Norman Podhoretz – created new journals together,[92] co-authored articles and, through their combined efforts, gave the movement significant momentum. The most important characteristic of the early neoconservatives was their scepticism about liberal social reform.[93] However, for all of their criticism of liberalism in the 1960s they were Democrats who took a hawkish foreign policy stance, believing in a strong military, fervent anti-communism, American exceptionalism and a strong commitment to Zionism.[94] These foreign policy views were held with even more conviction by the second generation of neo-conservatives. While the first two generations all started out as Democrats, by the 1970s and early 1980s they were by and large finding a new home in the Republican Party.[95] The second generation included four former Henry 'Scoop' Jackson aides – Richard Perle, Paul Wolfowitz, Elliott Abrams and Douglas Feith. These four men played significant roles in the Bush Jnr. administration. They were all strong advocates of invading Iraq during the late 1990s and pushed especially strongly for removing Saddam after the 9/11 attacks. Members of the third generation were, literally, often the children of first generation neo-cons, including William Kristol and John Podhoretz, and the Kagan brothers, Robert and Frederick. The demise of the Soviet Union opened up divisions within neoconservative thinking. Older neoconservatives like Irving Kristol and Jeane Kirkpatrick became hard to distinguish from orthodox Realists in the post-Cold War period.[96] Meanwhile, third generation neocons started advocating the case for US engagement in humanitarian intervention and democratisation efforts throughout the world; they also strongly advocated removing Saddam – something Irving Kristol and Kirkpatrick were less enthusiastic about.[97] By the 1990s neoconservatives were well-connected to key Republican political and policy circles with their voices being carried on a weekly basis via the *Weekly Standard* and elsewhere.[98]

The most noted neoconservative think-tank is often claimed to be the Project for the New American Century which in 1998 collected signatures from people like William Kristol, Robert Kagan, Paul Wolfowitz, R. James Woolsey, Elliot Abrams, John Bolton, Donald Rumsfeld, Francis Fukuyama, Zalmay Khalilzad, Richard Perle and Robert B. Zoellick, to send a letter calling on President Clinton to undertake the removal of Saddam Hussein's regime.[99] In presenting PNAC's case, the letter set out an understanding of and approach to Iraq that clearly informed the Bush administration:

> The policy of 'containment' of Saddam Hussein has been steadily eroding over the past several months. As recent events have demonstrated, we can no longer depend on our partners in the Gulf War coalition to continue to uphold the sanctions or to punish Saddam when he blocks or evades UN inspections. Our ability to ensure that Saddam Hussein is not producing weapons of mass destruction, therefore, has substantially diminished. Even if full inspections were eventually to resume, which now seems highly unlikely, experience has shown that it is difficult if not impossible to monitor Iraq's chemical and biological weapons production . . . As a result, in the not-too-distant future we will be unable to determine with any reasonable level of confidence whether Iraq does or does not possess such weapons . . .

The only acceptable strategy is one that eliminates the possibility that Iraq will be able to use or threaten to use weapons of mass destruction. In the near term, this means a willingness to undertake military action as diplomacy is clearly failing. In the long term, it means removing Saddam Hussein and his regime from power. That now needs to become the aim of American foreign policy.[100]

Hence, neoconservatism was clearly influential on the rhetoric, thinking and policies of the Bush administration, particularly NSS 2002 and Iraq policy. Judging by some of the commentary on the topic, the study of ideology and US foreign policy would seem to have found its perfect match with the neoconservatives and the Bush administration. For example, Patrick Buchanan has written that it was the "conversion of George W. Bush to neoconservative ideology that took America into the war" in Iraq.[101] Others have made similar claims about the influence of neoconservatism on the Bush White House. General Anthony Zinni claimed that the "neocons captured the president and vice president", while "Elizabeth Drew explained in the *New York Review of Books* that 'the neoconservatives . . . are largely responsible for getting us into the war against Iraq'."[102]

When did this supposed capture of the White House occur? The standard thesis is that after 9/11 the neoconservatives captured the imagination of White House speechmakers, key policy-makers and the President.[103] John Micklethwait and Adrian Wooldridge, in *Right Nation*, make this argument in a fairly sophisticated manner, writing:

after September 11, the neocon message, for better or worse, struck a mighty chord with the rest of the Right Nation. A neoconservative foreign policy soon became a conservative one.[104]

The Iraq War, it is regularly asserted, was a neoconservative war: sold by the neoconservatives first, loudest and ultimately convincingly to the Bush administration as a necessary war. Possibly the most authoritative voice on this topic, given his close connections with many conservatives, both within and outside the Bush administration, is that of Charles Krauthammer. "The remarkable fact that the Bush Doctrine is, essentially, a synonym for neoconservative foreign policy", wrote Krauthammer, "marks neoconservatism's own transition from a position of dissidence, which it occupied during the first Bush administration and the Clinton years, to governance."[105] The neoconservatives themselves generally tended to underplay their influence on the Bush foreign policy – for obvious reasons, but also because they believed that the Bush administration did not commit enough troops to Iraq for most of the war, at least until the troop surge of 2007. However, there were moments when they did assert their influence. Most striking in this regard is Richard Perle's statement that: "The President of the United States on issue after issue, has reflected the thinking of neoconservatives."[106]

In terms of direct policy decisions, it is undeniable that the influence of the neocons waxed and waned during the Bush years because different ideas and agendas asserted themselves at different times. On the question of influence, Vaïsse writes that: "Bush himself was not a neoconservative, but he did incorporate numerous neoconservative ideas into 'an astonishing ideological cocktail,' whose other ingredients included his evangelical faith, his moralism, his profound conviction that he was right, and his stubborn insistence on adhering to a goal once set."[107] The biggest problem with the thesis that a neoconservative ideology took over the Bush administration's foreign policy after 9/11 is that it tends to ignore the vast scope and often contradictory nature of US foreign policy.

That said, the neoconservatives were crucial to making the *case* for the invasion of Iraq, but their influence was less evident thereafter. They wanted a larger invasion force and a more expansive transformational agenda than Donald Rumsfeld, who put into practice a new type of technologically driven warfare that required only a relatively small number of invading and occupying military personnel. Moreover, Rumsfeld planned for a short-term occupation. The rapid deposing of the Taliban government in Afghanistan led to hubris within the Defense Department about the capabilities of the US to quickly win wars and transform foreign societies. The neoconservatives were not immune to this overconfidence, and some of their criticisms of Rumsfeld's approach rely heavily on the advantages of hindsight. What the neoconservatives did provide in all phases of the Iraq War was a reservoir of rhetoric regarding the benefits of spreading freedom and democracy. These were arguments that had been particularly prominent in the writings of William Kristol and Robert Kagan. Neoconservative arguments became more evident in Bush's speeches after the search for WMD proved futile. During Paul Bremer's period in control of the CPA, a neoconservative and neo-liberal agenda was pursued. In the years after that, as the occupation reflected very poorly on the Bush administrations, the neoconservatives tried to distance themselves from Iraq policy. Typical of this was Richard Perle's claim in a 2006 *Vanity Fair* interview that the neoconservatives had very little influence over the Bush administration.[108] However, once Bush announced a surge in troop numbers in Iraq in 2007 the neoconservatives were again credited with being listened to.[109]

In conclusion, Iraq was a neoconservative war in the sense that no other ideology was anywhere near as important in providing the rhetoric and ideational justifications for the invasion and occupation. Neoconservative beliefs about Iraq were often misguided, unrealistic and destructive. However, these ideas and their advocates have never been fully called to account for the damage they wrought. In part this reflects their success in distancing themselves from the post-invasion chaos by claiming their ideas were poorly applied. What is ironic is that neoconservatism emerged as a new ideology in the 1960s with a founding and fundamental belief that governments needed to better recognise the limitations on their ability to socially engineer broad change. By the twenty-first century these warnings were largely dismissed by neoconservatives when it came to what the American government could supposedly achieve in the international arena, as a new generation of highly influential neoconservatives propagated an extremely hubristic version of American exceptionalism coupled with a belief in unending American primacy.[110] In the wake of the 9/11 attacks, an emotionally charged and militaristic American nationalism was animated by President Bush. Instead of attempting to moderate these tendencies, as Realists and liberals tried to do, neoconservative policy-makers and commentators used this time of fear to promote the case for invading Iraq as the best way to transform the Middle East and therefore eradicate terrorism. The people of that region have paid a terrible price for the Bush administration's adoption of these dangerous ideas.

NOTES

1 Thomas E. Ricks, *Fiasco: The America Military Adventure in Iraq* (New York: Penguin Books, 2006), p.6.
2 Conor Friedersdorf, 'Remembering Why Americans Loathe Dick Cheney', *The Atlantic*, 30 August 2011, www.theatlantic.com/politics/archive/2011/08/remembering-why-americans-

loathe-dick-cheney/244306/; Wil S. Hylton, 'The People v. Richard Cheney', *GQ*, 13 February 2007, www.gq.com/story/richard-cheney-vice-president-impeachment?printable=true.

3 Bob Woodward, 'Cheney was Unwavering in Desire to Go to War,' *Washington Post*, 20 April 2004, www.washingtonpost.com/wp-dyn/articles/A25550-2004Apr19.html.

4 G. John. Ikenberry, 'America's Imperial Ambition', in Foreign Affairs (eds.), *America and the World* (New York: W.W. Norton, 2002), p.376.

5 Rajiv Chandrasekaran, *Imperial Life in the Emerald City* (New York: Knopf, 2006); Rajiv Chandrasekaran, *Little America* (New York: Knopf, 2012).

6 BBC News, 'Black Hawk Down: The Somali Battle that Changed US Policy in Africa', 1 February 2017, www.bbc.com/news/av/magazine-38808175/black-hawk-down-the-somali-battle-that-changed-us-policy-in-africa.

7 BBC News, 'Rwanda: How the Genocide Happened,' 17 May 2011, www.bbc.com/news/world-africa-13431486; Outreach Programme on the Rwanda Genocide and the United Nations, 'Rwanda: A Brief History of the Country', *The United Nations*, www.un.org/en/preventgenocide/rwanda/education/rwandagenocide.shtml.

8 Bill Clinton, *My Story* (New York: Random House, 2004). p.593.

9 'Prospectives', *Strategic Survey*, Vol.102, No.1, 2010, pp.355–365.

10 George W. Bush during the Presidential Debate at Wake Forest University, 11 October 2000, www.ontheissues.org/George_W__Bush_Foreign_Policy.htm.

11 George W. Bush, President Discusses War on Terror, *The White House Archives* (Washington, DC: The White House,8 March 2005), https://georgewbush-whitehouse.archives.gov/news/releases/2005/03/20050308-3.html.

12 Bush's presidential approval ratings were certainly transformed. Before the 9/11 attacks his approval rating was at around 55 per cent; by the time of the invasion of Afghanistan in October 2001 his approval rating was roughly 85 per cent. See Gallup Wall Street Journal Research, 'How the Presidents Stack Up', *Wall Street Journal*, http://online.wsj.com/public/resources/documents/info-presapp0605-31.html.

13 Frank Bruni, 'A Nation Challenged: White House Memo', *New York Times*, 22 September 2001, www.nytimes.com/2001/09/22/us/nation-challenged-white-house-memo-for-president-mission-role-history.html.

14 George W. Bush, First Inauguration Address, 20 January 2001, www.aol.com/article/news/2017/01/19/president-george-w-bushs-first-inauguration-speech-full-text/21658303/.

15 George W. Bush, Address Before a Joint Session of the Congress on the United States Response to the Terrorist Attacks of September 11, *The White House Archives* (Washington, DC: The White House, September 20 2001), https://georgewbush-whitehouse.archives.gov/news/releases/2001/09/20010920-8.html.

16 See, Robert Jervis, *American Foreign Policy in a New Era* (New York: Routledge, 2005); Adam Quinn, *US Foreign Policy in Context: National Ideology from the Founders to the Bush Doctrine* (New York: Routledge, 2010).

17 Jervis, *American Foreign Policy in a New Era*, p.87.

18 Dueck, *Hard Line*; Robert Jervis, 'Understanding the Bush Doctrine', *Political Science Quarterly* Vol.118, No.3, 2003, p.87.

19 Justin Vaïsse, *Neoconservatism: The Biography of a Movement* (Cambridge, MA: Belknap Press, 2010), p.246; Gary J. Dorrien, *Imperial Designs: Neoconservatism and the New Pax Americana* (Abingdon: Routledge, 2004); James Mann, *Rise of the Vulcans: The History of Bush's War Cabinet*, (New York: Viking Press, 2004).

20 Ron Suskind, *The Price of Loyalty: George W. Bush, the White House, and the Education of Paul O'Neill* (New York: Simon & Schuster, 2004), p.75.

21 Edward Rhodes, 'Onward, Liberal Soldiers? The Crusading Logic of Bush's Grand Strategy and What is Wrong with It,' in Lloyd Gardner and Marilyn Young (eds.), *The New American Empire: a 21st Century Teach-in on U.S. Foreign Policy* (New York: The New Press, 2005), pp.236.

22 White House National Security Council, *The National Security Strategy of the United States of America* [henceforward White House, NSS 2002] (Washington, DC: The White House, September 2002), p.3. For an analysis that highlights continuities and differences across US NSS documents, see Aaron Ettinger, 'US National Security Strategies: Patterns of Continuity and Change, 1987–2015', *Comparative Strategy*, Vol.36 No.2 2017, pp.115–128.

23 Jervis, *American Foreign Policy in a New Era*, p.79.

24 Jervis, 'Understanding the Bush Doctrine', p.365.

25 Jervis, *American Foreign Policy in a New Era*, p.79.

26 White House, *NSS 2002*, p.1.

27 Oz Hassan, 'Bush's Freedom Agenda: Ideology and the Democratization of the Middle East', *Democracy and Security*, Vol.4, No.3, 2008, pp.268–289, at p.270.

28 See Dorrien, *Imperial Designs*.

29 Quinn, *US Foreign Policy in Context*, p.142; Rhodes, 'Onward, Liberal Soldiers?', p.233.

30 Kagan in an interview with George Packer, *The Assassins' Gate: America in Iraq* (New York: Thorndike Press, 2005), p.18.

31 Ikenberry, 'America's Imperial Ambition', p.372.

32 Jervis, *American Foreign Policy in a New Era*, p.83; Jervis, 'Understanding the Bush Doctrine', p.379; Brendon O'Connor, 'Back to the Future, Again', *Australian Journal of Politics & History,* Vol.47, No.4, 2001, pp.594–600; Brendon O'Connor, 'Beyond the Cartoon: George W. Bush and his Biographers', *Political Studies Review,* Vol.3, No.2, 2005, pp.163–174.

33 George W. Bush, President Sworn-In to Second Term, the Second Inaugural Speech from the Office of the Press Secretary, *The White House Archives* (Washington, DC: The White House, 20 January 2005), http://georgewbush-whitehouse.archives.gov/news/releases/2005/01/20050120-1.html.

34 George W. Bush, Remarks at the National Day of Prayer & Remembrance Service, *The White House Archives* (Washington, DC: The White House, 14 September 2001), https://georgewbush-whitehouse.archives.gov/news/releases/2001/09/20010914-2.html. Bush similarly claimed "My administration has a job to do and we're going to do it. We will rid the world of the evil-doers," in Manuel Perez-Rivas, 'Bush Vows to Rid the World of 'Evil-Doers', *CNN,* 16 September 2001, http://edition.cnn.com/2001/US/09/16/gen.bush.terrorism/.

35 George W. Bush, *Decision Points* (London: Virgin Books, 2010), Ch.1; O'Connor, 'Beyond the Cartoon'.

36 Paul Harris, 'Bush Says God Chose Him to Lead his Nation', *The Guardian*, 2 November 2003, www.theguardian.com/world/2003/nov/02/usa.religion.

37 George W. Bush, President Delivers "State of the Union", *The White House Archives* (Washington, DC: The White House, 28 January 2003), http://whitehouse.georgewbush.org/news/2003/012803-SOTU.asp.

38 George W. Bush, President Sworn-In to Second Term, the Second Inaugural Speech from the Office of the Press Secretary, *The White House Archives* (Washington, DC: The White House, 20 January 2005), https://georgewbush-whitehouse.archives.gov/news/releases/2005/01/20050120-1.html.

39 George W. Bush, Graduation Speech at West Point, released by Office of the Press Secretary, *The White House Archives* (Washington, DC: The White House, 1 June, 2002), http://georgewbush-whitehouse.archives.gov/news/releases/2002/06/20020601-3.html; Jervis, *American Foreign Policy in a New Era*, p.90.

40 Condoleezza Rice, Dr. Condoleezza Rice Discusses President's National Security Strategy, released by the Office of the Press Secretary in *The White House Archives* (Washington, DC: The White House, 1 October 2002), https://georgewbush-whitehouse.archives.gov/news/releases/2002/10/20021001-6.html.

41 John Judis, 'Clueless in Gaza', *The New Republic,* 19 February 2013, https://newrepublic.com/article/112456/george-w-bushs-secret-war-against-hamas.

42 George W. Bush, The First Inaugural Address, *The White House Archives* (Washington, DC: The White House, 20 January 2001), https://georgewbush-whitehouse.archives.gov/news/inaugural-address.html.

43 George W. Bush, Address to the Nation on Operations in Afghanistan, *The White House Archives*, (Washington, DC: The White House, 7 October 2001), https://georgewbush-whitehouse.archives.gov/news/reeases/2001/10/20011007-8.html.

44 George W. Bush, Remarks on the Future of Iraq, *The White House Archives* (Washington, DC: The White House, 26 February 2003), https://georgewbush-whitehouse.archives.gov/news/releases/2003/02/20030226-11.html.

45 Newt Gingrich, 'The Failure of US Diplomacy', *Foreign Policy*, July/August 2003, pp.42–48.

46 Daniel T. Rodgers, *Age of Fracture* (Cambridge, MA: Belknap Press, 2011), p.268.

47 Toby Dodge, 'The Ideological Roots of Failure: The Application of Kinetic Neo-Liberalism to Iraq', *International Affairs,* Vol.86, No.6, 2010, pp.1269–1286, at p.1274.

48 It is also worth noting the Halliburton and other firms that received defence contracts largely donated to the Republican Party and the Bush campaign rather than to his Democratic opponent John Kerry in 2004. See William D. Hartung and Michelle Ciarrocca, 'The Ties that Bind: Arms Industry Influence in the Bush Administration and Beyond', *World Policy,* October 2004, https://worldpolicy.org/report-ties-that-bind-arms-industry-influence-in-the-bush-administration-and-beyond/.

49 Anna Fifield, 'Contractors Reap $138 Billion from Iraq War', *Financial Times,* 19 March 2013, www.ft.com/content/7f435f04-8c05-11e2-b001-00144feabdc0.

50 David E. Rosenbaum, 'A Closer Look at Cheney and Halliburton', *New York Times,* 28 September, 2008: www.nytimes.com/2004/09/28/us/a-closer-look-at-cheney-and-halliburton.html.

51 Fifield, 'Contractors Reap S138 Billion from Iraq War'.

52 Dodge, 'The Ideological Roots of Failure', p.1286.

53 George W. Bush, Address to a Joint Session of Congress and the American People, *The White House Archives,* (Washington, DC: The White House, 20 September 2002), https://georgewbush-whitehouse.archives.gov/news/releases/2001/09/20010920-8.html.

54 Ibid.

55 Ibid.

56 Rodgers, *Age of Fracture.*

57 John F. Kennedy, President Kennedy's Inaugural Address, *John F. Kennedy Presidential Library,* 20 January 1961, www.jfklibrary.org/Research/Research-Aids/Ready-Reference/JFK-Quotations/Inaugural-Address.aspx.

58 Eric Foner, 'American Freedom in a Global Age', *American Historical Review,* Vol.106, No.1, 2001, pp.1–16.

59 Robert N. Bellah, Richard Madsen, William M. Sullivan, Ann Swidler and Steven M. Tipton, *Habits of the Heart: Individualism and Commitment in American Life,* (Berkeley, CA: University of California Press, 1996), p.23.

60 Michael Foley, *American Credo: The Place of Ideas in US Politics* (Oxford: Oxford University Press 2007), p.19.

61 Herbert McClosky and John Zaller, *The American Ethos: Public Attitudes Toward Capitalism and Democracy* (Cambridge, MA: Harvard University Press, 1984), p.18.

62 Henry Nau, *Conservative Internationalism: Armed Diplomacy Under Jefferson, Polk, Truman and Reagan* (Princeton, NJ: Princeton University Press, 2013), p.208.

63 Rodgers, *Age of Fracture,* p.18.

64 Ibid.

65 Foley has written that: "The difficulties posed by attempting to translate a protean concept [as freedom] into a single thematic construction of a complex and contested history are not so much surmounted as habitually dismissed or transcended." Foley, *American Credo,* p.24; See also, Lieven, *America Right or Wrong,* p.73.

66 George W. Bush, President Bush Discusses Freedom in Iraq and Middle East, *The White House Archives* (Washington, DC: The White House, 6 November 2003), https://georgewbush-whitehouse.archives.gov/news/releases/2003/11/20031106-2.html.

67 George W. Bush, President Bush Announces Major Combat Operations in Iraq Have Ended, *The White House Archives* (Washington, DC: The White House, 1 May 2003), https://georgewbush-whitehouse.archives.gov/news/releases/2003/05/20030501-15.html.

68 Lieven, *America Right or Wrong,* p.64.

69 Rhodes, 'Onward, Liberal Soldiers?' p.232.

70 Lieven, *America Right or Wrong,* p.74.

71 Condoleezza Rice, Remarks by Dr. Condoleezza Rice, *The White House Archives* (Washington, DC: The White House, 26 June 2003), https://georgewbush-whitehouse.archives.gov/news/releases/2003/06/20030626.html.

72 See, Francois Heisbourg, 'A Work in Progress: The Bush Doctrine and its Consequences', *The Washington Quarterly,* Vol.26, No.2, 2003, pp.75–88; Henry Shue and David Rodin (eds.), *Preemption: Military Action and Moral Justification* (Oxford: Oxford University Press, 2007).

73 Quinn, *US Foreign Policy in Context,* p.143.

74 George W. Bush, Introductory Letter in National Security Council, *The National Security Strategy of the United States of America* (Washington, DC: The White House, September 2002), p. vi.

75 White House, *NSS 2002,* p.29.

76 A good overview of the weapons inspections process and debate over Iraq in 2003 can be found in: Peter Beinart, 'Iran Hawks are the New Iraq Hawks', *The Atlantic*, 8 May 2018, www.theatlantic.com/international/archive/2018/05/iraq-war-iran-deal/559844/.

77 George W. Bush, President Bush Meets with Prime Minister Blair, *The White House Archives* (Washington, DC: The White House, 31 January 2003), https://georgewbush-whitehouse. archives.gov/news/releases/2003/01/20030131-23.html.

78 George W. Bush, Introductory Letter, p.v.

79 White House, *NSS 2002*, p.15.

80 Chaim Kaufmann, 'Threat Inflation and the Failure of the Marketplace of Ideas: The Selling of the Iraq War', *International Security*, Vol.29, No.1, 2004, pp.5–48, at p.6. See also, James P. Pfiffner and Mark Phythian (eds.) *Intelligence and National Security Policymaking on Iraq: British and American Perspectives* (Manchester: Manchester University Press, 2008).

81 George W. Bush, Introductory Letter.

82 George W. Bush and Tim Russert, 'Interview with President Bush', *Meet the Press*, broadcast on NBC, 8 February 2004.

83 Melvyn Leffler, 'The Foreign Policies of the George W. Bush Administration: Memoirs, History and Legacy', *Diplomatic History*, Vol.37, No.2, 2013, pp.190–216.

84 David Corn and Michael Isikoff, *Hubris: The Inside Story of Spin, Scandal and the Selling of the Iraq War* (New York: Three Rivers Press, 2007); Peter Beinart, *The Icarus Syndrome: A History of American Hubris* (New York: HarperCollins, 2010).

85 See also, Jonathan Monten, 'The Roots of the Bush Doctrine: Power, Nationalism, and Democracy Promotion in U.S. Strategy', *International Security*, Vol.29, No.4, 2005, pp.112–156, at p.112.

86 Kenneth Zagacki, 'Constitutive Rhetoric Reconsidered: Constitutive Paradoxes in G. W. Bush's Iraq War Speeches", *Western Journal of Communication*, Vol.71, No.4, 2007, pp.272–293 at pp.281–282.

87 Dodge, 'The Ideological Roots of Failure'.

88 William B Caldwell, 'Not at all Vague', *Washington Times*, 8 February 2007.

89 This reminds one of Daniel Patrick Moynihan's famous statements that: "Everyone is entitled to his own opinion, but not his own facts." George F Will, 'The Wisdom of Pat Moynihan', *The Washington Post*, 3 October 2010, www.washingtonpost.com/wp-dyn/content/article/2010/10/01/AR2010100105262.html?noredirect=on.

90 When asked about Osama bin Laden after the 9/11 attacks, Bush said that "there's an old poster out West . . . I recall, that said, 'Wanted, Dead or Alive.'": CNN, 'Bush: bin Laden "Prime Suspect"', *CNN*, 17 September 2001, http://edition.cnn.com/2001/US/09/17/bush. powell.terrorism/ .

91 Max Boot, 'Think Again: Neocons', *Foreign Policy*, 1 January 2004, www.foreignpolicy. com/articles/2004/01/01/think_again_neocons; Vaïsse, *Neoconservatism*, p.14.

92 They established the *Public Interest* in 1965 and the *National Interest* in 1985.

93 Danny Cooper, *Neoconservatism and American Foreign Policy: A Critical Analysis* (New York: Routledge, 2011), p.35.

94 All three generations of neoconservatives have had a particularly strong commitment to Zionism. Some see this as the best explanation of why the neocons advocated the 2003 invasion of Iraq. See, Jacob Heilbrunn, *They Knew They Were Right: The Rise of the Neocons* (New York: Doubleday, 2008).

95 There were exceptions to this ideological migration from left to right, the most interesting being Moynihan who worked for John Kennedy and Lyndon Johnson, and then for Richard Nixon and Gerald Ford, but returned to his liberal roots to become the Democratic Senator for New York from 1977–2001.

96 For example, Irving Kristol's foreign policy views rarely differed from the Realist views of Owen Harries, the editor of Kristol's journal *The National Interest*.

97 Justin Vaïsse 'Was Irving Kristol a Neoconservative?' *Foreign Policy*, September 2009, www.foreignpolicy.com/articles/2009/09/23/was_irving_kristol_a_neoconservative; Geoffrey Wheatcroft, 'Friendly Fire', *The New York Times Book Review*, 2 September 2007, www. nytimes.com/2007/09/02/books/review/Wheatcroft-t.html; and Sidney Blumenthal, 'Mugged by Reality', *Salon*, 14 December 2006, www.salon.com/2006/12/14/jeane_kirkpatrick/. "Once the warrior queen of neoconservatism," argues Blumenthal, "Jeane Kirkpatrick died a critic of Bush's unilateralism. Her death illuminates the conflicting legacies of the movement she helped found." See also, Jeane J. Kirkpatrick, *Making War to Keep Peace* (New York: HarperCollins, 2007).

98 "Magazines and journals such as *The Weekly Standard* and *Commentary*," argues Danny Cooper, "are the repository of neoconservative ideas." Cooper, *Neoconservatism and American Foreign Policy*, p.17.

99 Elliott Abrams, Richard L. Armitage, William J. Bennett, Jeffrey Bergner, John Bolton, Paula Dobriansky, Francis Fukuyama, Robert Kagan, Zalmay Khalilzad, William Kristol, Richard Perle, Peter W. Rodman, Donald Rumsfeld, William Schneider, Jr., Vin Weber, Paul Wolfowitz, R. James Woolsey and Robert B. Zoellick, 'Letter to the President of the United States,' *The Project for the New American Century*, 26 January 1998, www.newamericancentury.org/iraqclintonletter.htm.

100 Ibid.

101 Patrick J. Buchanan, *Day of Reckoning: How Hubris, Ideology, and Greed Are Tearing America Apart* (New York: Thomas Dunne Books/St. Martin's Press, 2007) George Packer has written that the "Iraq war will always be linked with the term 'neoconservative.'" Packer, *The Assassins' Gate*, p.15.

102 This is Francis Fukuyama citing Elizabeth Drew; Fukuyama, *America at the Crossroads: Democracy, Power, And the Neoconservative Legacy* (New Haven: Yale University Press, 2006), p.12.

103 Vaïsse, *Neoconservatism*, p.14. See also Lieven, *America Right or Wrong*.

104 John Micklethwait and Adrian Wooldridge in *The Right Nation: Conservative Power in America* (New York: Penguin Press, 2005). See also, Buchanan, *Day of Reckoning*.

105 Charles Krauthammer, 'The Neoconservative Convergence', *Commentary*, July – August 2005, pp.21–26, at p.22.

106 Cited in *Panorama*, 'The War Party' broadcast on BBC 1, 18 May 2003. Transcript available at: www.informationclearinghouse.info/article8581.htm.

107 Vaïsse, *Neoconservatism*, p.14.

108 David Rose, 'Neo Culpa: Please Don't Call Them "Architects of the War": Richard "Prince of Darkness" Perle, David "Axis of Evil" Frum, Kenneth "Cakewalk" Adelman, and Other Elite Neoconservatives Who Pushed for the Invasion of Iraq are Beside Themselves at the Result', *Vanity Fair*, January 2007, www.vanityfair.com/politics/features/2007/01/neocons200701; Cooper, *Neoconservatism and American Foreign Policy*, p.45. Vaïsse, *Neoconservatism*, p.257. Richard Perle makes the case for exaggeration in his article, 'Ambushed on the Potomac', *The National Interest*, No.99, January–February 2009, https://nationalinterest.org/article/ambushed-on-the-potomac-2953. See also, Dana Milbank, 'Prince of Darkness Denies Own Existence', *Washington Post*, 20 February 2009.

109 Justin Vaïsse, 'Why Neoconservatism Still Matters' [Policy Paper], *Foreign Policy at Brookings*, May 2010, www.brookings.edu/wp-content/uploads/2016/06/05_neoconservatism_vaisse.pdf, p.8.

110 This point is well made in Fukuyama, *America at the Crossroads*.

8 Ideological framings of American foreign policy: the domestic legacy

The analysis offered in this book can be extended by turning to aspects of the lasting domestic legacy of the ideological crusades of American foreign policy. Presidents stood at the public apex of foreign policy in the USA during the period covered by this book, their rhetoric the most publicised component of vast ideological mobilisations. Presidents played the biggest role in setting the agenda, framing the debates and legitimising actions in foreign policy. They spoke with the authority of the office and as representatives of the nation. They were presumed to possess an insider's knowledge of the matters on which they pronounced. None of them could be mistaken for original thinkers but they drew on ideas supplied by those around them, from their long careers in politics and from the common fund of beliefs and values which make up the American political culture. Theirs are the most prominent voices in American politics but far from being the only ones. On many issues they faced robust criticism from within the political elite, including on matters of foreign and defence policy. But on the Cold War essentials a strong consensus was quickly formed in the late 1940s which set the parameters of controversy and established right-thinking on foreign policy and much else for the next four decades. The ideological campaign which Truman led rapidly expanded to involve millions of people.

The competitive scare-mongering of anti-communism which the political elite indulged in, and in which the Republican Party excelled, also legitimated and fuelled organised efforts to seize the agenda and turn it down routes which attacked the elites themselves. Truman set the world a binary choice in March 1947 between freedom and rule by minorities controlled from Moscow. The threat to freedom was conducted by conspiracies. Some of the conspirators were active inside the USA. The threat took the form of a God-less, immoral, ruthless Leviathan controlling ubiquitous agents. George Kennan, though he later recanted – describing his Long Telegram as akin to "one of those primers put out by alarmed congressional committees or by the Daughters of the American Revolution"[1] – provided much of the rationale that the Washington political class became wedded to.[2] Containment became the cover – suggesting a defensive response – for American global expansion into every region of the world outside the communist bloc.[3] National security was the popular and permanent justification for this growing world role which continued after the collapse of the Soviet Union. Mobilisation of the public behind the cause of security, freedom and Christian morality – American values – repeated old themes of the anti-socialist Right; the association of foreigners with subversion, the key role of organised conspirators, the need for loyalty checks and the depiction of the socialist left as unpatriotic and even criminal. The so-called 'paranoid style' in American political culture, conspicuous among Republican activists, was reinforced by mainstream politicians prominent in both political parties. America's primary economic interest in the global preponderance of capitalism, and of American capitalism within it, was broadcast less often as the primary guide to foreign policy, though strenuous propaganda efforts were made at home and abroad to identify capitalism with freedom. In practice such faith was compatible with the promotion of ruthless right-wing dictatorships throughout the Third World, where freedom and democracy were conspicuously absent.

The growth of television – 86 per cent of American homes owned one by 1959 – assisted the dissemination of the official line as network news divisions were enlisted to support the cause as early as 1948. Though the efficacy of propaganda in shaping public opinion was taken for granted – especially if key slogans and assertions went unchallenged – it was seen to be much more effective if the job was also done by private agencies, including news networks.[4] Network news divisions acted as unofficial state propagandists, sacking anyone suspected of left-wing views and requiring loyalty oaths from the rest of their employees.[5] They aired programmes that were "produced, scripted, and approved by the White House and the Departments of States and Defense as news and public affairs programs."[6] The outright collaboration practiced between 1948 and 1954 "shaped the institutional relationship between the defense establishment and the television news for decades."[7] A particular view of the Cold War was passed off as objective truth. By the time McCarthy came on to the national scene the print press itself had been won over to the prevailing version of anti-communism to such an extent that it was unable to expose the Senator as a fraud and a liar and unable to see that it mattered that it should do so.[8]

The mass media were not the only agencies outside the formal political system which played a role in disseminating and elaborating the dominant discourse. Church attendance grew by 20 per cent in the 1950s and many of the most prominent evangelists enthusiastically joined the anti-communist campaign. Politicians meanwhile made greater use of God and faith.[9] The culture industries were mobilised, as has been shown in numerous studies devoted to the subject.[10] The scope of politics, defined as an activity of groups seeking to influence public policies, is far broader than the formal political system. Within this field of contestation ideologies are refined, adapted, sometimes generated, and made relevant to special interests, broader publics and current affairs. Failure in this struggle will render an ideology marginal or even moribund. The more ideologically sophisticated activist element, much smaller than the electorate of course, has to connect with broader publics, as well as appealing directly to the holders of public office by finding politicians (and other "second-hand traders in ideas", as Hayek called them) who will promote their world-view and policies by affecting (if possible, controlling) the public conversation.[11] "Concrete ideologies are the creation of three different groupings: professional political thinkers, political organizations such as parties and interest groups, and mass populations that entertain politico-cultural assumptions which percolate into more specific receptacles of political ideas."[12] Schematically the multi-level domestic political world, suggested here, can be represented as in Figure 8.1, below, bearing in mind that the divisions it depicts are porous and interconnected in the ways we have indicated throughout this book.

Activists are more effective, *ceteris paribus*, if they have money and other power resources (such as prestige and expertise), an insider status and an ability to represent themselves as speaking for widely held values. Business lobbies are normally among the most successful special interests for all these reasons. They played an active role in Cold

FIGURE 8.1 Ideological innovation: the multi-level domestic political context

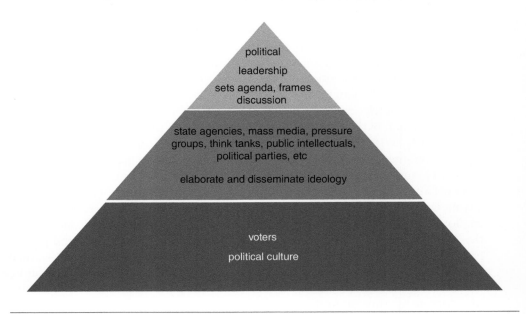

War politics. But while state-industry collaboration in anti-communism was acceptable to many business organisations – such as the Business Council, the National Association of Manufacturers and the Committee For Economic Development – they also strove to discredit organised labour and New Deal social reforms.[13] Many businesses thus linked their support for US foreign policy to the promotion of free enterprise inside the USA and opposition to organised labour and New Deal liberalism.[14] In some quarters within the USA the New Deal itself had always represented a socialist threat to 'American values' and stood in violation of the American constitution, and had done so since its inauguration in the 1930s.[15] The interests that took this view needed little encouragement to blame advocates of the New Deal for weakness, even betrayal, in the face of the communist global threat. A Democrat administration had raised the hue and cry concerning the ideologically driven Soviet quest for world domination, "impervious to logic or reason", but it had also, according to its critics, surrendered Eastern Europe. It had then lost China. Mao was simply an instrument of Stalin's foreign policy. China was to become part of the Soviet empire. Only American weakness and the perfidy of persons occupying high office could explain the mess. Yet another conspiracy was discovered. At this point McCarthy entered the fray, but so did Dulles, Eisenhower and Nixon.

Some State Department officials and experts might question the idea that all communists were Soviet agents – though there was no effort to make the doubts public – but the idea of "a highly coordinated, conspiratorial, malevolent force became encoded in the image of a 'communist monolith' – arguably the most dominant representation of international Communism during the height of the Cold War."[16] It had the virtue of simplicity and excluded the idea of complicating (and competing) national communisms. It entered the popular imagination and stayed there in the face of both the Yugoslav and Chinese splits with Moscow. It became part of the public culture of the USA – "the arena in which social and political conflict is played out and in which consensus is forged, manufactured and maintained . . . Its contours . . . shaped by innumerable agents, including social and business organisations, educational and political institutions, and the mass media."[17] Thus when Mao came to power in October 1949 "both print and radio comment took it for granted that all Communist gains, including those of the CCP, translated into victories for the Kremlin . . . By mid-December, five out of every six Americans believed that the Chinese Communists took their orders from Moscow."[18] Truman administration officials "routinely" encouraged this perception.

While McCarthy found popularity exaggerating and inventing aspects of communist subversion within the USA, General MacArthur emerged as a popular hero for wanting to extend the Korean War into an all-out victory over Red China. As Truman's popularity sank to a historic low the insurgencies associated with McCarthy and MacArthur provided pointers back to the White House for those seeking the Republican nomination. Eisenhower – remembered now for 'moderate Republicanism' – said that he saw socialism in the New Deal, denounced the Yalta agreements and blamed Truman for the loss of China. His running mate, Richard Nixon, pandered to the heartlands of McCarthyism and talked of the need for all-out war in Korea and China. Dulles repeated the charge of subversion and betrayal in high places and promised a crusade to liberate the captive peoples under communism. This 'policy of boldness' served to reinforce the sense of peril from abroad and strengthen the conviction in right-wing circles that the US had to adopt the most extreme measures to defeat the 'Communist Evil'. Dulles talked up America's readiness to use nuclear weapons and saw all international issues through a Cold War lens. These tropes were broadcast in numerous mass circulation publications and digested by millions of American citizens. And it was during the Eisenhower administrations that a dense network of right-wing organisations began to demand actions commensurate with the official rhetoric.

Various lobbies, think-tanks, foundations, newspaper columnists, academics and others contributed to the elaboration of the dominant themes.[19] But they also adapted them to serve a variety of interests. Opponents of the New Deal, like the du Pont brothers, are a case in point. As early as 1934 they framed their opposition to Roosevelt's reforms in terms of a defence of the Constitution and promoted their argument via the American Liberty League and the National Association of Manufacturers. Few paid much attention at first. But the "free market movement that had started in the 1930s grew and gained momentum against the backdrop of McCarthyism and the broader climate of anti-Communist politics."[20] Some businessmen endorsed McCarthy accordingly, and took "the nightmarish fears inspired by anticommunism and turned them against the entire liberal state."[21] The communist threat helped them equate the dismantling of welfare with the defence of freedom: "Years after McCarthy had been repudiated they continued to fight for the market using the tropes they had developed when anticommunism was at its zenith."[22] They were also assisted by the spread of evangelical Protestantism from the 1930s and by successful campaigns to align it with free market capitalism. The money for these programmes of campaigning, lobbying and propaganda was donated by the likes of Chrysler, Colgate-Palmolive, General Motors, Gulf Oil, Sears Roebuck and US Steel and had ready takers such as the popular evangelist Billy Graham.[23] By the late 1950s this anti-communist/anti-New Deal lobby could expect a sympathetic hearing for their argument about the erosion of states' rights from among those opposed to Civil Rights for black Americans.

The USA has more voluntary associations of every kind than any other political system, partly because the federal structure of political institutions provides so many points of access for pressure groups and special causes wishing to influence policy. Those with money and power are best able to exploit the system. It was in the context provided by the anti-communist consensus that

> a large number of more or less extreme movements . . . proliferated in the 1950s and 1960s [which], taken together, came to be known as the Radical Right . . . a whole structure of crusades, campaigns, radio stations, newsletters, magazines, storefronts, action groups, committees, lecture bureaus, lobbies and assorted voluntary organi-sations of every kind devoted to warning the citizens, in a tone of voice that rarely fell below the decibel level of the primal scream, about the dangers of communism, foreign and domestic.[24]

One reason for its success was its ability to exploit the huge racist constituency alarmed by the threat of black Civil Rights. For what could be better evidence of encroaching domestic socialism than Federal corrosion of states' rights and what could be better evidence of the communist threat than the Civil Rights movement itself? These threats could be added to the established narrative in Republican grassroots circles in which big government and international communism were already identified as the enemies of American freedom. William F. Buckley, editor of the influential journal *National Review* (founded in 1955), saw these connections and duly justified opposition to black Civil Rights in the pages of his journal. Conservative intellectuals like Buckley also laboured to mobilise the religious convictions of millions of Americans. Anti-communism provided the essential centre for this constellation of beliefs as preached by Goldwater, Reagan and the numerous groups forming the conservative 'movement' that was pitched against liberalism by the mid-1960s.

Ronald Reagan was just one of its many activists in the 1950s. His early political career was that of a zealot for laissez-faire capitalism and anti-communism, working for General Electric (GE), a company that demanded the utmost conformity from its own employees, including Reagan himself who accepted censorship of the television shows and speeches he made for GE. Lemuel Boulware, GE's vice-president in the years 1954–1962, nurtured Reagan, and helped finance other militants sharing his views, such as Buckley and the *National Review*. Reagan claimed to have visited all 135 GE plants in the USA, warning employees that only a handful of businessmen were holding back the spread of socialism in the country during the Eisenhower years. The speech he gave was honed during many repetitions and by the early 1960s his central message of the apocalyptic Soviet threat and the creep of socialism within the USA was often to be heard in Republican ultra-right strongholds, such as Southern California. Reagan was one of numerous propagandists operating at the level of Republican activists. They drew on values and beliefs deep within the American political culture such as anti-statism, religiosity, support for free enterprise, individual advancement and freedom to make their case. Hodgson sees "the turmoil and tension of the period from 1945 to 1960" – a period more frequently regarded as an era of consensus – as being "due to the connection some made, and others as passionately denied, between the unmistakable challenge of communism abroad and domestic radical-ism."[25] But it would be more accurate to say that in this, the period of the anti-communist consensus, any turmoil and tension in the system was caused by the architects of that consensus, like Truman, and exacerbated by demagogues, like McCarthy and Nixon, and those who found them useful, such as the leaders of the Republican Party and much of the mainstream news media. This was the fertile political soil Hodgson refers to "in which a new conservatism was to grow."[26] The witch-hunters and zealots were effective because the climate of fear had already been created and mainstream politicians were as keen to exploit it as the news media were reluctant to question it.[27]

Liberals were in the ascendancy when the Cold War began and believed that they could compete with Republicans on the salient matters – national security, military spending, military interventions abroad, patriotism and so on. Others saw an opportunity for the Right. The Harvard academic Samuel P. Huntington perceived the special value of anti-communism to conservatism before 'the movement' emerged as a national force and when the 'moderate Republicanism' of Eisenhower still seemed secure. In 1957 he argued that conservatism only gained strength, purpose and coherence when it was faced with a social challenge. But, he added, "the only threat extensive enough and deep enough to elicit a conservative response today is the challenge of communism and the Soviet Union to American society as a whole."[28] This was what was already understood by business interests opposed to the New Deal, the intellectual advocates of laissez-faire, the local oligarchs defending states' rights (as in Virginia) and the racists worried by the growth of Civil Rights and demands for equality. The main problem these groups had in the 1950s was that the mixed economy created by the New Deal was popular – because it seemed successful as the US economy continued to expand and deliver a new era of consumerism. The case against the New Deal was blunted by that fact. That would change in the 1970s. In the meantime the zealots of laissez-faire had to make the best of anti-communism and racism – two dispositions that already commanded millions of supporters upon which other political projects could be built.

This is what Senator Barry Goldwater set out to do. His book *The Conscience of a Conservative* (1960), ghost-written by William F Buckley's brother-in-law L. Brent Bozell, popularised his battle against the twin socialist evil, at home and abroad, and welded it to resistance against school integration and the erosion of states' rights. America's own leaders, or so the argument ran, were guiding the country to disaster by their appeasement of the Soviet Union and support for the growth of the Federal state. It was the common message of Reagan, Goldwater, the John Birch Society, self-styled 'moral conservatives' like Phyllis Schlafly and many other agitators of the Right. The old north-eastern Republican Party leadership was out of touch with the grassroots, according to the radicals, and had to be removed. The fact that the arguments of the ultras produced best-sellers like Schlafly's *A Choice Not an Echo* (1964) showed that there was an enthusiastic audience for these views even when they argued that international communism was winning the Cold War because America's media and political elites were themselves pro-communist, as in John A. Stormer's *None Dare Call It Treason* (1964). Such views were routinely dismissed as those of the paranoid lunatic fringe of course. The 1950s ended with bitter disappointment among Republican activists and right-wing intellectuals, persuaded that the promise of militant action against the communists had come to nothing. Neither the communists nor New Deal institutions had been 'rolled back'. Pragmatism had prevailed over rhetoric in the estimation of the Republican Right. Nevertheless, the anger of the 'betrayed' could be vindicated and fuelled even by the claims of their Democratic opponents in the 1960 presidential election campaign. For according to Democratic presidential candidate John F. Kennedy the US had actually fallen behind the Soviet Union militarily. A missile gap had opened to America's disadvantage. A decade in which the US economy had grown by 37 per cent was now portrayed as one in which the Soviets had taken the lead in science and technology. Goldwater's supporters needed no encouragement to believe such arguments, which could only deepen their anger at the elites responsible for America's weakness.

The claims of military and economic decay were false. But they supported the convictions of those who felt that the USA was not using its strength in the key international struggle. The Kennedy administration itself continued to depict that struggle as a Manichean conflict of Good and Evil, chiming with the extremists it professed to despise. The evil Soviets were behind every development of which Washington disapproved, from Cuba to Vietnam. The primary purpose of much of this rhetoric was to win elections and criticise opponents, of course. It was therefore chiefly concerned to appeal to a domestic audience. For this to be effective the ideas in question had to have broad appeal, however exaggerated or even false they might be, such as the scare about Soviet economic and military superiority in the late 1950s, or the idea that the Soviet Union was principally motivated by a desire for world domination in the late 1940s. When broad masses of American voters showed enthusiasm for McCarthy, however, Cold War liberals, like Hofstadter and Daniel Bell, tried to explain it in social-psychological terms as the manifestation of status anxiety and the 'paranoid style' among poorly educated misfits, rather than a response and supplement to the concerns of the political mainstream.[29] But this theorising from some of the assumptions of the post-war 'consensus' was wrong. Empirical research has shown, to the contrary, that right-wing activists who embraced the scare stories most enthusiastically were more likely to be well-educated, well-paid, upwardly mobile and Republican.[30] Such concerned citizen-activists could point to the words of leading politicians across the political spectrum to establish the gravity of the present danger and show the distance between their words and their lack of proportionate action.

Anti-communism was the bond that drew the various elements of the Right together and kept them together in the 1950s and early 1960s, whatever ideological differences there were between so-called libertarians opposed to New Deal 'socialism', racists worried about Civil Rights and religiously-inspired moralists. With sufficient ingenuity these different concerns might be woven into a persuasive whole and intellectuals associated with *National Review*, such as William F. Buckley and Frank Meyer, did their best to fuse the disparate elements under the twin causes of fighting both international communism and domestic liberalism/socialism. State spending on the military was fine – in fact it was rarely sufficient – but government expenditure on social and welfare programmes was an affront to economic efficiency, personal freedom and morality. Wealthy backers such as the Texas oil millionaire H. L. Hunt financed the movement; television and radio broadcasts and best-selling books propagated its ideas.[31] All this, it has been observed by Horwitz, "points to the importance of the institutions that mediated between elite and base." Horwitz gives examples: journals like *The Freeman* and *National Review*; intellectual forums like the Mont Pelerin Society; think-tanks like the American Enterprise Association; the mass distribution of books like Hayek's *The Road to Serfdom* (by *Reader's Digest* and other networks); and the proliferation of many far-right organisations like the Christian Anti-Communism Crusade and the John Birch Society in the context of an intense, broad-based anti-communism in American society.[32] Little attention was given to these connections by the many American political scientists who saw domestic politics as essentially pragmatic.[33]

Advocacy of a more militant, militarist nationalism in combat with international communism was justified by mainstream politicians, while opposition to Civil Rights was mainstream thinking on the Right of American politics. Opposition to New Deal 'socialism', by contrast, was marginalised until the Keynesian full employment boom of the post-war years became mired in stagflation in the 1970s. The Keynesian-New Deal consensus unravelled in the course of that decade. By the 1980s it had almost become axiomatic that reinvigorating the economy was to be achieved by tax cuts, deregulation of business and an end to welfare dependency. The stagflationary context brought the ideas of intellectuals like Friedrich Hayek, Ayn Rand and Milton Friedman to the fore; but it was also the long-term work of many other right-wing ideologues, such as James M. Buchanan,[34] that combined neo-liberal economics with both a moralistic cultural critique of 1960s America and ideas of American exceptionalism in foreign policy. Blue-collar workers and religious fundamentalists were brought into this coalition in the 1970s. As Horwitz observes "conservatives of every stripe tended, over time, to support the foreign policy purview of the president in ways that undercut Congress' role and that justified the concentration of power in the executive branch."[35] This culminated in the Nixon presidency but most of the foundations of the imperial presidency had been established by Democratic administrations since Roosevelt and much of the groundwork for Nixon's victory in 1968 had been done by Goldwater's supporters.

Goldwater's bid for the presidency had emerged before all these elements were in place. In that sense, as Buckley remarked, his campaign was premature. He had stood for victory over communism, with nuclear weapons if necessary, opposition to both Civil Rights and the big government that would lead to socialism. 'Better Dead than Red' summed up the argument of his widely distributed *The Conscience of a Conservative*. President Johnson's supporters had little difficulty in persuading themselves and others that Goldwater was 'nuts'. The collapse of the Republican vote in the North East was taken as proof of his supporters' marginality. But Goldwater had proved popular in the Deep South. His presidential campaign had won a majority of white Southern votes. It also made a star of Reagan in grassroots Republican circles after 'The Speech' was broadcast to the nation on 27 October 1964. What if the block of voters Goldwater represented were to desert the Democrats for ever? Johnson's conduct of the Vietnam War, the opposition it generated, his domestic welfare and Civil Rights reform programme, were among the factors that began the disintegration of the coalition of voters who elected him in 1964. Meanwhile Radical Right organisations, think-tanks and foundations such as the Hoover Institution, American Enterprise Institute and the John Olin Foundation continued to funnel money and propagate ideas designed to oust the 'moderate Republicanism' associated with Eisenhower and capitalise on the polarisation and realignments that were taking place. Nixon's presidential victories in 1968 and 1972 harnessed a 'silent majority', particularly strong in the South, appalled by domestic opposition to the war in Vietnam, the perceived denigration of the armed forces and the weakening of American power, outraged by Civil Rights, the expansion of welfare under Johnson and the moral decay which all this was supposed to signify.

But many of the activists who had supported Nixon were disappointed by his domestic and foreign policies, just as they had been disappointed by Eisenhower. Nixon was charged with presiding over a "deteriorated military position" in the pages of *National Review*.[36] The sense that American power in the world was receding because of timorous or treacherous policy choices had been a staple on the Right since the end of the Second World War. The theme was taken up by the 'Moral Majority' that emerged at the end of the 1970s. In Reagan's run for the Republican nomination in 1976 the proposed Panama Canal Treaty (handing control of the canal to Panama) symbolised the alleged weakening of America, which Reagan staunchly opposed. Under Jimmy Carter's presidency the list of perceived setbacks only increased as stagflation continued at home; the Iranian hostage crisis and the Soviet invasion of Afghanistan were simply the most publicised examples. The Soviet Union was emerging as the dominant military power. The 'Finlandization of

America' beckoned, according to influential scaremongers. Neoconservatives like Norman Podhoretz felt obliged to warn, once again, that the Soviet Union was an ideologically driven state determined to refashion the international order, just as Kennan had analysed it in 1947. Once again, according to Podhoretz, America found itself weakened by policies of appeasement. Nixon and Kissinger had presided over retreat, calling it détente, while the dynamic 'forward surge' of Soviet imperialism took on the world.[37] Much was made of the Soviet Union's rapid bid for military superiority in the 1970s – as publicised by groups such as the Committee on the Present Danger and the right-wing 'experts' who composed Team B, organised by CIA Director George H. W. Bush. All their contentions about the new Soviet military threat were false, but such warnings had the desired effect in helping to discredit Carter and elect Ronald Reagan to the White House.[38]

Reagan's victory in 1980 heralded a 'Second Cold War' according to some analysts, such was the increase in Cold War rhetoric as military spending increased massively, Cruise and Pershing missiles were deployed in Western Europe, and the new President took measures to destroy the left-wing government of Nicaragua.[39] Reagan also took action against domestic 'socialism' by cutting taxes and welfare benefits and weakening trade unions. The national debt tripled to $2.8 trillion by 1989. The Christian Right supported Reagan's military build-up and wanted confrontation with the 'communist' threat in Central America, Africa and Afghanistan, invoking biblical prophecy of the 'end times' and Armageddon as it did so. The "union of theological certitude and militant nationalism" came to "typify the foreign policy agenda of the Christian right" for the next 30 years. When George W. Bush took the decision to invade Iraq in 2003, 87 per cent of white evangelical Christians supported his decision, compared to 62 per cent of the US population as a whole.[40] The Cold War had been over since 1991, but the mentality it promoted lived on.

God had never been far away in American politics. "For us there are two kinds of people in the world", John Foster Dulles once explained. "There are those who are Christians and support free enterprise, and there are the others."[41] Garry Wills only states the obvious when he says that "nothing has been more stable in our history, nothing less budgeable, than religious belief and practice."[42] Forty per cent of the population was calling itself 'born again' according to surveys conducted in 1989, but the mainstream of American religious life had always been evangelical and elements such as revivalism, biblical literalism and millennial hope had always 'profoundly influenced' US politics.[43] Religious ideology had informed much of the militant opposition to domestic socialism and the New Deal in the inter-war period but when Godless communism emerged as an existential threat in the 1940s it could be a mobilising force behind foreign policy. In the mind of Dulles, and the millions of Americans who thought like him, Christian faith and the conviction that America stood for the very best that humanity had to offer, were interwoven beliefs. The United States was an instrument of divine providence to spread freedom, above all economic freedom. Only bad people refused to see this and they could be overcome by the righteous use of force. By the time Dulles had quit the scene the Republican Party had become the principal champion of military spending within the party system; and by the 1980s evangelicals were solidly in support "spurred on by Christian Right organizations" that became prominent during the decade.[44] Reagan, like most of his predecessors in the White House, made extensive use of religious imagery, linking it to American exceptionalism. Under George W. Bush "the association of exceptionalism with unilateralism" in foreign policy carried divine sanction for millions of Republican voters.[45] This version of exceptionalism "became virtually the watchword of the campaign for the 2012 Republican nomination."[46]

At the grassroots it had been expressed in the patriotic ranks of the Tea Party, which developed after Barack Obama became president in 2009. Some of the nationalist and anti-leftist discourses of the Tea Party bore a predictable resemblance to those of McCarthyism; its supporters also showed strong attachment to the Republican Party, resentment against immigrants and opposition to welfare programmes and liberal values on moral issues such as abortion and gay rights.[47] The divinely inspired Constitution of the US had been betrayed. The leading 'Teavangelical' – Sarah Palin, vice-presidential candidate in 2008, and a believer in "divine providence, miracles and hearing God's voice" – readily mixed politics and religion, Christianity and patriotism, in the campaign against President Obama's ruination of America by 'socialism'. The movement she led combined strong belief in American exceptionalism with free market capitalism and minimal government.[48] Conservative think-tanks such as the Cato Institute and right-wing media such as Fox News played a significant role in shaping its ideology.[49] So did radio right-wingers with audiences numbered in tens of millions – such as Rush Limbaugh, Sean Hannity, Michael Savage, Glenn Beck and Laura Ingraham – websites like the *Drudge Report* and *Breitbart* and billionaires like the Koch brothers demanding laissez-faire economics. About 30 per cent of US adults were favourably impressed by the Tea Party by late 2009 and roughly 46 million Americans, two-fifths of voters, told exit pollsters in 2010 that they supported the Tea Party in the midterm elections.[50] The entire field of candidates for the Republican presidential nomination in 2016 – Rick Santorum, Rick Perry, Bobby Jindal, Carly Fiorina, Ted Cruz, Dr Rand Paul, Jeb Bush, Mike Huckabee, John Kasich, Marco Rubio and others – was composed of people who shared many Tea Party convictions.[51] It was from this field that Donald Trump emerged triumphant with his slogan 'make America great again' and it is a mark of the relationship of religious faith to the other things Trump stood for that white evangelical and Catholic Americans supported him as strongly as they had supported earlier Republican candidates for the White House.[52] One year into his presidency they continued to do so with approval ratings of 90 per cent among Republicans.[53] What remained of the familiar grassroots Republican ideology in Trump's rhetoric was its populism, its anti-establishment rancour, its nationalism, its opposition to domestic liberalism/socialism, its strident Us vs Them tone, its authoritarian streak, its militarism and its appeal to the true, moral, long-suffering Americans threatened by privileged minorities and corrupt elites. Trump thinks of himself as a winner and in his campaign for the presidency he bet on a rhetoric that he had strong reason to think would mobilise the winning coalition. If that rhetoric has resonance it is because the fears, resentments, hatreds and ways of thinking it appeals to have been decades in the making and have millions of adherents.

NOTES

1 George Kennan, *Memoirs 1925–50* (New York: Pantheon Books, 1967), p.294.
2 See Marc J. Selverstone, *Constructing the Monolith: The United States, Great Britain and International Communism, 1945–1950* (Cambridge, MA: Harvard University Press, 2009). The USA's part in the global propaganda war that followed is covered in Nicholas J. Cull, *The Cold War and the United States Information Agency* (New York: Cambridge University Press, 2008); Reinhold Wagnleitner, *Coca-Colonisation and the Cold War: The Cultural Mission of the United States in Austria after the Second World War* (Chapel Hill NC: University

of North Carolina Press, 1994); Frances Stonor Saunders, *Who Paid the Piper? The CIA and the Cultural Cold War* (London: Granta Books, 1999).

3   Melvyn Leffler, 'The American Conception of National Security and the Beginnings of the Cold War, 1945–48', *American Historical Review*, Vol.89, No.2, 1984, pp.346–381.

4   Nancy E. Bernhard, *US Television News and Cold War Propaganda, 1947–1960* (Cambridge: Cambridge University Press, 1999), pp.43–45, 67–68, 85.

5   Ibid., p.3

6   Ibid., p.2

7   Ibid.

8   Ibid., p. 156–158. See also David Greenberg, *Republic of Spin: An Inside History of the American Presidency* (New York: Norton, 2016), pp.270–276.

9   See Dianne Kirby, 'The Cold War and American Religion', *Oxford Research Encyclopedia of Religion*, May 2017, http://religion.oxfordre.com/view/10.1093/acrefore/9780199340378.001.0001/acrefore-9780199340378-e-398; T. Jeremy Gunn, *Spiritual Weapons: The Cold War and the Forging of an American National Religion* (Westport, CT: Praeger, 2009).

10 For example, Stonor Saunders, *Who Paid the Piper?*; David Caute, *The Dancer Defects: The Struggle for Cultural Supremacy During the Cold War* (Oxford: Oxford University Press, 2003). Tony Shaw has pointed out how in the "1940s and 1950s Hollywood's eight major film studios . . . supported the fight against communism mainly out of political conviction and economic self-interest, not because they felt beholden to officialdom." Tony Shaw, 'Ambassadors of the Screen: Film and the State-Private Network in Cold War America', in Laville and Wilford (eds.), *The US Government, Citizen Groups and the Cold War*, pp.157–172, at p.159.

11 Nancy MacLean, *Democracy in Chains: The Deep History of the Radical Right's Stealth Plan for America* (London: Scribe, 2017), pp.83–88, 116–118. MacLean points out that thinkers like Buchanan, Hayek and Buckley were well aware of the long-term nature of their project.

12 Freeden, *Ideologies and Political Theory*, p.123.

13 See Kim McQuaid, *Big Business and Presidential Power: From FDR to Reagan* (New York: William Morrow, 1982); Elizabeth A. Fones-Jones, *Selling Free Enterprise: The Business Assault of Labor and Liberalism, 1945–60* (Urbana, IL: University of Illinois Press, 1995).

14 Bernhard, *US Television News*, p.25.

15 Organisations such as The American Liberty League, the National Association of Manufacturers, the Hearst press, industrialists like du Pont, politicians like Robert A. Taft, Congressional opponents of Civil Rights and strong labour unions.

16 Selverstone, *Constructing the Monolith*, pp.113, 2.

17 Ibid., p.6.

18 Ibid., pp.147–148.

19 The contributions of academics were often directly funded by the state or by wealthy foundations funded by big business. But they brought their own enthusiasms to the table too. For academics in the behavioural sciences see Ron Robin, *The Making of the Cold War Enemy: Culture and Politics in the Military-Industrial Complex* (Princeton, NJ: Princeton University Press, 2001). For US political science see Ido Oren, *Our Enemies and US: America's Rivalries and the Making of Political Science* (Ithaca, NY: Cornell University Press, 2013).

20 Kim Phillips-Fein, *Invisible Hands: The Businessmen's Crusade Against the New Deal* (Norton: New York, 2010), p.58.

21 Ibid., pp.58–60.

22 Ibid., p.60.

23 Ibid., pp.75–77.

24 Godfrey Hodgson, *The World Turned Right Side Up: A History of the Conservative Ascendancy in America* (New York: Houghton Mifflin, 1996), p.62.

25 Ibid., p.52.

26 Ibid., p.54.

27 Nelson Polsby, 'Towards an Explanation of McCarthyism', *Political Studies*, Vol.8, No.3, 1960, pp.250–271.

28 Samuel P. Huntington, 'Conservatism as an Ideology', *American Political Science Review*, Vol.51, No.2, 1957, pp.454–473, at p.445.

29 See Daniel Bell (ed.), *The Radical Right* (New York: Anchor Books, 1964) and for a convincing refutation of the arguments contained within this classic of Cold War liberalism see M. P. Rogin, *The Intellectuals and McCarthy: The Radical Specter* (Cambridge, Mass.: MIT Press, 1967), pp. 59, 86, 99, 103, 157, 215–216, 224–228, 242–243.

30 Rogin, *The Intellectuals and McCarthy*; Lisa McGirr, *Suburban Warriors: The Origins of the New American Right* (Princeton, NJ: Princeton University Press, 2001).

31 Dionne, *Why the Right Went Wrong*, pp. 40–43.

32 Robert B. Horwitz, *America's Right: Anti-Establishment Conservatism from Goldwater to the Tea Party* (Cambridge: Polity Press, 2013), pp.42–43.

33 For example, Clinton Rossiter, *Parties and Politics in America* (Ithaca, NY: Cornell University Press, 1960), p.1.

34 See MacLean, *Democracy in Chains*.

35 Horwitz, *America's Right*, p.40.

36 Dionne, *Why the Right Went Wrong*, p.73.

37 Norman Podhoretz, 'The Present Danger', *Commentary*, 1 March 1980; see also his *The Present Danger* (New York: Simon & Schuster, 1980).

38 Tim Weiner, *Legacy of Ashes: The History of the CIA* (New York: Allen and Lane, 2007), pp.351–353.

39 Halliday, *The Making of the Second Cold War*.

40 Horwitz, *America's Right*, pp.109, 106–111.

41 Quoted in Kinzer, *The Brothers*, pp.320–321.

42 Gary Willis, *Under God: Religion and American Politics* (New York: Simon & Schuster, 1990), pp.15–16.

43 Ibid., pp.19–20.

44 Philip Schwadel, 'The Republicanization of Evangelical Protestants in the United States: An Examination of the Sources of Political Realignment', *Social Science Research*, Vol.62, 2017, pp.238–254, 240.

45 Mark Silk, 'American Exceptionalism and Political Religion in Republican Politics Today', *The Review of Faith and International Affairs*, Vol.10, No.2, 2012, pp.33–40, at p.36.

46 Ibid., p.38.

47 See Ritchie Savage, 'From McCarthyism to the Tea Party: Interpreting Anti-Leftist Forms of US Populism in Comparative Perspective', *New Political Science*, Vol.34, No.4, 2012, pp.564–584. See also Patrick Fisher, 'The Tea Party and the Demographic and Ideological Gaps Within the Republican Party', *Geopolitics, History, and International Relations*, Vol.7, No.2, 2015, pp.13–31, at p.21.

48 Anthea Butler, 'From Republican Party to Republican Religion: The New Political Evangelists of the Right', *Political Theology*, Vol.13, No.5, 2012, pp.634–651, see pp.634–636.

49 Theda Skocpol and Vanessa Williamson, *The Tea Party and the Remaking of Republican Conservatism* (New York: Oxford University Press), pp.131, 172.

50 Ibid., pp.21–22.

51 See Eliot Weinberger, 'They Could Have Picked . . .' *London Review of Books*, Vol.38, No.15, 28 July 2016.

52 See the Pew Research Center analysis at www.pewresearch.org/fact-tank/2016/11/09/how-the-faithful-voted-a-preliminary-2016-analysis/.

53 Cited by Adam Shatz, 'American Carnage', 2 July 2018, www.lrb.co.uk/blog/2018/07/02/adam-shatz/american-carnage/.

Index